Discover Yorkshire's Wildlife

Your guide to Yorkshire
and Sheffield Wildlife
Trusts' nature reserves

Discover Yorkshire's Wildlife

ISBN 978-0-9509460-3-0

Published by Yorkshire Wildlife Trust.

For more copies of this book, please email: info@ywt.org.uk. Tel: 01904 659570
Designed by United by Design www.ubdstudio.co.uk
Printed in Great Britain by Mick Cherry – www.thatprintbloke.co.uk

The production of this book has been generously supported by the following companies. Yorkshire Wildlife Trust would like to thank them for their support.

Acknowledgements

This book is the culmination of a project that commenced in autumn 2011 and has taken a year to complete. It would not have been possible without the generous contributions of many people, notably those who took the time to write sections about the Yorkshire Wildlife Trust nature reserves for which they have a special love and deep knowledge. Whilst we have been constrained by a limited number of pages, we hope we have managed to capture a flavour of their passion for these wonderful places and their wildlife.

All of the photographs used in this book have been provided free of charge by a large number of talented people and we feel really bring to life the stunning wildlife and landscape of Yorkshire. In addition, massive thanks must go to our colleagues at the Trust who despite being incredibly busy, have found the time to write many of the words you will find within these pages. We hope this joint effort has resulted in a book which inspires you to get out there and enjoy this beautiful county and gives you a taste of what the staff, volunteers and supporters of Yorkshire Wildlife Trust are so committed to looking after.

Editors

Jonathan Leadley and Joanna Richards
Yorkshire Wildlife Trust, October 2012

Editorial and writing team

Tim Bailey, Caroline Comins, Ian Jelley

Contributors

Nabil Abbas – Sprotbrough Flash
Chris Alder – Globe Flower Wood, Grass Wood
Judith Allinson – Brae Pasture, Salt Lake Quarry, South House Pavement
Derrick Bateman – North Cliffe Wood
Roger Bird – Potteric Carr
Michael Brook – Upper Park Wood
David Burtell – Agden Bog
Charles Clarkson – Jeffry Bog, Kirkham Wood
Dame Judi Dench
Alastair Fitter – Askham Bog
Andrew Gibson – Kilnsea Wetlands, Spurn, Welwick Saltmarsh
Keith Gittens – Garbutt Wood
Julie Gough – Sheffield Wildlife Trust nature reserves
Barry Greenacre – Saltmarshe Delph

Christine Handley – Woodhouse Washlands
Astrid Hanlon – Peatlands
Tom Hayek – Water voles, Farmland
Anthony Hurd – Coast, Marine
Claire Jackson – Otters
John Lawton – Foreword
Harriet Linfoot – Urban
John MacArthur and Rob Wilkinson – Adel Dam
Stephen Martin – North Cave Wetlands
Tony Martin – Paull Holme Strays
Stephen Meays – Badgers
Deborah Millward – Seata Quarry, Semer Water
Peter Nash – Denaby Ings
Roger Neale – Southerscales
Helen Pedley – Broadhead Clough
Martin Phillips – Wharram Quarry
Jonathan Proud – Allerthorpe Common

Elizabeth Round – Burton Riggs, Chafer Wood, Ellerburn Bank, Fen Bog, Garbutt Wood, Harland Mount
Gordon Scaife – Rifle Butts Quarry
Dale Scott – Low Wood
Fiona Shipp – Leeds sites
Joyce Simmons – Brockadale
John Smith – Yelland's Meadow
Jim Staveley – Maltby Low Common
Rob Stoneman – Foreword
Mary Sykes – Moorlands
Mick Townsend – Thorpe Marsh
Jon Traill – Snakeholm Pastures, Otters
Peter Treloar – Staveley Nature Reserve
Don Vine – Kirkstall Valley
Jonathan Watkins – Leyburn Old Glebe
Jack Whitehead – Filey Dams
David Woodmansey – Flamborough Cliffs

Thanks to

Hayley Cox, Phillip Whelpdale, Lizzie Dealey and Martin Batt for their input into this book and Jessica Thompson and Di Leadley who assisted in the final stages of the publication, and Annabel Eager and Owen Turner at United by Design for all their ideas, patience and creativity.

Design by

United by Design
Branding & design agency

www.ubdstudio.co.uk

Contents

Introduction

Yorkshire is a fantastic place to discover wildlife – whether a seasoned naturalist or a beginner taking your first steps into the wonderful world of wildlife, the county has plenty to offer everybody. What makes Yorkshire so special is the incredibly varied landscape and climate, with a corresponding range of habitats and wildlife.

Yorkshire Wildlife Trust is the largest charity dedicated solely to nature conservation in the county and over several decades, with the support of local people and funding bodies, has safeguarded an impressive number of wildlife havens, representing many of the habitats and wildlife characteristic of the county. The majority of these nature reserves can be found within the pages of this book. Many of the sites are owned by the Trust, but some are managed in partnership with various landowners. A small handful of fragile or tiny sites have been added as footnotes to entries for nearby nature reserves. Finally, there are also a few Trust nature reserves which have not made it into this book as they have been deemed to be hazardous to visitors or there may be access restrictions in place.

Sheffield Wildlife Trust manage a range of sites and have worked in partnership with Yorkshire Wildlife Trust in the production of this book in order to provide readers with a comprehensive picture of the Wildlife Trust nature reserves in the county. These sites are included with the South Yorkshire nature reserves, but bear the Sheffield Wildlife Trust logo.

Together with a review of key habitats, a small selection of Yorkshire's most charismatic species have been included among the nature reserve pages which will hopefully provide insight to readers. With space for only a tiny number of species, selection was extremely difficult and those entered were chosen through a public poll early in 2012.

Both Yorkshire Wildlife Trust and Sheffield Wildlife Trust are actively implementing the Wildlife Trusts' vision for Living Landscapes and Living Seas. Nature reserves and other protected areas are key parts of this vision, but for wildlife to have a more secure future conservation must work at a landscape scale. For more information about this vision, please visit ywt.org.uk or wildsheffield.com.

Discover Yorkshire's Wildlife will hopefully inspire you to don your walking boots, grab your hand lens or binoculars and get out into Yorkshire's countryside. For those less mobile, or who visit the county only occasionally, the book may help you reminisce about Yorkshire's fabulous wildlife.

Love Yorkshire, Love Wildlife

Foreword by John Lawton

John Lawton

Yorkshire has been described as "God's own county". It is. Not only is Yorkshire the largest county in England, it hosts two National Parks (the North York Moors and the Yorkshire Dales), with a third (the Peak District) creeping across the south west county boundary.

The geology of Yorkshire literally underpins the county's wonderful wildlife, with rocks from every geological period from the Ordovician to the Cretaceous. Rifle Butts Quarry reveals a major unconformity between the Lower Jurassic and the Upper Cretaceous near Market Weighton. The North Sea coast is spectacular (and among the most rapidly eroding in the UK), the relentless erosion providing the material for Spurn Point. The last great run of the English chalk thrusts out into the sea at Flamborough Head, with its spectacular sea-bird cliffs.

The Yorkshire Naturalists Trust (as it was originally known) was founded in 1946 – the second Naturalists Trust in the UK after Norfolk. In 1944, two blocks of relict fen-woodland at Askham Bog (just outside York) became available for sale, and were bought by the 'chocolate barons' Sir Francis Terry and Arnold Rowntree; Yorkshire Wildlife Trust was founded with the primary objective of receiving Askham Bog as a gift, which was duly completed in 1946. The Trust did not complete its ownership of Askham (a nice touch) until its Golden Jubilee in 1996. From this small beginning (a single nature reserve and eleven 'subscribers' plus Terry as President and Rowntree as Vice-President) the Trust has grown steadily so that today we have over 90 nature reserves and approaching 35,000 members. On the way we became the Yorkshire Wildlife Trust in 1983. The

Trust's first public appeal for money was in 1955, to raise £500 to purchase Moorlands (a woodland) near York as our second nature reserve. The Trust acquired Spurn from the War Office in 1959 thanks to the unstinting efforts of Dr Edward Wilfred Taylor the then (honorary) President. The Trust's first paid Executive Officer, Lt. Col. John Newman, was not appointed until 1968. Now we have 100 staff.

The remarkable and exciting growth of the Trust reflects the huge interest that exists in the UK in natural history and the environment. It is also necessary because threats to wildlife and wild places continue unabated. The Trust's precious nature reserves are a fundamental (but by no means the only) part of our efforts to protect the county's natural heritage. And what superb nature reserves we have. The chain of nature reserves is important, and you will find them all described in this book. But some are more notable than others, and are of national and international significance. They include Spurn, Fen Bog (an upland valley mire), Strensall Common (heathland on the Vale of York), Potteric Carr (a fantastic wetland complex near Doncaster), Wheldrake Ings (ancient lowland hay-meadows in the Lower Derwent Valley), Southerscales (limestone pavements on Ingleborough), and Flamborough Cliffs. No other county in England can boast such a rich variety of nationally important sites. But many smaller, less well-known nature reserves are gems in their own right, and all are worth a visit.

Enjoy them, and love Yorkshire and her wonderful wildlife.

Prof. Sir John Lawton,
Chairman,
Yorkshire Wildlife Trust
November 2012

Foreword by Rob Stoneman

Rob Stoneman

Nature conservation in Britain has a long pedigree. Nearly a thousand years ago the Normans introduced the idea of reserves of wildlife for hunting; great medieval forests that even today have resonance in the wild places of, for example, Hatfield Moor near Doncaster. The then radical concept of nature reserves, however, began with the brilliant naturalist Charles Rothschild in 1912. He was concerned that some of the best places for wildlife were already being degraded and formed a Society for the Promotion of Nature Reserves (SPNR). He and other distinguished colleagues scoured the country to come up with the best wildlife sites – a list of 284 sites neatly catalogued in blue linen envelopes each containing a detailed map and site description.

Early successes were Woodwalton Fen in Cambridgeshire famed for its large copper butterflies, Meathop Moss in Cumbria and Holkham Marshes in Norfolk, the latter given over to the National Trust.

The SPNR also arranged the purchase of Norfolk's Cley Marshes and formed a new organisation to manage the Marshes – the Norfolk Naturalists Trust – the first of the Wildlife Trusts. With Rothschild's death in 1924, the SPNR foundered but regrouped as the war loomed with the redoubtable Herbert Smith leading plans for nature conservation once the war ended. This culminated in the 1949 National Parks Act, which also created the Nature Conservancy (forerunner of Natural England), NNRs and SSSIs. Meanwhile, another Trust was founded here in Yorkshire (1946) and in Lincolnshire (1948). Lincolnshire Naturalist Trust

founder – Ted Smith (still President today) – then worked with the SPNR to create a network of Naturalist Trusts across Britain.

In the beginning, the Trusts were almost exclusively focused on nature reserve acquisition. However, it was not long before the Trusts broadened their remit into volunteering, education, survey and monitoring. The SPNR meanwhile redefined itself as the central charity to the Naturalist Trusts, receiving a Royal Charter in 1971, to become the Royal Society for Nature Conservation. In the 1980s, RSNC facilitated another wing of the movement: the urban wildlife partnership, the largest of these urban wildlife groups becoming Wildlife Trusts in their own right – in Sheffield, Birmingham, Middlesborough and London.

By the 1990s, the Wildlife Trusts (as they were by then

known) were very different – typically employing a professional staff backed up by hundreds of volunteers with many thousands of members. Your local Wildlife Trust could be found fighting battles of international significance or campaigning for a local wildlife site, or working with a local farmer or taking children pond-dipping, as well as managing nature reserves.

Yet, despite the growth and size of the Wildlife Trusts and other conservation organisations, wildlife still declined. Intensification of agriculture and inappropriately sited development continued to take its toll. Britain's wildlife was now so fragmented that species were gradually lost. The Wildlife Trusts' response is Living Landscapes – an ambitious new philosophy to rebuild and restore Britain's wildlife across landscapes; building out from the nature

reserves to create a better quality of life for all. With climate change looming and impacting already, never has such an approach been timelier.

The challenge on land is mirrored by the challenge out at sea, where our marine wildlife has been hugely diminished by industrial fishing and pollution. A decade of campaigning led to the Marine and Coastal Access Act in 2009, the legislative platform to begin the restoration of our seas and create Living Seas.

In 2012, the Wildlife Trusts collectively employ 1,200 staff, working with over 70,000 volunteers and are supported by nearly 850,000 members. They manage over 2,500 nature reserves so that in most parts of Britain, you are never more than 10 miles from a Wildlife Trust nature reserve. It is a movement that Rothschild would be hugely proud of – a movement to restore the wildlife of the UK.

Dr. Rob Stoneman
Chief Executive,
Yorkshire Wildlife Trust
November 2012

Enjoy your visit!

A guide to visiting nature reserves

Visitors at Garbutt Woo...

Yorkshire Wildlife Trust nature reserves provide excellent opportunities for you to experience some of Yorkshire's best wildlife and landscapes, and to learn more about our natural heritage. It is worth remembering that nature reserves are wild places and conditions can be hazardous at times. Also, visiting a nature reserve can be frustrating if you visit at a time of day when wildlife is less active or in a season when the specialities are not present. These pages will give you some information and tips about visiting the Trust's sites safely and responsibly, and how to get the most from your visit.

Access

Yorkshire Wildlife Trust is keen for people to visit its nature reserves and tries hard to make them accessible by creating paths, installing boardwalks, viewing hides, car parking, kissing gates, interpretation and signage. However, some of the sites by their very nature can be challenging to access, due to their isolated location, the difficult terrain such as wet ground, steep slopes or dense vegetation or the fragility of their habitats. We work with disability groups to provide access for less mobile people where practical and when funding allows. Check the icons at the top of the pages to see what access is available.

Planning your visit

To ensure a safe and enjoyable visit please go properly equipped with good walking shoes or wellies and sensible clothing for the weather conditions, plus sun screen and insect repellent if appropriate. Binoculars, cameras, field guides and other equipment may enhance your visit. You can visit the Trust's shop at Potteric Carr or the online shop ywt.org.uk/shop to purchase some of these items.

Before you visit make sure you are familiar with the access information for the nature reserve you intend to visit, where you can park or what public transport is available. The factfile, postcode, grid references and maps in this guide should help. If visiting an isolated site on your own, make sure you tell somebody where you are going and when you will be back. Please make sure that you do not leave valuables on display in your car. Also, make sure you are aware of the facilities available on or close to the site. The vast majority of Yorkshire Wildlife Trust nature reserves do not have toilets, refreshments or shelter, so please make allowances for this.

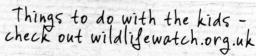

Things to do with the kids -
check out wildlifewatch.org.uk

- Collect autumn leaves and make a collage
- Try bark rubbing
- Do a bug hunt
- Spot and identify animal tracks and signs

Help Yorkshire Wildlife Trust keep its nature reserves havens for wildlife and people, by following this code:

- Dogs disturb wildlife by their mere presence. Please check that dogs are permitted to visit and if so please keep your dog under control (preferably on a short lead) at all times, taking particular care during spring and summer, and when grazing animals or ground nesting birds are present.
- Please clean up after your dog and take this and any litter away with you.
- Please do not remove any plants or animals from nature reserves.
- Sheep, ponies and cattle are often used to graze our nature reserves. Please avoid disturbing these animals and take great care when in the vicinity of grazing animals if you have a dog with you.

- Please keep to the paths wherever possible.
- Please be considerate to other visitors to the site. This is particularly important in viewing hides – respect the quiet!
- Close all gates and avoid trespass or disturbance to adjacent property.
- Take care to avoid disturbing birds or other animals especially during the spring and early summer when they are breeding.
- Some sites are subject to flooding following heavy rainfall or snowmelt, so please take special care at these times.
- Do not light fires – some habitats, especially heathlands, can be very vulnerable.
- If you wish to report an incident or injured grazing animal please call 01302 570077.

When should you visit?

Visiting a nature reserve hoping to see a particular plant or animal can often lead to disappointment and even when species such as otters are present you have to be very lucky to see one. Timing your visit to when few other visitors are present such as dawn and dusk, during the week, or even when the weather is not so good, could mean that there has been less disturbance and could lead to that once in a lifetime sighting. Even more importantly, check whether the wildlife you hope to see is present at the time of year you plan to visit. Many insects, birds and plants are seasonal and may only be found for a short period of time and visiting outside of their season will mean you won't find them. Weather conditions can also play a role. For example, sites such as Spurn and Flamborough Cliffs can be exceptional for watching migrating birds, but this spectacle is much influenced by the weather.

Upland peatlands

Mossdale Common

Yorkshire's upland peatlands are unique, evoking a sense of unrivalled wildness. In Yorkshire alone there are nearly 70,000 ha of peatlands. These habitats overlay deep blanket peat which supports a variety of wonderful species.

Peatlands burst with colour throughout the year; from purple heather in late summer to a blanket of white winter snow. Closer inspection reveals a patchwork of reds, golds, pinks, browns and greens of sphagnum mosses without which there would be no peatland. Peatlands are enormously valuable habitats not only for their unusual wildlife but as the world's biggest land carbon stores, as purifiers of the water we drink and for the fascinating cultural heritage they preserve stretching back to the Iron Age.

Peatlands are home to rare and wonderful wildlife; the call of curlew and the acrobatics of lapwing characterise the landscape. Not to be overlooked are the smaller species such as the huge array of invertebrates, lichens and, as previously mentioned, sphagnum mosses. They host specialist species such as sundew, cranberries and cloudberries as well as the unmistakeable red grouse.

Red grouse

Sphagnum capillifolium

Bilberry

SPECTACLE

Visit the uplands in August to witness the rolling purple haze – heather flowering at its best.

Common lizard

Peatland habitats are vulnerable. The action of people over the centuries has increased their vulnerability; 80% of the UK's peatlands are damaged, which means that peat is eroding away, releasing vast amounts of carbon dioxide, worsening climate change and threatening wildlife. Through careful management, damage is being reversed, drains that were cut into the landscape are being blocked and vegetation is being introduced to bare areas. With these measures, the survival of these vital and evocative landscapes can be ensured.

Round-leaved sundew and Sphagnum papillosum

Woodlands

Bluebells at North Cliffe Nature Reserve

Woodlands are rarely wall to wall with trees. The best woods consist of a patchwork of mature trees interspersed with patches of scrubby bushes, young trees and open areas where grasses and wildflowers flourish.

This mosaic of glades, rides, thickets and stands of large trees create a varied habitat and changing conditions, very different from the dark commercial forests we see in the uplands. The mass of plants, both living and dead, provides food for many different species of insect and other invertebrates, providing food in turn for birds and small mammals, especially bats.

Woodlands change dramatically with the seasons. They can be quiet, gloomy places in winter, punctuated by roving flocks of tits and twittering flocks of finches such as siskin and lesser redpoll. In spring sleeping woods burst into life as bright wood anemone, lesser celandine and early purple orchid cover the floor and the air is filled with birdsong. The breathtaking spectacle of a haze of bluebells under the vibrant green new leaves of hazel and oak is a sight not to miss and several Yorkshire Wildlife Trust nature reserves host this wonder annually.

Summer is a tranquil time as the view is blurred with many shades of green leaves, with a backdrop of the buzzing of hoverflies and chirp of crickets. Butterflies abound, though many of our fritillary species have declined in parallel with traditional management practises. Autumn sees frenetic activity as jays, wood mice and grey squirrels mop up the harvest of seeds and nuts,

Stoat

Hart's tongue fern

SPECTACLE
Sunny summer afternoons can be a great time to watch woodland butterflies nectaring on bramble and thistle flowers along woodland rides.

creating a larder for the winter ahead. Fungi replace wildflowers, covering all surfaces in a dazzling array of form and colour.

In many parts of Yorkshire, woodland would be the natural vegetation if nature was left to its own devices. The woodland we see today is either very recently planted or is semi-natural, with a history of exploitation by people. Woodlands have long been a valuable resource, with the most obvious products being timber and fuel. Woodlands were also valued for hunting, with glades used for grazing livestock.

Great spotted woodpecker

Speckled wood

Grasslands

Brockadale

Grasslands are one of our most colourful habitats. Wherever you are in Yorkshire you can find some of this semi-natural habitat not far from your doorstep.

Move from the close cropped acidic grassland of Yorkshire's uplands, through the calcareous grasslands found on our rolling hills to lush lowland meadows found along our rivers and the weather beaten coastal grasslands hanging on to the cliff tops along the Yorkshire coastline.

Species rich grasslands would once have covered huge tracts of our Yorkshire landscape but, over the last century or so, human activity has caused huge losses to these habitats through agricultural intensification and development. Today, some of these natural habitats are preserved in relatively small areas, many of which are managed as nature reserves by Yorkshire Wildlife Trust or others – and very much worth a visit.

Acidic grassland in the Yorkshire Dales, the Moors and the Peaks, is often found amongst bog and heath. It is also associated with lowland

heaths in the Vale of York. Packed with delicate little plants, these often short, well grazed grasslands need a close look to appreciate their value. Vivid yellow tormentil flowers are scattered with the tiny white heads of heath bedstraw, and the orangey-red spikes of sheep's fescue. Grasses include fescues and wavy hair-grass, whose flowers form an amazing pink haze over this grassland in mid-summer.

Calcareous grassland can be seen on our Yorkshire Wolds grassland nature reserves, along the 'spine' of the county on the magnesian limestone ridge and also on

Marbled white

Pyramidal orchid

Skylark

the fixed dunes at Spurn. These grasslands are very showy starting in spring with cowslip and violet, through summer's display of orchids including pyramidal, bee and fragrant, to autumn's show of pinks and purples in various species of scabious, knapweeds and autumn gentian. Some rare species are also found within these grasslands including thistle broomrape, autumn ladies tresses and rare spring sedge. Not to mention the clouds of butterflies you can see feeding on the flowers including common blue, marbled white and ringlet.

Neutral grassland remains along some of our river valleys in Yorkshire and is found in areas where management has changed very little for centuries, with hay cutting and grazing being key to their continuing diversity. Large tracts of species rich wet grassland occurs at Wheldrake Ings and along the River Derwent and in smaller pockets at Fen Carr and Owston Meadow near Doncaster. Not only do these meadows have stunning shows of flowering plants but are also home to breeding birds including curlew, snipe, redshank and lapwing.

Bee orchid

Farmlands

SPECTACLE

Any winter stubble or weedy set aside is worth looking at for flocks of larks, finches and buntings. Scan from your car or behind a hedge to avoid disturbance.

Corn bunting

Often overlooked as a valuable habitat, farmlands are essential for Yorkshire Wildlife Trust's Living Landscapes Vision, allowing species under increasing pressure from development and climate change to move across the countryside.

Yorkshire's widely varied topography and geology means that the character of our farmland also varies across the county from the highly productive arable land of the Humberhead Levels and South Yorkshire through to the much less intensive sheep and cattle grazed areas of uplands, in the Yorkshire Dales and South Pennines.

Increased uptake of government grants such as Entry/Higher Level Stewardship (ELS/HLS) and English Woodland Grant Scheme (EWGS), which provide funding for environmental work on farms and in woodlands has encouraged and enabled landowners to work with nature rather than seeing it as a barrier to commercial gain.

Beef shorthorn cattle

These schemes can produce a wide range of benefits to the countryside from relatively simple habitat gains such as taking the edges of fields out of production (known as field margins) to more complex works such as creation of large wetland areas or species rich flower meadows. Yorkshire Wildlife Trust has an established tradition of working in close co-operation with farmers across the county from smallholders right up to the much larger landed estates that can cover huge swathes of land. We believe strongly that these areas of land are vital to the development of a sustainable countryside and that the people who manage them are key stakeholders in their future. Farmlands managed with wildlife in mind can hold a huge array of bird, mammal and invertebrate species, so next time you are planning a walk, why not find a route with Public Rights of Way through the farmed landscape and see what sights and experiences await?

Harvesting potatoes

Grey partridge

Urban landscapes

Fox

The villages, towns and cities of Yorkshire may look like hostile places for wildlife, but look a little closer and a wealth of plants and animals can be found.

Over one million acres of gardens exist across the UK and this mosaic of vegetable patches, lawns, flower borders and compost heaps provide a really valuable wildlife habitat. As such, gardens, along with ex-industrial sites ('brownfield' sites), river corridors, footpaths and road verges are vital in

Yorkshire Wildlife Trust's vision for a Living Landscape. Towns and cities can be barriers to wildlife movement, but by improving areas for wildlife within urban areas we can reconnect the landscape. These urban oases can act as corridors for wildlife to disperse along or as stepping stones.

Some of our top predators such as foxes, otters and peregrines are now a frequent sight in some of our urban areas. This is testament to the improving fortunes of some of these species in the wider countryside thanks to

Raking cuttings at Foss Islands, York

Blue tit

Buff-tailed bumblebee

Hedgehog

conservation efforts. It is also a hint at how adaptable wildlife can be, as animals and plants exploit new opportunities.

Many of the species living in gardens would have originally inhabited the woodland edge, where trees and shrubs exist side by side with grasslands and other open areas. Undoubtedly, gardens have provided an excellent substitute habitat for blackbird, hedgehog and pipistrelle bats.

Many of us live in urban areas and can all do our bit to help wildlife. Even a window-box planted with nectar-rich flowers can help the local bees and butterflies. Those with a slightly larger plot can help wildlife in a wide range of ways, from digging a pond, erecting a nestbox or planting native shrubs and trees.

As the pressure mounts on wildlife in rural areas, gardens and other urban habitats will become increasingly important sanctuaries for both people and wildlife.

Wetlands

Potteric Carr

Yorkshire, like many counties of England would have once hosted vast floodplain wetlands including the impenetrable marshes in the Vales of York and Pickering and the vast peatlands of the Humberhead Levels.

A combination of drainage and improvement has transformed lowland Yorkshire. Apart from the island that is the Thorne and Hatfield Moors National Nature Reserve, only isolated fragments of wetlands remain. That is not to say Yorkshire has no wetlands. The activities of people have created modern wetlands which will never replace native habitats but do provide homes to many species. Swathes of sand and gravels along the river valleys have been exploited through quarrying and left chains of new wetlands, many of which have been set up and managed with wildlife in mind. North Cave Wetlands, just west of Hull, is a working example. As extraction finishes the land is redesigned and landscaped for wildlife, before being handed to Yorkshire Wildlife Trust. This has created a mosaic of wet grassland, open water, reedbed, fen and damp woodland, which in turn hosts a wealth of species. Dragonflies thrive in this landscape, whilst avocet, lapwing and little ringed plover all breed. Large numbers of ducks pass through or winter on the site and the occasional marsh harrier or black tern enlivens a spring or autumn day.

Other sites, such as Potteric Carr, have evolved through mining subsidence, with sinking land levels allowing wet conditions to re-establish. Along our river valleys, particularly the Lower Derwent near York and Selby, the valley still floods during the winter attracting internationally-important numbers of wildfowl and waders. These seasonal wetlands have changed

Dipper

Emerald damselfy

SPECTACLE

Wetlands are exciting places throughout the year as different bird species pass through on migration. For the biggest numbers of wintering wildfowl, visit between November and February.

little with the centuries and traditional management in some areas such as at Wheldrake Ings ensure the flourishing of the rare floodplain meadows once the water recedes each spring.

Water courses and bodies in upland areas seem comparatively lifeless, though look more closely and despite the lack of nutrients reducing their natural productivity, they still host much wildlife. The white-breasted bobbing dipper and citrine-bellied grey wagtail vie for the best stones protruding from foaming streams as they seek out larval or adult caddis flies which prosper in the clean, oxygen-rich water.

North Cave Wetlands

Great crested newt

The Yorkshire Coast

Flamborough Cliffs

Yorkshire has a varied and dramatic North Sea coastline, stretching south from the rugged, rocky coast near Whitby in North Yorkshire to the 'great white cape' of Flamborough Head and along the crumbling, soft, low-lying Holderness coast to the unique, sinuous dune-encrusted peninsula of Spurn, jutting out over the mouth of the Humber Estuary.

This variety provides Yorkshire with a staggering array of marine and coastal wildlife – among the best in the world.

Here are a few highlights:

Seabird frenzy
Seabirds need two things; safe breeding areas free from predators and a good feeding ground. In Yorkshire we have both and as a consequence every spring and summer we host one of the most impressive mainland wildlife spectacles in the UK. The breathtaking sheer vertical chalk cliffs of Flamborough Head provide a home to tens of thousands of gannets, fulmars, kittiwakes, guillemots, razorbills and everyone's favourite, puffins. The birds occupy the narrowest of ledges on the cliff faces, stacks, caves and nooks to bring up their families. Offshore lies the second main requirement – fish! Yorkshire waters teem with fish and the large, shallow, sandy offshore area known as the Dogger Bank attracts many of Flamborough's seabirds to feed.

Mud glorious mud!
As far removed from the towering cliffs of Flamborough as you could get are the horizonless expanses of mud and sand in the Humber Estuary. One of the most important estuaries for migrating and wintering birds, this landscape is rich in life. The mud is home to a staggering number of

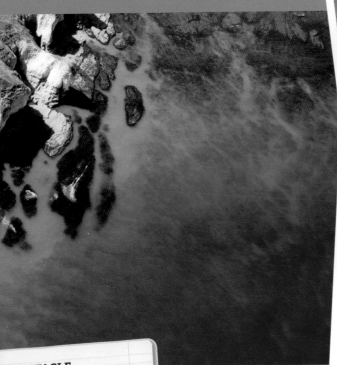

Common lobster

Gannets

invertebrates, from large ragworms, lugworms and razorclams to tiny bivalves and shrimps. It is this proliferation of unseen life that supports the vast flocks of wading birds and wildfowl that make the Humber their home for at least part of the year.

Out of sight

Whilst the coastal habitats may be the most visible, what is even more spectacular are the habitats that lie beneath the sea along Yorkshire's coast. We get a glimpse of this magical environment during each low tide, in that no-man's land known as the intertidal zone. Rocky shores are best, so the northern Yorkshire coastline is the place to look. Rockpools can

simply teem with life – orange starfish pause among bright red beadlet anemones, whilst in the shadows several species of crab lurk, peering out from nooks and crannies. Look closer and you may spot a tiny, yet exquisite sea slug, feeding on encrusting sea mats. Like many other habitats, the intertidal changes with the season, so you will need to come back again to see what's new. If you can dive or snorkel then a whole new world will be opened up. The chalk reefs and caves off Flamborough Head provide home to colourful fish, such as ballan wrasse, alongside lobsters, sponges and the soft coral dead man's fingers.

Dunlins

Living Seas Centre

This page is sponsored by Centrica Storage Lt

Mud magic

Rockpooling

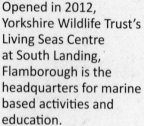

Opened in 2012, Yorkshire Wildlife Trust's Living Seas Centre at South Landing, Flamborough is the headquarters for marine based activities and education.

The North Sea is home to a fantastically diverse set of creatures from kelp forests to spiny starfish and with a visit to the centre you can learn all about these and everything else that lives under the waves, along the shoreline and on the beach, as well as the seabirds that make the most of the bountiful seas.

As well as providing innovative interpretation and education materials, the Living Seas Centre is the base for a wide range of marine-themed events including beach cleans, Shoresearch, snorkel safaris and boat trips.

A small office also enables the Living Seas team to further their work in marine advocacy, awareness and research.

For more information on the centre and events run from there check our website ywt.org.uk or visit the Living Seas Facebook page facebook.com/YWTLivingSeas.

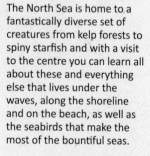

Shoresearch

Pearson Park Wildlife Garden

Veg patch

Bee keeping

Bat detecting

There is a hidden gem in Hull's city centre, which is well worth a visit at any time of the year. Yorkshire Wildlife Trust's Pearson Park Wildlife Garden is just off Princes Avenue in Hull and is a base for many of the educational activities and events that the Trust carries out in the area.

20 years ago this fabulous wildlife garden was covered in concrete, but the hard work of local people transformed it into an inner city wildlife habitat to be enjoyed by all. The Trust took over the lease in 2009 and staff and volunteers have been busy there ever since.

The wildlife garden boasts a meadow, ponds, wooded area, vegetable patch and herb garden. There are also several bee hives there, with staff trained to take care of these buzzing friends.

For more information about events held at Pearson Park Wildlife Garden and in the surrounding area then take a look at our website ywt.org.uk, or visit Pearson Park's Facebook page facebook.com/YWTPearson or drop into the office on site.

Stirley Community Farm

Harvest time

A young volunteer

Stirley Community Farm is an exciting venture into the world of food and farming for Yorkshire Wildlife Trust. The farm near Huddersfield was taken on by the Trust in 2011 and has moved at an unrelenting pace since then, with the aim of demonstrating that farming and wildlife can exist hand-in-hand, whilst sustaining itself as a viable social enterprise.

Once again a busy, working farm following dereliction after failing as a diary farm, the Trust has introduced a herd of beef shorthorn cattle, developed a thriving vegetable garden, planted an orchard and begun work on a forest garden.

A jam packed events programme exists from regular gardening clubs where individuals can come to learn more about growing their own, to guided walks around the farm and surrounding areas to show how it is possible to manage a species rich landscape even if agricultural.

Plans are afoot to convert one of the barns into an education centre where formal training and school visits can be accommodated. The farm has been welcomed by the local community, with great support for what the Trust is trying to achieve and a team of dedicated volunteers helping to shape it.

For more information on events held at Stirley Community Farm visit our website ywt.org.uk or the farm's Facebook page facebook.com/YWTStirley.

Veg box

Painting

Green crafts

Yorkshire Wildlife Trust's flagship nature reserve in Doncaster is a base not only for staff working on projects in the local area but also a dedicated education and events team. With facilities including a pond dipping platform, classroom, and equipment including butterfly nets and identification guides, the Trust is able to run a diverse and exciting events programme at the nature reserve.

Activities run throughout the year, and there are events suitable for all ages and all abilities. Events vary from pond dipping sessions and bat walks, to wild foraging and moth trapping to name but a few. A particularly busy programme runs during the school holidays, with events suitable for families running most days.

Make sure you leave plenty of time either side of an event to explore this fantastic nature reserve; with over six miles of pathway, a shop and café, and scores of wildlife to see.

For more information on what's going on at Potteric Carr see our website ywt.org.uk or the nature reserve's Facebook page facebook.com/YWTPotteric or alternatively have a word with the staff on reception.

Pond dipping

ADEL DAM

Adel Dam, a tranquil nature reserve tucked out of sight, has emerged from a centuries-old working dam and the surrounding land. A rare combination of wet and dry woodland surrounds a lake and pond frequently visited by kingfishers – the number one attraction. Masses of bluebells and fungi in season are also exceptional.

This woodland nature reserve straddles Adel Beck which runs through a shallow valley, with the former dam central. Mature native and exotic trees can be found in the mixed woodland, with as many as 36 species. Alder and willow dominate the wet woodland, with sphagnum moss on the ground. Oak, birch, holly, rowan, yew and ash are found in the dry woodland, alongside introduced species like Corsican pine.

Broad buckler ferns and brambles cover the floor with fine showings of bluebells and marsh marigolds in spring and foxgloves in the summer. A stop off at Marsh Hide to look over the pond and feeding station will reward you with sightings of chaffinch, nuthatch and great spotted woodpecker. Moorhen, coot and mandarin can be seen bringing up their families in summer from the Lake Hide.

Kingfishers – Adel Dam's main attraction – have bred here; if you are lucky you will catch a flash of their bright blue. Elusive species include water rail and lesser spotted woodpeckers. Birds of prey also frequent the site, with resident sparrowhawk and visits from red kites and buzzards. Fungi flourish amongst the standing and lying dead trees. Badgers and roe deer visit the site, and a family of foxes have made the nature reserve their home.

The site has been noted for its special ecology since 1830 and has been a nature reserve since 1968. Once an operational dam, it fell into disuse with the gradual demise of the water industry. It then became a central feature of a Victorian garden, around which many additional trees were planted. The dam was later breached in the 1930s, allowing water to escape to form the current lake. A loyal supporters group work hard on site, carrying out general maintenance tasks. Plans are in place to increase diversity in the dry woodland, by reducing sycamores and replanting with low to mid canopy shrubs and trees, as well as developing some reed beds.

NEAREST POSTCODE
LS16 8BX

GRID REFERENCE
SE 272 414

RESERVE SIZE
7.77 ha

PUBLIC TRANSPORT
Take a bus from Leeds or Otley, alight at Golden Acre Park

DIRECTIONS
Take underpass from Golden Acre car park (off A660) into the park, then follow the footpaths to the bridle path. Follow this to the nature reserve entrance. There are wheelchair-friendly paths from car park to the nature reserve and to Marsh Hide, a RADAR key is required by wheelchair users at the nature reserve entrance.

OTHER INFORMATION
Café and toilets in adjacent Golden Acre Park. Limited wheelchair access, paths are more rugged and muddy after the Marsh Hide. Covered entrance lobby with seating for picnics.

Top tip...

For a peaceful walk come to Adel Dam – a joy to visit in any season. Spring flowers put on a wonderful show, and a couple of kingfishers might be chanced upon at any time.

Golden Acre Park

Arthington Road →

← A660

Bridlepath

Adel Beck

N

0   100yds

Bakery Café & Toilets
Golden Acre Park
Arthington Road
Otley
A660
Leeds
Bridlepath
Hotel
Adel Dam
N

kingfisher

Can be seen fishing

Sphagnum squarrosum

Covers the ground in the wet woodland area

SPRING
Bluebell
Marsh marigold
Blackcap
Frog spawn

SUMMER
Dragonflies
Damselflies
Bats

AUTUMN
Fieldfare
Siskin
Lesser redpoll
Fungi

WINTER
Teal
Goosander
Little grebe

AGDEN BOG

Situated in the beautiful Bradfield Dale, on the north west corner of Agden Resevoir, Agden Bog Nature Reserve is a classic example of a type of bog that has now mostly disappeared from our landscape following the draining of the land for agriculture. Rich in flora, colour springs forth from purple moor-grass and heath spotted orchids. Birds, mammals and amphibians all thrive in this exceptional place.

NEAREST POSTCODE
S6 6LJ

GRID REFERENCE
SK 252 930

RESERVE SIZE
1.92 ha

PUBLIC TRANSPORT
A bus runs from Hillsborough to Bradfield, 1km from the nature reserve.

DIRECTIONS
Access from the A6102, taking the High Bradfield road at Oughtibridge. From High Bradfield turn right, half-way down the hill to Low Bradfield. Drive round Agden Resevoir and park off-road on the left just before right-hand bend and opposite the houses.

The nature reserve is most notable for its botanical interest, with vegetation varying from sphagnum beds, purple moor-grass dominated wet grassland, extensive bracken beds to birch woodland. Round-leaved sundew and cranberry are common amongst the moist sphagnum beds, whilst in the early summer hundreds of flowering heads from heath spotted orchids poke up, brightening the landscape. These are followed by the golden spikes of bog asphodel, and later in the season, the purple-blue globes of devil's-bit scabious. A patch of adder's tongue fern may also be found.

The site is also good for spotting a number of mammals including brown hare and roe deer. Birds including nightjar, spotted flycatcher, siskin, lesser redpoll and common sandpiper have all been recorded nesting nearby, and black grouse may be seen. Common toads, common frogs and common lizards also make the nature reserve their home. Less common are golden-ringed dragonflies which breed on the mire and can sometimes be seen hawking over the site, or sunning on the tops of vegetation clumps.

Yorkshire Wildlife Trust is hoping to initiate a grazing regime; this would reduce the area of purple moor-grass and bracken, which will encourage expansion of the sphagnum beds. Common butterwort once grew amongst these beds and it is hoped grazing may enable its return. The site is currently managed with the kind assistance of Wharncliffe Heathlands Trust.

Tormentil and cross-leaved heath

Devil's-bit scabious

An important late summer nectar source

LOCATION

Agden Dyke

Agden Bog

Stone wall

Smallfield Lane

Huddersfield
A616
Stocksbridge
A6102
A629
A61
35A
A61
35
A629
Agden Bog
High Bradfield
Oughtibridge
B6087
M1
Low Bradfield
Sheffield
N

← **Bradfield Dale**

P

Agden Reservoir

N

0 — 400yds

Low Bradfield ↓

High Bradfield & Low Bradfield →

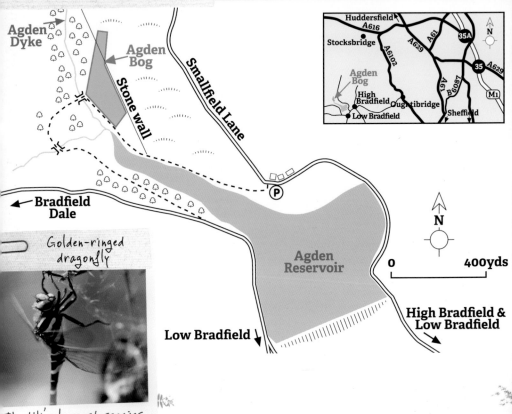

Golden-ringed dragonfly

The UK's largest species can be found here

Top tip...

Don't forget to take a magnifying glass on your visit so that you can fully appreciate the beauty of the sphagnum mosses and sundews.

SPRING	SUMMER	AUTUMN	WINTER
Cuckoo	Dragonflies	Starling roost	Peregrine
Swallow	Damselflies		Merlin
Sedge warbler	Marsh orchid		Barn owl
Reed warbler	Devil's-bit		
Heath spotted orchid	scabious		

ALLERTHORPE COMMON

Bees buzzing around sweet smelling purple spikes of heather, a green woodpecker 'yaffling' from the woodland edge, an adder shyly slithering into the undergrowth below prickly coconut-scented gorse bushes – all make up the sights, sounds and smells of Allerthorpe Common.

Allerthorpe Common is alive with wildlife throughout the year and supports a surprising range of habitats for such a small pocket of lowland heath – wet heath, dry heath, acid grassland, woodland, scrub and open water are all waiting to be discovered.

The lowland heath habitat found here once stretched right across the Vale of York, but now only remains in isolated fragments. This habitat and the wildlife it supports are now rare across the UK. Much of the flat, fertile land it is found on has been used by humans over time for agriculture and development, meaning nationally we have lost over 80% of this habitat since 1800 – making those areas we have left even more important.

Ling heather, tormentil, sheep's fescue and wavy hair-grass grow on the drier areas of the site. In spring listen out for the song of woodlark. Cross-leaved heath, purple moor grass and the locally rare St John's-wort grow in the damper areas as well as nationally rare May lily. Patches of gorse scrub provide shelter for birds and their network of roots support a healthy population of adders. Areas of mature birch and willow woodland add another dimension to the site – great spotted woodpecker may sometimes be seen. One large pool and several smaller ponds support numerous damselfly and dragonfly species including broad-bodied chaser and blue-tailed damselfly.

Sitting within Forestry Commission woodland, the site has historically been an oasis for wildlife typical of lowland heaths. One of the best areas on the Common, it was designated as a SSSI in 1965 and Yorkshire Wildlife Trust has managed the site since 1966. More recently the Forestry Commission has left open large tracts of coniferous forest felled for timber surrounding the nature reserve. This land is now returning to lowland heath allowing species from the nature reserve to colonise. On site grazing using rare breed longhorn cattle helps keep tree saplings and some of the coarse competitive grasses that can take over the heath in check. On top of this volunteers work regularly to control bramble and bracken that can become a problem and remove any birch saplings that the cattle have missed.

NEAREST POSTCODE
YO42 4RU

GRID REFERENCE
SE 761 475

RESERVE SIZE
5.57 ha

PUBLIC TRANSPORT
York – Hull buses stop at Barmby Moor village, 2.3 miles away.

DIRECTIONS
Turn south off the A1079 near Barmby Moor signed Sutton-on-Derwent and Thornton. Take the next left signposted Thornton, and parking is in a Forestry Commission car park 0.5 miles along this road on the right. From here cross the road and follow the forest track until you come to a line of pylons. Turn right and the nature reserve is a short distance along on your right.

SITE DESIGNATION
SSSI

OTHER INFORMATION
Do not get too close to the adders, they have a venomous bite if threatened. Paths are unsurfaced.

LOCATION

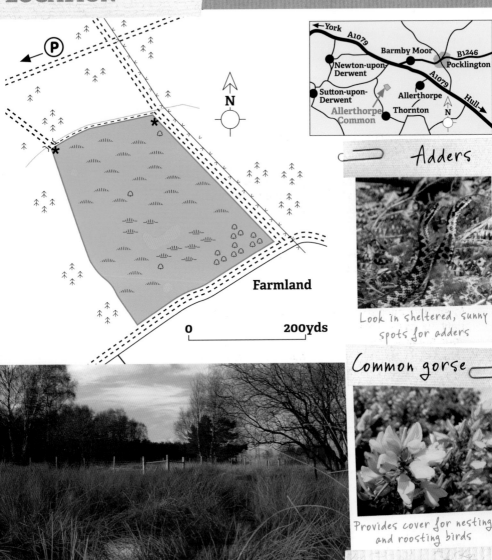

Farmland

0   200yds

(inset map) York — A1079 — Barmby Moor — B1246 — Pocklington — Newton-upon-Derwent — Sutton-upon-Derwent — Allerthorpe — A1079 — Hull — Thornton — **Allerthorpe Common**

Adders

Look in sheltered, sunny spots for adders

Common gorse

Provides cover for nesting and roosting birds

Top tip...

Visit early on a sunny morning between February and April and you are almost guaranteed close-up views of basking adders. **Do not get too close though as adders do have a venomous bite if threatened.**

SPRING	SUMMER	AUTUMN	WINTER
Adder	Tormentil	Woodcock	Jay
Woodlark	Ling heather	Tit flocks	Coal tit
Common frog	Marsh cinquefoil	Siskin	Treecreeper
Willow warbler	Damselflies	Lesser redpoll	
Yellowhammer	Dragonflies		

Adder

Vipera berus

Adder

☑ SPRING ☐ WOODLAND
☑ SUMMER ☑ MOORLAND
☐ AUTUMN ☑ LOWLAND HEATH
☐ WINTER ☐ FARMLAND

Yorkshire's only venomous snake is common in suitable habitats throughout the county and its confiding habits mean it is more frequently seen than our other snake species; the grass snake.

Adders are not aggressive and usually only bite if handled or trodden on. They are dangerous to dogs and small children, but nobody has died in the UK from an adder bite for many years. Early spring is an excellent time to watch adders emerge from their winter hibernation sites and bask in the weak spring sunshine to warm up. Look along sheltered south-facing banks in suitable areas.

When temperatures increase, adders are very active and the males compete vigorously for females in bouts of wrestling. Unlike grass snakes, which lay eggs, female adders give birth to live young, usually around late summer. The young adders are tiny copies of the adult snake, about the size of an earthworm. As winter approaches, adders make their way back to traditional underground hibernation sites, following scent trails laid down by other snakes over several years.

Adders are easy to distinguish from grass snakes as they have an inverted 'v' on their neck and a strong zigzag or diamond shaped markings down the length of their backs. Grass snakes are more uniform with a distinctive pale whitish collar just behind their heads. Adders vary in colour with males tending to be pale grey or whitish with the black zigzag, females pale brownish, although some individuals are black.

Adders are most frequently found in lowland heath sites, such as Allerthorpe Common and Calley Heath, but also in moorland areas of the Dales and North York Moors. As with all reptiles adders are protected by law, so please do not interfere with them if discovered – and keep your distance to avoid a painful bite!

Badger
Meles meles

- ☑ SPRING
- ☑ SUMMER
- ☑ AUTUMN
- ☐ WINTER

- ☑ WOODLAND
- ☑ PASTURELAND
- ☐ WETLAND
- ☑ FARMLAND

Protected since 1992

Badgers are part of the weasel family, Mustelidae, which all have musk-bearing glands under their tails and includes otters, polecats, stoats, weasels and pine martens.

Badgers grow up to 75cm and weigh around 10–12kg, about the same as an average one-year-old human baby. Female badgers, or sows are smaller than the male or boar. Badgers have black and white fur but this often gives them a greyish look at a distance. Their instantly-recognisable black and white striped head is very distinctive and is used as the logo of The Wildlife Trusts. Badgers live in woodlands and copses, especially where these are attached to pastureland.

With powerful front legs and sharp claws, badgers are great at digging and construct their underground homes in well-drained soil. These 'setts' are often the first indicator that badgers are present, along with small dung pits that are used to mark territorial boundaries. Setts have a horizontal, rugby ball shaped hole with a large heap of disturbed soil around the entrance. Clans of badgers living in a sett usually comprise of about 15 animals, though this can vary. Badgers do not hibernate, but their emergence from below ground becomes much more erratic during the winter. Occasionally other species may be tolerated within the same sett complex, such as foxes.

Badgers are widespread throughout the UK and although generally nocturnal can be seen during the day, especially in periods of dry weather when food is scarce. Badgers are omnivorous and very opportunistic feeders. They will eat earthworms, mice, frogs, voles and snails but also roots, fruits, acorns, beech mast and peanuts left out for garden birds. Badgers are protected under the 1992 Protection of Badgers Act.

ASHBERRY

One of the finest ancient woodlands in Yorkshire, which is bordered by flower-rich limestone grassland on the valley sides and a marshy valley bottom through which a crystal-clear stream flows.

The habitats within the nature reserve are heavily influenced by the underlying geology of the site. Glacial melt water carved out the steep sided valley, cutting through different rock layers. The valley forms part of a system of small steep sided valleys in this area with tributaries of the River Rye running through them.

The very thin soils on the upper slopes of the valley support areas of unimproved limestone grassland and woodland with a very high diversity of specialised plant species. The middle and lower slopes of the valley are also wooded and contain a range of bird species including nuthatch, treecreeper and wood warbler.

In the valley bottom there are areas of neutral grassland, mire and carr woodland. Where the calcium rich springs that flow through the site reach the valley bottom extensive areas of marsh exist, with many rare plant and insect species associated. These include bird's-eye primrose, globe flower, marsh hawk's-beard and grass of Parnassus. Black bog-rush occurs in two of the larger areas of springs, and common butterwort and marsh lousewort (or red rattle) are widespread. Red, fallow and roe deer are present in the area and an early morning visit could be rewarded with a sighting of them grazing the grassland along the steeply wooded valley sides. Freshwater shrimps and white-clawed crayfish are found in the stream that runs through the site.

NEAREST POSTCODE
YO62 5LE

GRID REFERENCE
SE 568 845

RESERVE SIZE
51.85 ha

PUBLIC TRANSPORT
A bus service runs to nearby Helmsley from Scarborough, Malton and York. In the summer months Moorsbus run a service between Helmsley and Rievaulx.

DIRECTIONS
½ mile west of Rievaulx and about 3 miles north west of Helmsley. If approaching from Helmsley, take the B1257 Stokesley road for approximately 1½ miles and take a left hand turning onto Scawton road. Descend through the woods, turn left across the river Rye and turn right towards Old Byland after a further ¼ mile. Very limited road side parking, access to the nature reserve is via a small gate.

SITE DESIGNATION
SSSI

OTHER INFORMATION
Dogs are allowed on the public right of way on leads. Bikes allowed on bridleway only.

Wood anemone

Fallow deer stag

Top tip...
Visit early in the morning for a chance of glimpsing herds of fallow deer.

LOCATION

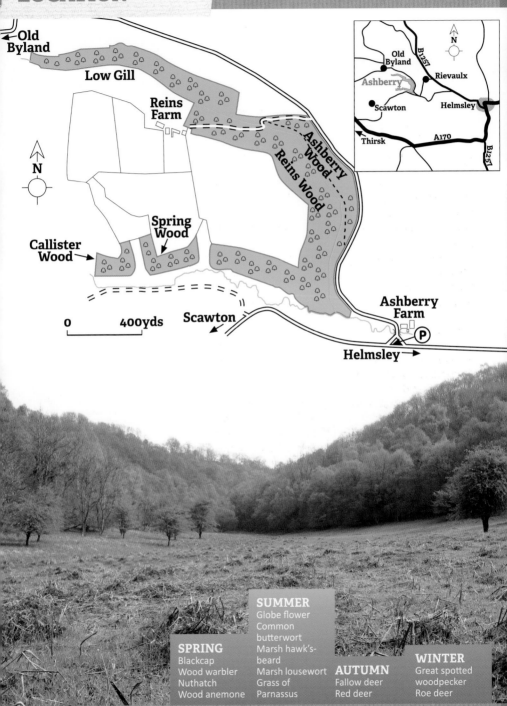

Old Byland

Low Gill

Reins Farm

Ashberry Wood

Reins Wood

N

Spring Wood

Callister Wood

N
Old Byland
B1257
Rievaulx
Ashberry
Scawton
Helmsley
Thirsk
A170
B1257

0   400yds

Scawton

Ashberry Farm

P

Helmsley →

SPRING
Blackcap
Wood warbler
Nuthatch
Wood anemone

SUMMER
Globe flower
Common butterwort
Marsh hawk's-beard
Marsh lousewort
Grass of Parnassus

AUTUMN
Fallow deer
Red deer

WINTER
Great spotted woodpecker
Roe deer

ASKHAM BOG

Magnificent royal ferns, rare gingerbread sedge and spectacular displays of water violets are to be found in this mosaic of fen, woodland and meadow.

Askham Bog is a remarkable survivor of the ancient fenlands of Yorkshire. It occupies the site of an ancient lake, left behind by a retreating glacier 15,000 years ago – the low hill to the south of the Bog, along which the A64 road runs, is the terminal moraine from that glacier. Since Roman times it has been used by local communities as a source of peat for fuel, resulting in a mosaic of habitats and a legacy of ditches, probably originally used for peat extraction.

The edges of the Bog are kept base-rich by water draining from the moraine and harbour the greatest diversity of plants and insects, including marsh orchids, marsh violet and meadow thistle. The colony of gingerbread sedge in Far Wood is the largest in England and some of the royal ferns are huge and probably very old.

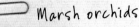

Marsh orchids

Flower in the fen areas in June and July

Siskin

Twittering flocks feed
on alder cones in winter

Yellow flag iris

Large numbers grow
in the wetter areas

SPRING
Brimstone
Chiffchaff
Willow tit
Water violet
Four-spotted
chaser

SUMMER
Grasshopper
warbler
Emperor
dragonfly
Yellow flag iris
Meadow rue
Marsh valerian

AUTUMN
Roe deer
Fieldfare
Redwing
Royal fern

WINTER
Woodcock
Lesser redpoll
Siskin
Goldfinch

ASKHAM BOG

Water violet

The site was once renowned for water beetles and though some rare species still occur, many were lost when the adjacent Challoner's Whin was used as a municipal dumping ground early in the 20th Century. However, the moth fauna is still exceptional, with rare species such as fen square-spot. Birds are abundant, including woodcock, buzzard, willow and marsh tits, grasshopper and reed warblers. In winter huge twittering flocks of goldfinch, lesser redpoll and siskin feed on birch and alder seeds. Roe deer and foxes are seen regularly and the pond is a great place to watch water voles, while overhead many dragonflies including the spectacular emperor can be seen on warm summer days.

In 1946, the Bog was purchased by the famous sweet manufacturers Francis Terry and Arnold Rowntree and the Yorkshire Naturalists' (now Wildlife) Trust was formed to receive it as a gift: Askham Bog therefore holds a special place in the history of nature conservation in Yorkshire. Decades of active management, including cutting meadows for hay and grazing by Exmoor ponies, have restored its biodiversity.

A dazzling display in the ditches and ponds in spring

NEAREST POSTCODE
YO23 2UB

GRID REFERENCE
SE 575 481

RESERVE SIZE
43.87 ha

PUBLIC TRANSPORT
Buses stop adjacent to the nature reserve on the A64 and in the nearby village of Copmanthorpe. A cycle track links to both York and Tadcaster.

DIRECTIONS
Approaching York on the eastbound A64 take the A1036 turn off and then turn sharp left into the car park just after the first set of traffic lights.

SITE DESIGNATION
SSSI

Royal fern

Large examples can be seen from the boardwalk

Top tip...

A real feeling of wildness only a few miles from a city centre and metres from a main road. Try an early morning visit for best chance of an encounter with roe deer, water vole and some of the rarer bird species. Don't miss the spectacular royal ferns!

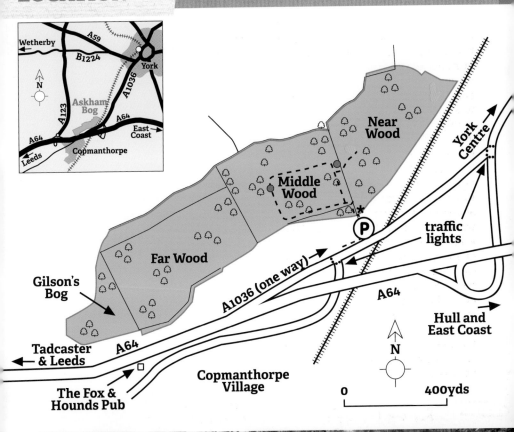

Wetherby

A59

B1224

York

A1036

N

Askham Bog

A123

A64

East Coast

A64

Leeds

Copmanthorpe

Near Wood

York Centre

Middle Wood

Far Wood

Gilson's Bog

traffic lights

P

A1036 (one way)

A64

Tadcaster & Leeds

A64

Hull and East Coast

Copmanthorpe Village

The Fox & Hounds Pub

N

0   400yds

BISHOP MONKTON (RAILWAY CUTTING)

A small haven for wildlife tucked away in an intensively agricultural landscape. Cut into the magnesian limestone belt, this stretch of the now disused London and North Eastern Railway line provides ideal conditions for lime-loving plant species. The rich abundance of flowers and sheltered nature of the site provides sun traps for basking insects, particularly for a number of butterfly species.

Part of the Harrogate to Ripon line of the London and North Eastern Railway, this section became disused in 1967. Once the railway went out of use nature began to take the site over, with flourishing wildflowers and the gradual establishment of trees and scrub around the boundaries of the site. The site now comprises an area of increasingly rare, unimproved neutral and calcareous grassland, supporting a good range of plants, including cowslip, wild marjoram, ox-eye daisy, bird's-foot trefoil, lady's mantle, salad burnet and St John's-wort, creating an attractive swathe of colour in May, June and early July.

Whilst the line was active a railway workers' hut with a garden was located by the side of the track and a number of garden plants have survived and are still in evidence on the site today. Whilst not native, these plants provide additional food sources for insects within the nature reserve and give tantalising glimpses into the industrial past of the site.

The perimeter is bounded by a dense belt of scrub, providing an important habitat for birds, mammals and invertebrates. This scrub is particularly significant in the local area, as the nature reserve is surrounded by arable farmland that provides few such habitats.

In managing this nature reserve, Yorkshire Wildlife Trust aims to maintain the extent and quality of the grassland, along with its margin of scrub.

NEAREST POSTCODE
HG3 3QD

GRID REFERENCE
SE 312 660

RESERVE SIZE
1.85 ha

PUBLIC TRANSPORT
A bus route passes through the village of Burton Leonard (although the nature reserve is some distance outside the village).

DIRECTIONS
The nature reserve lies west of the village of Bishop Monkton. From Harrogate take the Bishop Monkton turning off the A61 Ripon road, continue over the hump back bridge towards the village. Turn round and return to park on the left hand verge, well away from the bridge, which is 'blind' and used by fast traffic. Entrance to the site is through the farm gate close to the bridge and a kissing gate approximately 20m down the edge of the field.

Lesser whitethroat

Listen out for their rattling song in spring

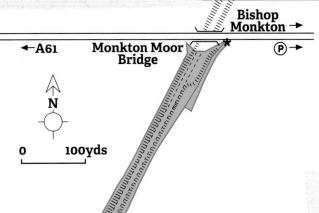

Bishop Monkton →

Monkton Moor Bridge

← A61

P

N

0   100yds

Ripon

Bishop Monkton

P

Bishop Monkton Railway Cutting

Wormald Green

A61

Burton Leonard

Harrogate

N

Gatekeeper

Top tip...

With over 70 species of moths recorded, try visiting in the evening to find some of them yourself!

Seen basking in the sun in sheltered areas

SPRING
Cowslip
Bird's-foot trefoil

SUMMER
Common spotted orchid
Ringlet
Gatekeeper
Comma

BLACKA MOOR

This magnificent moorland of 180 ha provides breath-taking scenery and forms part of a much larger internationally important wild landscape.

Blacka Moor provides spectacular views from the moorland overlooking the City of Sheffield below. This large nature reserve contains a range of upland species and is a great place to watch red deer rutting in the autumn, when the bellows of the impressive stags can be heard across the landscape.

Unique features on Blacka Moor include the varied heather, the gradual transition from woodland to open moor and its population of bilberry bumblebees, *Bombus monticola*. This small upland species is declining and can be seen mainly in the summer months, though queens emerge as early as April. The bumblebees have a short tongue and feed on the nectar of bilberry and heather flowers.

Blacka Moor's diverse migrant bird population includes willow warbler, blackcap, cuckoo, wheatear, stonechat and whinchat. The ease and regularity of seeing red deer on site - the UK's largest land mammal - is also a major bonus. To help the development of this rare heathland habitat, Sheffield Wildlife Trust has reintroduced cattle grazing on site.

Blacka Moor is full of archaeological features, especially in the woodlands, which illustrate its past. Charcoal platforms, white coal kilns, spoil tips, banks and hollow ways are all evidence of the ways in which the woods were used as an integral part of the local economy. This has led to the Trust rejuvenating parts of the woods by restarting some of these woodland activities. A programme has been put together for felling small groups of trees, thinning through some parts of the woodland, coppicing, controlling non-native rhododendrons and installing bird nestboxes. This work will improve the wood not only for birds, but also insects and woodland plants.

Sheffield & Rotherham

NEAREST POSTCODE
S17 3AH

GRID REFERENCE
SK 277 806

RESERVE SIZE
180 ha

PUBLIC TRANSPORT
From Sheffield take the A625 towards the Fox House Inn. The nature reserve is before the Inn.

DIRECTIONS
From Sheffield take the A625 towards Frogatt. The nature reserve is at Fox House, before you reach Frogatt. Car parking is available on Hathersage Road, just before the road splits to Calver and Foxhouse.

SITE DESIGNATION
SSSI, LNR

Antler moth

Top tip...

Visit early in the morning or in the evening for the best chance of seeing red deer.

LOCATION

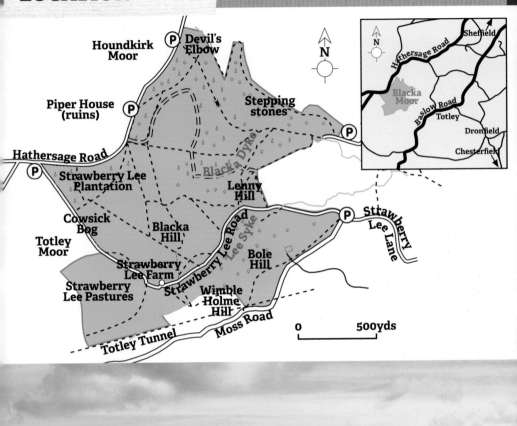

Houndkirk Moor

Devil's Elbow

Piper House (ruins)

Stepping stones

N

Hathersage Road

Blacka Dyke

Strawberry Lee Plantation

Lenny Hill

Cowsick Bog

Blacka Hill

Strawberry Lee Road

Lee Syke

Bole Hill

Totley Moor

Strawberry Lee Farm

Strawberry Lee Pastures

Wimble Holme Hill

Moss Road

Totley Tunnel

Strawberry Lee Lane

Hathersage Road

Sheffield

N

Blacka Moor

Baslow Road

Totley

Dronfield

Chesterfield

0   500yds

SPRING
Willow warbler
Wheatear
Cuckoo
Green hairstreak
Orange
underwing

SUMMER
Curlew
Stonechat
Heather
Bilberry
bumblebee

AUTUMN
Red deer
Fungi

BOLTON-ON-SWALE LAKE

Created through sand and gravel quarrying, this is one of the few large areas of open water in this part of North Yorkshire and attracts a wide range of breeding and wintering waders and wildfowl.

Once a working sand and gravel quarry, Bolton-on-Swale Lake has been landscaped and allowed to flood to provide suitable habitat for a wide range of wetland bird species. Additional planting of trees and bushes at the edge of the lakes and sympathetic management of the surrounding farmland has provided further wildlife friendly habitats.

During the winter months numbers of ducks, geese and waders can be very high, with nationally significant numbers of wigeon using the site. Smaller numbers of goldeneye, pochard, tufted duck and teal can also be seen here. Overwintering waders such as lapwing, curlew and golden plover rely on the permanent grasslands surrounding the lake for food and this is taken into account in the management of these grasslands as part of a working farm.

The large assemblages of wetland birds can sometimes hold more unusual visitors; passage migrant species on site regularly include common sandpiper and occasionally curlew sandpiper, little stint, ruff and whimbrel. Merlin, pink-footed goose and several species of tern have also been recorded on site.

The nature reserve is managed by an agricultural tenant and as such access to the site is limited to the hide adjacent to the site car park, which provides excellent views out over the lake and surrounding fields.

NEAREST POSTCODE
DL10 6AH

GRID REFERENCE
SE 248 987

RESERVE SIZE
34.65 ha

PUBLIC TRANSPORT
A bus route goes through Bolton-on-Swale

DIRECTIONS
From the A1 travelling north enter Catterick and continue north on the A6136 keeping the racecourse on your left. Cross Catterick Bridge and after approximately ½ mile turn right at the cross roads onto the B6271 towards Bolton-on-Swale. Continue for 1½ miles to a road on the right, this is Back Lane which leads to the nature reserve car park. From Northallerton follow the B6271. Pass the signpost to North and South Ellerton on the left, continue for ½ mile to a signpost (Ellerton to Scorton). Fork left down Back Lane to reach the nature reserve car park.

Shoveler

Goosander

Look out for this large duck in winter

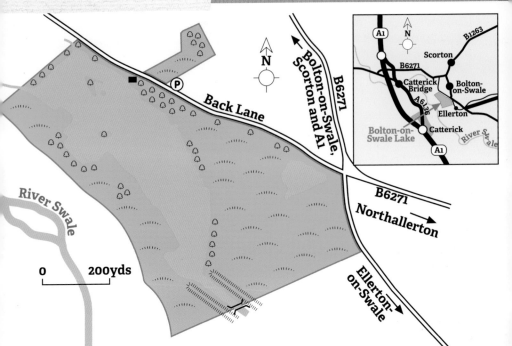

Back Lane

B6271
Bolton-on-Swale,
Scorton and A1

River Swale

0   200yds

B6271
Northallerton →

Ellerton-
on-Swale →

A1
N
Scorton
B1263
B6271
Catterick
Bridge
Bolton-
on-Swale
A6136
Ellerton
Bolton-on-
Swale Lake
Catterick
A1
River Swale

Top tip...

Check out the winter roost of gulls, which can often contain a rarity such as a glaucous or Iceland gull, particularly in late winter.

SPRING
Shoveler
Little ringed plover
Oystercatcher
Sand martin
Yellow wagtail

SUMMER
Great crested grebe
Little grebe

AUTUMN
Teal
Common sandpiper
Green sandpiper
Ruff
Merlin

WINTER
Wigeon
Tufted duck
Pochard
Goldeneye
Golden plover

BRAE PASTURE

Visit Brae Pasture Nature Reserve for breathtaking views across the Ribble Valley. In summer, experience a multitude of plants and flowers, with an expanse of yellow rock-rose in June and the rare Alpine bistort, found here in one of its most southerly locations.

Whilst only covering two fields there is a considerable mix of habitats on this nature reserve including limestone pavement, acid grassland, calcareous flush and a wooded cliff gill. In these habitats over 150 plant species have been recorded including the uncommon Oeder's apple moss (so called as its capsules look like miniature apples), as well as early purple orchid, violet and primrose. Butterflies like the small skipper and common blue thrive feeding off rock-rose, whilst curlew and snipe use the surrounding fields and may be spotted from the nature reserve.

SITE DESIGNATION
Part of Ingleborough SSSI and National Nature Reserve

NEAREST POSTCODE
BD24 0HU

GRID REFERENCE
SD 790 741

RESERVE SIZE
8.58 ha

PUBLIC TRANSPORT
Nearest train station is in Horton-In-Ribblesdale.

DIRECTIONS
Head north from Horton-in-Ribblehead village on B6479. Pass under a railway bridge and travel on for ¾ mile. Once you pass a public footpath sign pull in shortly on your left. Access to the nature reserve is via a stone stile along the public footpath.

Nearby site

SOUTH HOUSE PAVEMENT

A narrow strip of limestone pavement in good condition, over half a mile long and 50m wide, South House Pavement offers magnificent scenery and interesting plant life; from ferns and grasses to rich mosses and lichens.

Surrounded by dry stone walls, typical in the Yorkshire Dales National Park, South House Pavement Nature Reserve is a fantastic example of a limestone pavement. A great site for the sure-footed, the mosaic of narrow clints (blocks) and grykes (fissures) does mean it can be rather difficult to venture across, particularly in wet weather when it is best avoided.

An excellent site for limestone grassland species you can find ferns including rigid buckler fern and hart's tongue fern. Herbs such as meadowsweet and spear thistle grow in the grykes, whilst small trees and shrubs like rowan, bird cherry and hawthorn are scattered across the nature reserve. There are some patches with thicker soil where heather is found. Beautiful pink hairy stonecrop grows at the edge of pools that form in depressions on the clint surface when it rains, or where the soil borders the bare rock.

NEAREST POSTCODE
BD24 0HU

GRID REFERENCE
SD 776 744

RESERVE SIZE
5.16 ha

PUBLIC TRANSPORT
Train (Settle-Carlisle line) station and occasional buses at Horton-in-Ribblesdale 2.5 miles away.

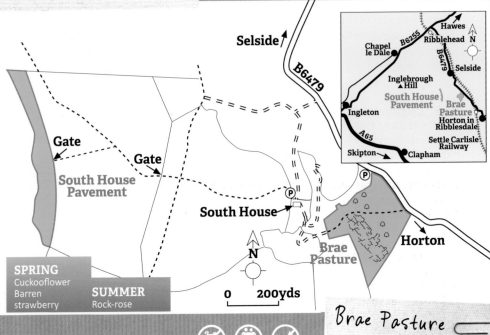

Selside

B6479

Gate

Gate

South House
Pavement

South House

Brae
Pasture

Horton

N

0   200yds

Hawes

Chapel
le Dale

B6255

Ribblehead N

B6479

Selside

Inglebrough
Hill

South House
Pavement

Ingleton

Brae
Pasture

Horton in
Ribblesdale

A65

Settle Carlisle
Railway

Skipton

Clapham

SPRING
Cuckooflower
Barren
strawberry

SUMMER
Rock-rose

Brae Pasture

DIRECTIONS
Take the B6479 Horton
to Selside Road and turn
off for South House. The
nature reserve lies beyond
South House on the lower
slopes of Simon Fell, east
of Ingleborough Hill. There
is limited roadside parking.
Enter the nature reserve by
a small gate in the wall.

SITE DESIGNATION
Part of Ingleborough
National Nature Reserve

Limestone
pavement

South House Pavement
was once grazed, the rocky
areas cleared in previous
centuries. However the
grykes in the pavement
make it a dangerous
site for livestock and
there is no water supply.
Management is now
focussed on maintaining
the dry stone walls and
occasionally removing
sycamore seedlings and
rosebay willowherb which
would otherwise grow and
shade out the rich ground
flora. The land here is now
part of the Ingleborough
National Nature Reserve.

Top tip...

The summer flowers in
the meadow and around
the limestone pavement
areas are exceptional;
visit in June to see them
at their best.

SPRING
Wheatear
Meadow pipit
Blue moor-grass

SUMMER
Hairy stonecrop

BROADHEAD CLOUGH

Broadhead Clough offers a spectacular Pennine landscape with a dramatic past. This deep valley lies in the bottom of Bell Hole and was better known in the 18th Century for the notorious Cragg Vale Coiners than its wildlife. Within a fair distance you can experience open, windswept moors and explore the boggy mires of the valley bottom.

The most important habitat of this diverse site is the rare wet woodland bog areas. A number of small streams flowing through the site spread out to form boggy areas known as mires, undermining tree roots and causing them to crack or the trees to fall prematurely.

Fallen wood combined with the underlying peat soils, leaves and sphagnum moss rots away to form more peat bog. There are 65 species of moss and liverwort here, which include sphagnum and star mosses, with tufts of rush and other wetland plants and fungi. This provides ideal conditions for the larvae of many invertebrates, which provide food for many charismatic birds including curlew, cuckoo, woodpeckers and finches that rely on the nature reserve for food or shelter.

Managing this area is a delicate operation. Too many trees can dry out the wetter areas and can also shade out sunlight from reaching the plants beneath. Too few trees results in dead and rotting wood being removed from the food chain. Trust staff and volunteers work hard to selectively allow light to reach the woodland floor whilst maintaining moist conditions. The path network and drains are kept clear and bracken kept at bay to ensure that visitors can take in the site's beauty without damaging the fragile mires. Following the main footpath to the moorland commons above gives a stunning view onto the mires and across the whole nature reserve down the valley. If you like social history it is well worth arranging a visit to Coiners' Barn while you are there to find out more about the Cragg Vale Coiners, an infamous gang of local criminals.

Curlew

NEAREST POSTCODE
HX7 5RT

GRID REFERENCE
SE 001 250

RESERVE SIZE
22.38 ha

PUBLIC TRANSPORT
Mytholmroyd has a station and regular buses from Halifax and Burnley. National Cycle Route 66 crosses the B6138: for cyclists who like a challenge this road is the longest continuous climb in England.

DIRECTIONS
Take the B6138, signposted Littleborough until ½ mile from Mytholmroyd, the houses on the right give way to fields. Visitors' vehicles are not allowed to use the track to the nature reserve and should be parked on the roadside. Immediately before the road swings left and right to cross Dauber Bridge, there is a track on the right, with a public footpath sign to Frost Hole. Walk along the track for about a ¼ mile, fork left onto the concrete road until you reach the main entrance (0.6 miles from the road).

SITE DESIGNATION
SSSI

OTHER INFORMATION
Not suitable for pushchairs. Height gain 215m from road to top of nature reserve with some steep climbs and steps. The paths are slippery when wet. To arrange refreshments and education facilities at Coiners' Barn visit bellhousecoiners.com

LOCATION

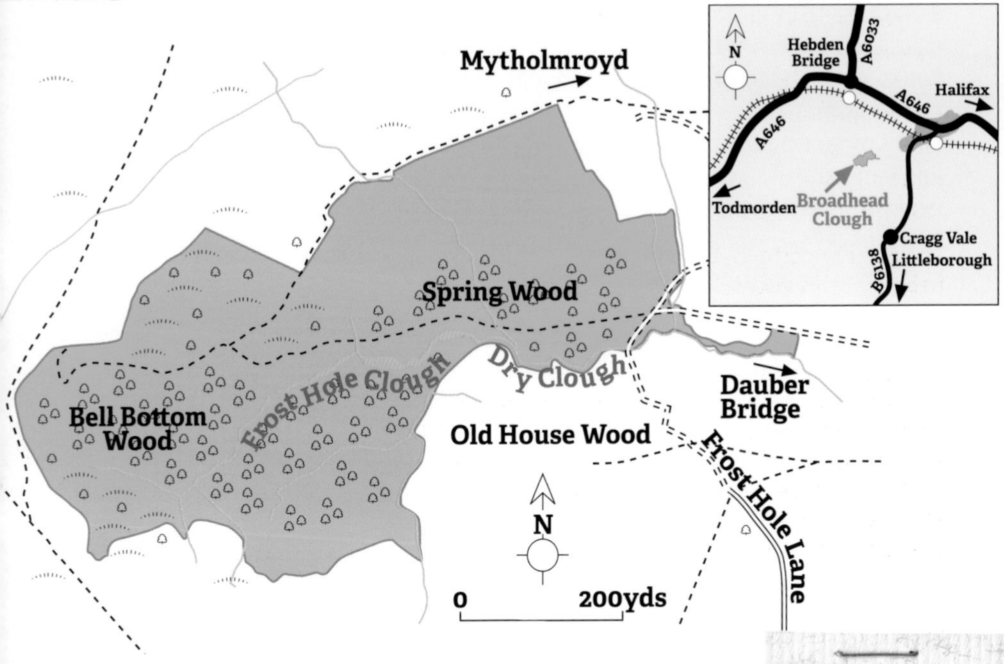

Mytholmroyd
Spring Wood
Bell Bottom Wood
Frost Hole Clough
Dry Clough
Old House Wood
Dauber Bridge
Frost Hole Lane
N
0
200yds
N
Hebden Bridge
A6033
Halifax
A646
A646
Todmorden
Broadhead Clough
Cragg Vale
Littleborough
B6138

Top tip...

This nature reserve has a variety of habitats nestled together in a wider moorland landscape. See semi-mature clough woodland, bogs, meadows and heath in one day with easy access on foot from public transport.

Marsh violet

SPRING	SUMMER	AUTUMN	WINTER
Cuckoo	Marsh orchid	Jay	Woodcock
Blackcap	Cotton grass	Fungi	Tawny owl
Curlew	Heather	Redwing	Long tailed tit
Wood sorrel	Harebell	Fieldfare	Red grouse
Marsh violet	Bird's-foot trefoil		Brown hare

BROCKADALE

This page is sponsored by Wentbridge House Hot...

There is always something to see at Brockadale Nature Reserve, although for the best experience visit in spring and summer. The woodland in springtime offer carpets of wood anemone, bluebell, primrose, violet and early purple orchid before being shaded out by new leaf growth in the canopy above. Whilst in the summer, the flower-covered slopes are alive with a jewel-case of butterflies and other insects.

NEAREST POSTCODE
WF8 3LJ

GRID REFERENCE
SE 513 173

RESERVE SIZE
58.7 ha

PUBLIC TRANSPORT
There is an infrequent bus service from Pontefract to Doncaster which stops at either Wentbridge, Kirk Smeaton or Little Smeaton.

DIRECTIONS
From A1 take Wentbridge and Kirk Smeaton turn. Drive east to Kirk Smeaton, go through the village to Little Smeaton and head north west up New Road. Once out of the village turn left down Leys Lane to the car park at the end.

SITE DESIGNATION
SSSI

Brockadale is in the valley of the River Went as it flows through a craggy, steep-sided gorge formed after the last ice-age when glacial melt-water burst through the magnesian limestone rock. Now the river meanders along the flat-bottomed valley. The nature reserve is particularly important for its flowery slopes, which have never been ploughed. This grassland habitat is now rare, with magnesian limestone only existing in a narrow band stretching from Nottingham to Durham, its soil producing excellent farmland. The site's flowers only survive because the valley sides are too steep to cultivate.

Around 350 species of plants grow on the nature reserve, some of which are scarce. Early flowers such as cowslip, common dog-violet and spring cinquefoil, well suited to the limestone soil, can be seen in spring. Native plants such as rock-rose follow, as well as orchids, salad burnet, yellow-wort, betony, field scabious and, in August, a profusion of clustered bellflower. Butterflies abound in the meadows, with the spectacular marbled white and dark green fritillary unmissable in July. Day-flying moths like six-spot burnet and chimney sweepers are common, with close to 300 species of moths having been identified on site.

The mixed woodland covers the cool, damp valley floor and dry limestone hills. Woodland butterflies like speckled wood and white-letter hairstreak live here. Around 40 species of bird breed on the nature reserve. Great spotted and green woodpeckers, nuthatch and long-tailed tit are resident, whilst warblers such as chiffchaff, willow warbler, blackcap and whitethroat are summer visitors. Yellowhammer and bullfinch are frequently seen in the hedgerows, kingfisher can be spotted along the river, and buzzard and kestrel may pass overhead.

The nature reserve was initially purchased by Yorkshire Wildlife Trust in 1966, but has since increased in size following the purchases of additional land. The Trust manages the grassland by grazing long-horned cattle and sheep in the winter months, and has support from local volunteers.

LOCATION

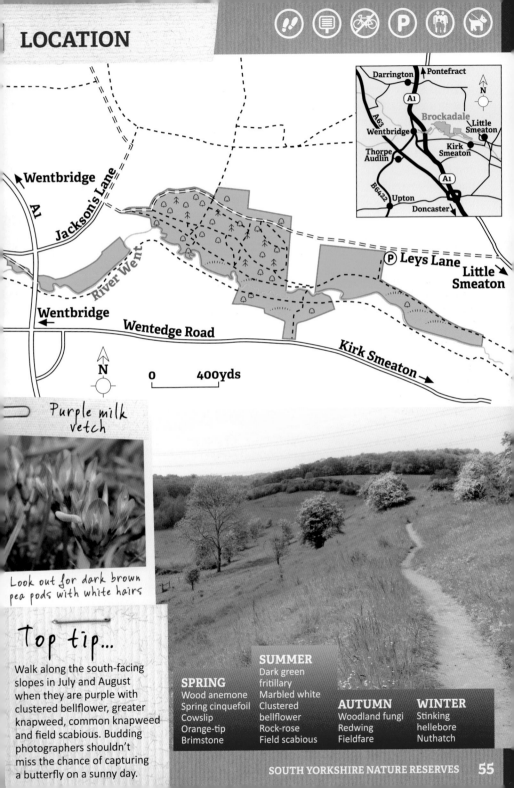

Inset map
Darrington → Pontefract
A1
A63
Brockadale
Wentbridge
Little Smeaton
Kirk Smeaton
Thorpe Audlin
A1
B6422
Upton
Doncaster →
N

Main map
→ Wentbridge
A1
Jackson's Lane
River Went
→ Wentbridge
Wentedge Road
Kirk Smeaton →
P Leys Lane
Little Smeaton →
N
0   400yds

Purple milk vetch
Look out for dark brown pea pods with white hairs

Top tip...
Walk along the south-facing slopes in July and August when they are purple with clustered bellflower, greater knapweed, common knapweed and field scabious. Budding photographers shouldn't miss the chance of capturing a butterfly on a sunny day.

SPRING
Wood anemone
Spring cinquefoil
Cowslip
Orange-tip
Brimstone

SUMMER
Dark green fritillary
Marbled white
Clustered bellflower
Rock-rose
Field scabious

AUTUMN
Woodland fungi
Redwing
Fieldfare

WINTER
Stinking hellebore
Nuthatch

BURTON LEONARD LIME QUARRIES

Once a limestone quarry, this nature reserve is now an oasis for scrub, woodland and grassland plant species. Butterflies bask in the sun and other insects may be found seeking shelter in this quiet spot. The site's industrial past is still evident, with a number of lime kilns found throughout the nature reserve.

Burton Leonard Lime Quarries comprises of a mixture of broadleaved woodland, scrub and open glades of magnesian limestone grassland. This special mix of habitats encourages a rich combination of plant species, some of which are locally rare including burnet rose and autumn gentian. Two small populations of the nationally scarce spring sedge are also present in the grassland areas.

The shallow lime-rich soils are nutrient-poor, yet support the most botanically diverse magnesian limestone grassland communities with species including wild thyme, salad burnet, small scabious, rough hawkbit, fairy flax and bird's-foot trefoil. The screes merit individual recognition due to the differing plant communities they support, including squinancywort, eyebright, betony, field scabious, wild basil, hairy violet, harebell, greater knapweed, clustered bellflower, cowslip and carline thistle. Woodland and calcareous scrub of hawthorn, elder and hazel has developed around the margins of the disused quarries leaving large exposed, sparsely vegetated cliff faces. Ash woodland is developing in several areas below the quarry faces.

The bottoms of the sheltered quarries provide ideal habitats for many butterflies, including green-veined white, meadow brown, ringlet and speckled wood. White-letter hairstreak are also occasionally seen around the elm trees.

The site was an active limestone quarry from the 19th Century through to 1941, with the worked stone being burnt in the lime kilns on site to produce quick lime. This material had a wide variety of uses from construction to agriculture. The remains of four lime kilns can still be seen on site as evidence of the nature reserve's industrial past.

NEAREST POSTCODE
HG3 3TE

GRID REFERENCE
SE 323 629

RESERVE SIZE
3.06 ha

PUBLIC TRANSPORT
A bus service (Ripon-Knaresborough-Harrogate) passes through Burton Leonard Village.

DIRECTIONS
From Burton Leonard village walk along Lime Kiln Lane to the nature reserve. Approach Burton Leonard village from the A61 Harrogate-Ripon road.

SITE DESIGNATION
SSSI

Yorkshire Wildlife Trust leases the nature reserve from Mountgarrett Estates, and works to prevent encroachment of trees and shrubs onto the limestone grassland banks.

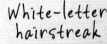

White-letter hairstreak

Often feed on thistle flowers in the afternoon

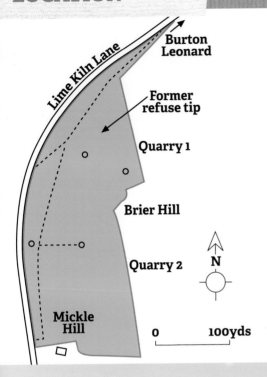

Lime Kiln Lane

Burton Leonard

Former refuse tip

Quarry 1

Brier Hill

Quarry 2

N

Mickle Hill

0   100yds

Ripon
River Ure
N
Bishop Monkton
Wormald Green
Burton Leonard
Burton Leonard Lime Quarries
Copgrove
Knaresborough
A61
Harrogate

Common spotted orchid

The variety rhodochila is found here

Top tip...

Visit in early to mid summer on a warm sunny day to see a fantastic display of limestone grassland flowers and the insects that they attract.

SPRING
Cowslip
Orchids

SUMMER
Squinancywort
Wild thyme
Eyebright
Fairy flax
Meadow brown

AUTUMN
Autumn gentian

WINTER
Red kite

BURTON RIGGS

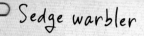
Sedge warbler

Inhabit marshy areas around the lakes and ponds

The large, open lakes at Burton Riggs make it a fantastic place to watch wildfowl and waders, particularly during autumn migration and over the winter months.

An unusual habitat in the Ryedale area, Burton Riggs is a 14 hectare site primarily consisting of clean freshwater lakes with some scrub, woodland and grassland. The wildlife of the site is enhanced during the winter when little egret, tufted duck and pochard are seen. The ponds surrounding the lakes have been home to great crested newt for a number of years.

in the 1970s for the construction of the adjacent A64, it is relatively young in wildlife terms, but already has a rich mix of habitats and species to its name. A public footpath runs through part of the nature reserve underneath the A64 road bridge and out into the industrial area to the east. Permissive paths run around the entirety of the site, one route around the smaller lake being specially designed for disabled access and the route around the larger lake being a rougher track with steps and boardwalks surmounting boggy and hilly parts.

Wildlife management includes keeping ponds clear from silting up, rotational coppicing of willow around the lakes and increasing the area of woodland so that there is a step-up from two to three patches around the site. The scrub is a vital habitat for small birds and mammals, and is retained as much as possible, only being cut back along the footpaths.

Burton Riggs is bounded mainly by industrial land and housing, which makes it a valuable oasis for wildlife and local people alike. As an artificial site created by gravel quarrying

Common darter

Fly late into the autumn and can regularly be seen sunbathing

NEAREST POSTCODE
YO12 4QE

GRID REFERENCE
TA 029 832

RESERVE SIZE
13.83 ha

PUBLIC TRANSPORT
Regular bus and train services into Scarborough.

DIRECTIONS
The nature reserve is situated just off the A64 out of Scarborough on the opposite side of the roundabout to the supermarket.

Tufted duck

Flocks of tufted ducks can be seen throughout the winter

LOCATION

Scarborough

Pedestrian
access over
level crossing

Morrisons
pub

Footpath
under A64

A64

P

N

0   200yds

Scarborough

Crossgates

B1621

Eastfield

Filey

Seamer

Burton
Riggs

A64

N

Top tip...

Burton Riggs is a must
during the autumn and
winter, with regular
sightings of migratory
birds stopping off for days
of rest, including ducks
and other species such as
short-eared owls.

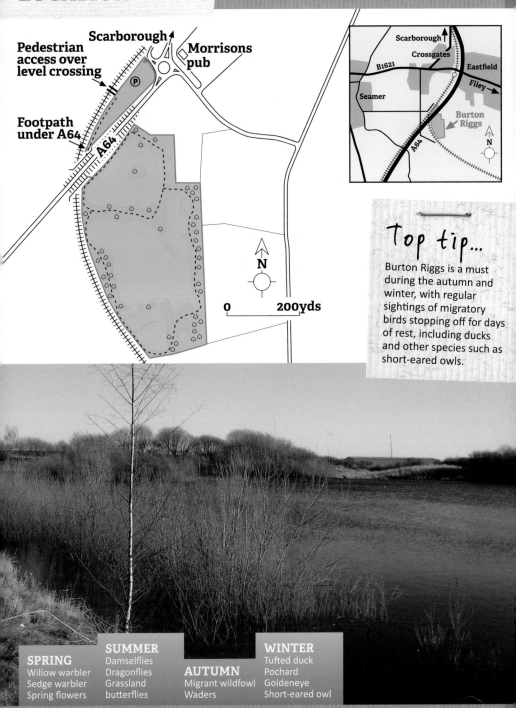

SPRING
Willow warbler
Sedge warbler
Spring flowers

SUMMER
Damselflies
Dragonflies
Grassland
butterflies

AUTUMN
Migrant wildfowl
Waders

WINTER
Tufted duck
Pochard
Goldeneye
Short-eared owl

CALLEY HEATH

This page is sponsored by Power Health Products Ltd

On a walk round Calley Heath you'll soon discover it is not your typical nature reserve, but a diamond in the rough. On close inspection you will be delighted by the detail of tiny flowering plants in the short rabbit-grazed sandy grasslands, or the numbers of common butterflies feeding on flowering grass and willowherb heads in the old allotments.

Calley Heath is an area of grassy heath – a habitat rare in Yorkshire. Tiny flowering plants can be seen in the grassland including bird's-foot trefoil, dove's-foot cranesbill and common stork's-bill – all typical of these sandy soils. Hare's-foot clover is worth looking out for, named for its fluffy-looking flower heads. Shepherd's cress, recorded in only three other places in Yorkshire, also grows well here.

Parts of the site support rough grassland which is valuable for a huge number of insects. Over 370 fly species alone have been recorded here and the site is also important for beetles and bugs too. One fly species – *Hilara gallica* – was thought to be extinct in Britain until it was re-discovered here recently; the nature reserve is now its UK stronghold.

There are small areas of oak woodland in the drier parts of the site, with alders and willow fringing the ditches and in some of the wetter spots rushes and yellow flag iris grow.

At the time of the gold rush in America, when people travelled west to California to make their fortune, Calley Heath was granted to the poor of Barmby Moor by a local Trust – so the people here similarly travelled west to make their fortune – hence the area became known as Calley (or California) Heath.

When the Trust took on the nature reserve in 2003 parts of the site were agricultural set-aside. Since then work on site has concentrated on removing invading scrub, bracken and bramble in order to restore the acidic grassland habitat. The two fields which had been previously farmed were re-seeded with a species mix to recreate the natural grasslands. A true success story, as restoration is really working on site, with one of the seeded grasslands now species rich.

NEAREST POSTCODE
YO41 5PF

GRID REFERENCE
SE 751 496

RESERVE SIZE
11.12 ha

PUBLIC TRANSPORT
Regular buses run between York and Hull and stop near the Steer Inn opposite the nature reserve

DIRECTIONS
On the north side of the A1079 York to Hull Road 9.5 miles east of York centre. Almost opposite the Steer Inn. Entrance via gate off the main road. Limited parking at nature reserve entrance.

OTHER INFORMATION
Dogs allowed only on leads on public footpath.

Top tip...
Come mid-summer equipped with a hand lens or small magnifying glass to appreciate the tiny grassland flowers in full bloom. Crouching down you may also spot battalions of ants busy working or some of the beautiful mosses.

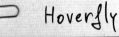

Hoverfly

Little Meadow

Sandy Acres

Carr Tongue

Carr Tongue

circular footpath

public footpath

A1079(T)

Black Dyke

Beck Farm

*

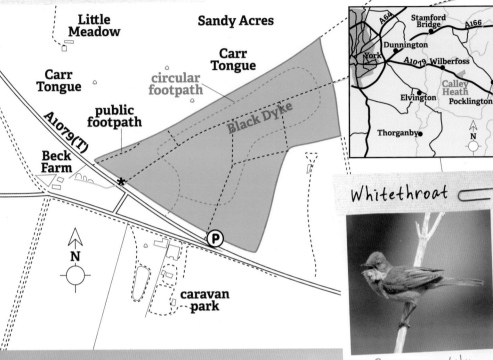

Stamford Bridge
A64
A166
Dunnington
York
A1079
Wilberfoss
Elvington
Calley Heath
Pocklington
Thorganby
N

N

P

caravan park

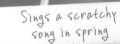

Whitethroat

Sings a scratchy song in spring

Hare's-foot clover

These fluffy flower heads can be seen in the grasslands

SPRING	SUMMER	AUTUMN	WINTER
Willow warbler	Toadflax		
Blackcap	Heath bedstraw		
Whitethroat	Musk mallow	Harebell	Red kite
Kestrel	Red admiral	Hare's-foot clover	Barn owl
Marsh marigold	Small copper		

CARBROOK RAVINE

This narrow valley used to form part of an extensive 2,500 acre deer park for the gentry of Sheffield. Although there are no deer now there is plenty of wildlife.

In the south east of Sheffield near the Manor Estate lies Carbrook Ravine. This small nature reserve is home to a wide range of threatened species like skylark, song thrush and bluebell. The locally rare golden male fern also grows in this nationally important wet woodland area, while ash, maple, aspen, sycamore and hazel can be found in the species rich north west of the site.

Sparrowhawk

Displaying pairs can be seen overhead in spring

The vast grassed areas are home to mice, voles and shrews which provide food for the local tawny owl and kestrel populations, whilst the large numbers of small woodland birds in turn attract sparrowhawk.

The Ravine is also important to the local community, providing a beautiful contrast to the predominantly man-made landscape. It is a great place to relax, explore and enjoy!

THE wildlife TRUSTS

Sheffield & Rotherham

NEAREST POSTCODE
S13 8FA

GRID REFERENCE
SK 393 857

RESERVE SIZE
11.35 ha

PUBLIC TRANSPORT
Buses between Sheffield city centre and Chesterfield stop at Woodhouse Road. The nature reserve is 1 mile walk from here. Train stations in Sheffield and Woodhouse.

DIRECTIONS
Take Junction 34 off the M1, and travel south on the A6102. Cross over the A57 and then turn right onto Castlebeck Avenue. Plenty of street parking nearby.

Song thrush

Present throughout the year

Sycamore leaves

Several tree species ca
be found in a small are

LOCATION

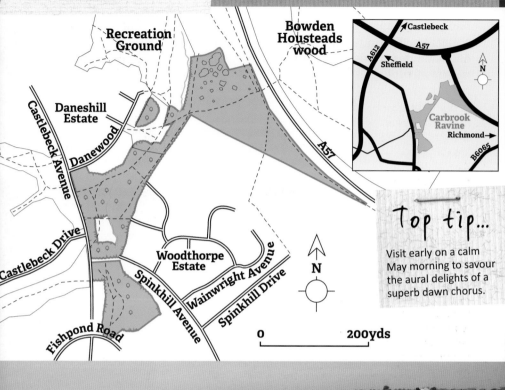

Recreation Ground

Bowden Housteads wood

Castlebeck
A57
A612
Sheffield
N
Carbrook Ravine
Richmond→
B6065

Daneshill Estate

Danewood

Castlebeck Avenue

Castlebeck Drive

Woodthorpe Estate

Spinkhill Avenue

Wainwright Avenue

Spinkhill Drive

Fishpond Road

A57

N

0   200yds

Top tip...

Visit early on a calm May morning to savour the aural delights of a superb dawn chorus.

SPRING
Skylark
Song thrush
Blackcap
Chiffchaff
Bluebell

SUMMER
Golden male fern

AUTUMN
Fungi

WINTER
Tawny owl

At Carr House Meadows, the old English style meadows have been maintained and create a lovely setting.

Flower meadow

Enjoy a tapestry of colour in summer

These meadows are a rare example of the flower-rich fields that were once a common sight in England. They abound with colour throughout the spring and summer; bluebells, yellow rattle and swathes of red and white clover early in the season, followed by field scabious and orchids, as well as the bright pink marsh-loving ragged robin, a rarity in the Sheffield area. In turn, meadow butterflies are plentiful with ringlets and meadow browns being particularly numerous.

Cattle are used to manage the meadows – grazing gives more delicate wildflowers the space to grow. They churn up the ground with their hooves creating niches for wet loving plants to seed and create an ideal habitat for insects.

Butterflies, beetles, spiders and grasshoppers all thrive in the rich foliage. The hedgerows and dry stone walls are home to still more insects, plus a dense population of songbirds including chiffchaff, willow warbler, bullfinch and goldfinch.

Noctule bat

This large bat can be seen flying high over the meadows at dusk

THE wildlife TRUSTS

Sheffield & Rotherham

NEAREST POSTCODE
S35 0DE

GRID REFERENCE
SK 282 954

RESERVE SIZE
15.7 ha

PUBLIC TRANSPORT
A bus runs between Sheffield and Stocksbridge, which is 4.5 miles from the nature reserve.

DIRECTIONS
Take Junction 36 from the M1, onto the A616. Turn left onto Manchester Road (A6102) for about four miles. Take Brightholmlee Lane on your right and travel towards More Hall Reservoir. The nature reserve is off Carr House Lane; please park considerately in the village.

SITE DESIGNATION
LNR

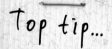

Top tip...

Enjoy a stroll on a sunny June afternoon to experience wildflower meadows at their best.

LOCATION

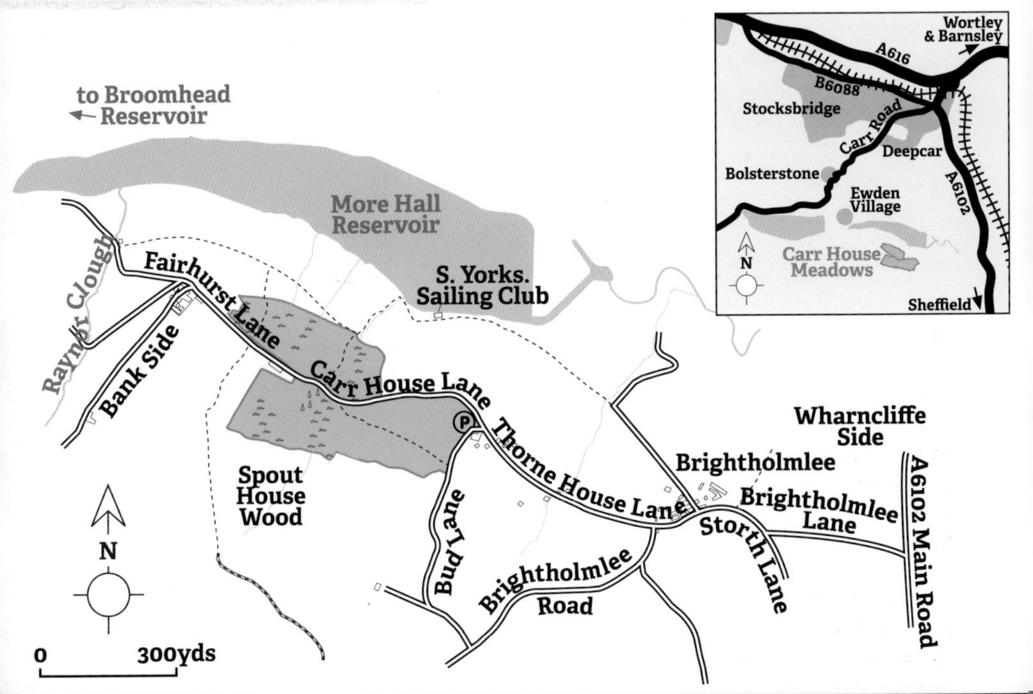
to Broomhead Reservoir
More Hall Reservoir
S. Yorks. Sailing Club
Rayner Clough
Fairhurst Lane
Bank Side
Carr House Lane
Thorne House Lane
Spout House Wood
Bud Lane
Brightholmlee Road
Wharncliffe Side
Brightholmlee
Brightholmlee Lane
Storth Lane
A6102 Main Road
N
0
300yds
Wortley & Barnsley
A616
B6088
Stocksbridge
Carr Road
Deepcar
Bolsterstone
Ewden Village
A6102
Carr House Meadows
Sheffield

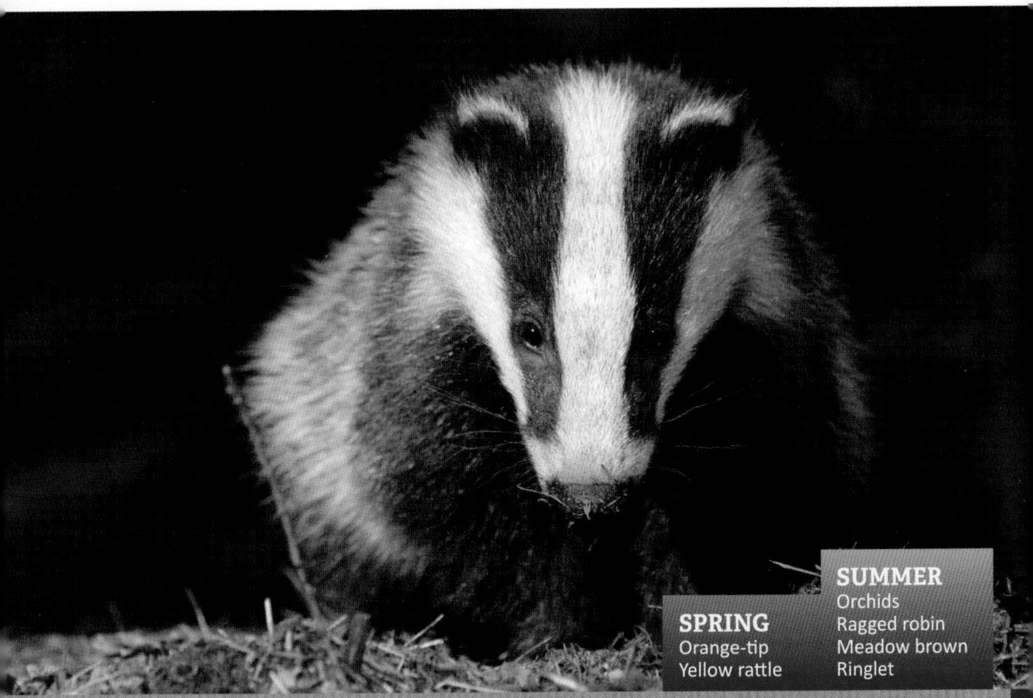
SPRING
Orange-tip
Yellow rattle
SUMMER
Orchids
Ragged robin
Meadow brown
Ringlet

CENTENARY RIVERSIDE

Since opening in 2009 a programme of planting and construction works has transformed this former steel works site into a magical urban wetland; a haven for wildlife.

Sheffield & Rotherham

Reed bunting

The dapper males sing a short refrain in spring

Footpaths and ponds have been created; trees, grasslands and wildflowers planted, seats, signage and sculptures installed. Eventually it is hoped that many native species, including otters, will recolonise the area.

The huge relics of the site's industrial past are being used with the sculpture, 'Steel Henge', on the flood defence bank, the concrete foundations adapted to create wildlife habitats; and the giant deckchair sculptures reflecting the increasing use of the River Don for leisure. As well as looking to the past, Centenary Riverside will contribute to the area's economic future. An important part of Rotherham's flood defences, this unique flood storage wetland means that adjacent land can be developed safely.

The site is a great place to visit or to unwind, particularly from the bustle of the city.

NEAREST POSTCODE
S60 1DS

GRID REFERENCE
SK 421 921

RESERVE SIZE
4.5 ha

PUBLIC TRANSPORT
Buses from Sheffield Interchange to Meadow Bank Road/Psalter Lane. Train, tram or bus from Sheffield Interchange/ Station to Meadowhall.

DIRECTIONS
Take the A6178 from the M1 into Rotherham city centre. The nature reserve is off Sheffield Road. Off road parking is available in Rotherham town centre and there is limited street parking on Riverside Way.

OTHER INFORMATION
This site has a picnic area.

Volunteers at work

Purple loosestrife

Top tip...

Visit early in the morning to enjoy the peace and wildlife of this inner city haven and you may be lucky enough to spot an otter.

LOCATION

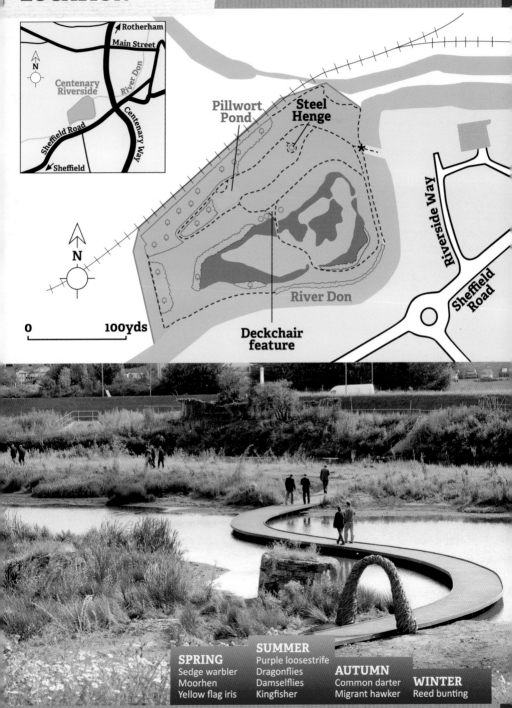

Rotherham
Main Street
N
Centenary Riverside
River Don
Sheffield Road
Centenary Way
Sheffield

Pillwort Pond
Steel Henge

N

River Don

Deckchair feature

Riverside Way

Sheffield Road

0   100yds

SPRING
Sedge warbler
Moorhen
Yellow flag iris

SUMMER
Purple loosestrife
Dragonflies
Damselflies
Kingfisher

AUTUMN
Common darter
Migrant hawker

WINTER
Reed bunting

CHAFER WOOD

Bluebells, ramsons and other woodland plants offer a tapestry of colour in this idyllic mixed broadleaved woodland nature reserve. The sounds of twigs snapping during an early morning stroll through this peaceful valley may alert you to passing roe deer. The views from the top of the wood across the Vale of Pickering are stunning.

NEAREST POSTCODE
YO13 9PA

GRID REFERENCE
SE 899 832

RESERVE SIZE
28.47 ha

PUBLIC TRANSPORT
The nearest train station is at Scarborough. A bus runs through Ebberston along the A170.

DIRECTIONS
Take the A170 Pickering road to the village of Ebberston. The nature reserve is north of the village, off a quiet lane.

Chafer Wood supports an interesting variety of habitats, home to a wide range of plants and birds. The shaded lower parts of the valley are rarely exposed to sunlight and are therefore covered in delicate ferns and mosses. By the stream running through the nature reserve, woodland plants such as bluebells, baneberry, goldilocks buttercup and leopard's bane can be found, whilst a carpet of wild garlic (ramsons) fills the air with an oniony fragrance during the spring.

Roe deer are very much in evidence on the site and may well be encountered on a quiet stroll. Rare species of cranefly also thrive, as conditions in the valley bottom create the perfect habitat in which to breed. Birds you might come across include nuthatch, redstart, blackcap, green and great spotted woodpeckers.

In addition to the woodland there are areas of limestone grassland that form small open glades within the trees.

Before Yorkshire Wildlife Trust took ownership of the site some areas had been used as a plantation, evident by small populations of introduced trees like sycamore and larch. Management by the Trust is focussed on removing these introduced tree species and replanting with native species which are then protected from deer and rabbit damage. Bracken is managed by cutting so it does not encroach and shade out other plants, whilst the open areas of limestone grassland are strimmed once or twice a year with the cuttings raked up to create habitat piles for insects to use.

Some historical interest remains on the site, including an ancient pinfold near the entrance which has been restored by the Trust. A 200 year old structure, known as King Alfred's Cairn also exists, although excavation in the 1950s of the cave beneath revealed human remains dating back to Neolithic times.

Cherry blossom

Dalby Forest

Netherby Dale Dykes (Scheduled Ancient Monument)

Quarry (disused)

Netherby Dale

Dalby Forest

N

Chafer Wood

Pickering

Ebberston

A170

B1415

Yedingham A64 Malton

B1258

Scarborough

King Alfred's Cairn

N

0 ———— 400yds

Pinfold

Ebberston & A170

Red campion

A delicate red flower seen on the woodland floor

SPRING
Wild cherry
Blackthorn
Bluebell

SUMMER
Pyramidal orchid
Green woodpecker
Craneflies
Rock-rose

AUTUMN
Roe deer
Fox

CRABTREE PONDS

In a very urban area, surrounded by roads, this handsome nature reserve provides much-needed green space and is a great place for bats.

Crabtree Ponds is part of a larger nature reserve and is mainly used for recreational purposes or as a cut-through by local residents. The nature reserve started life in the 19th Century as an ornamental pond for Crabtree Lodge and is now a large area of standing water abundant with aquatic life including several species of fish, such as rudd, roach, perch, crucian carp, three-spined stickleback and even eels. Several local biodiversity priority species, such as smooth and palmate newts, frogs and toads can also be found here.

The dense shrub layer provides an ideal habitat for fungi with 27 different species recorded on site. It also provides perfect shelter for hedgehogs and an ideal home for many insects. Common pipistrelle, Daubenton's and Leisler's bats all fly over from roosts in nearby Roe Woods to feed on insects at the ponds.

In the woods where sycamore, poplar and ash flourish. Many birds breed including treecreeper, great spotted woodpecker and several species of tits, some of which benefit from the nestboxes that have been put up.

Sheffield & Rotherham

NEAREST POSTCODE
S5 7BJ

GRID REFERENCE
SK 361 899

RESERVE SIZE
1.4 ha

PUBLIC TRANSPORT
Nearest train station is in Sheffield. Frequent buses run to the city centre.

DIRECTIONS
The nature reserve is off the Barnsley Road (A6135) in Sheffield city centre.

Top tip...

Visit at dusk on a summer evening to watch Daubenton's bats skimming low over the water like small hovercrafts and watch larger high-flying Leisler's bats seeking airborne insects.

Smooth newt

Can be found in the ponds or in other damp places

Common pipistrelle

See at dusk as they hunt for insects

LOCATION

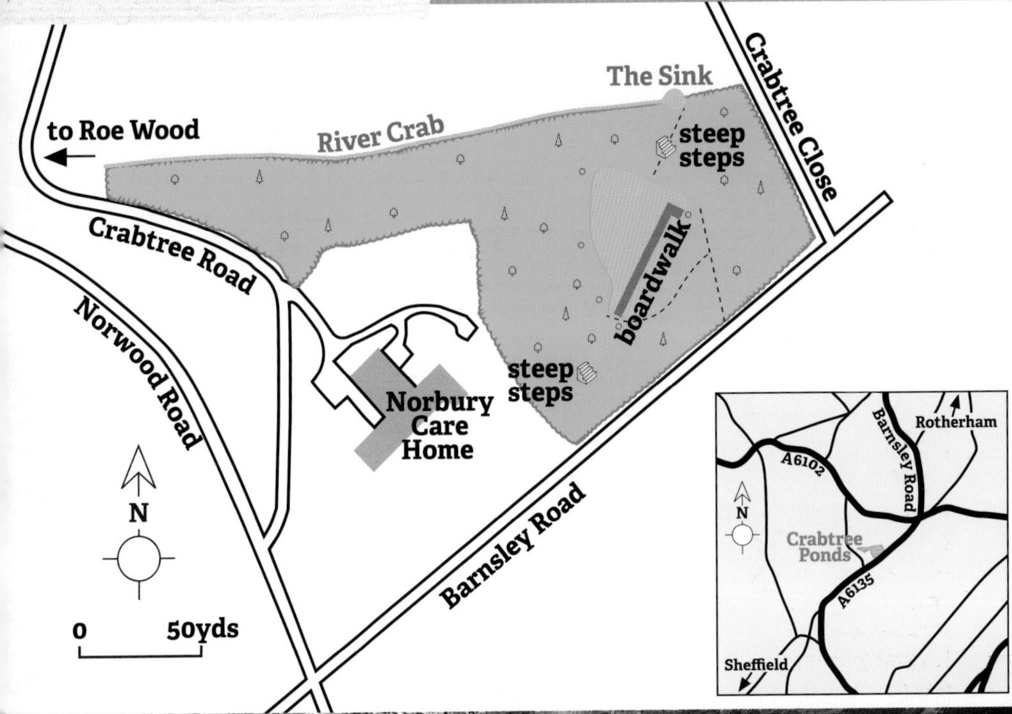

The Sink
River Crab
to Roe Wood
steep steps
Crabtree Close
Crabtree Road
boardwalk
Norwood Road
steep steps
Norbury Care Home
N
0
50yds
Barnsley Road
Rotherham
Barnsley Road
A6102
N
Crabtree Ponds
A6135
Sheffield

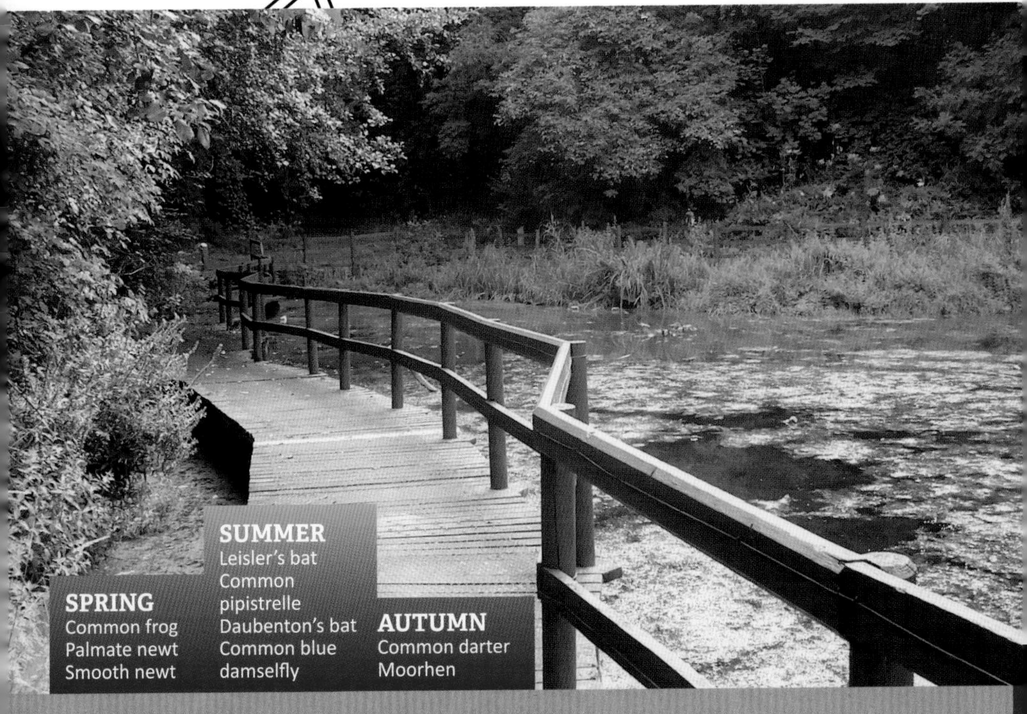

SPRING
Common frog
Palmate newt
Smooth newt

SUMMER
Leisler's bat
Common pipistrelle
Daubenton's bat
Common blue damselfly

AUTUMN
Common darter
Moorhen

DENABY INGS

Grass snake

Look out for the distinctive white collar

This wildlife haven – a fantastic mix of habitats from open water and riverside water meadows to woodland scrub and hedgerows – is in easy reach of the urban areas of Denaby and Mexborough. Bustling with wildlife including spritely kingfisher, elegant orchids and colourful pochard amongst others, Denaby Ings provides a much needed wildlife haven in a landscape scattered with farmland and housing developments.

Riverside meadows, dry meadows, open water, woodland scrub and hedgerow habitats are all found at Denaby Ings and support a diverse range of species. Grey herons sit by the river waiting to strike. In the meadows butterflies are abundant visiting the assorted wildflowers, whereas winter sees flocks of migrant birds including fieldfare and lesser redpoll.

To catch a sight of the wondrous wildlife here spend time in two of the viewing hides which overlook the main marsh and provide excellent sights over the open water of the Ings and the river valley to the wooded crags in the distance. Follow the raised embankment of the old Dearne Valley Railway to reach them. The railway, which was once used to transport coal from the local mines, is now full of the sound of birdsong during the spring and summer.

Close to the River Dearne, the site plays an important role in flood relief – the iron gates of the sluice allow water to escape into the water meadows on the nature reserve when there is severe flooding. Local volunteers and the Trust work to maintain the paths and to keep open areas free from scrub. The marsh and meadows are regularly mown and grazed to maintain the habitat for a diversity of species. The water levels in the Ings are monitored and controlled to provide a mix of reedbeds and muddy shoreline attractive to the birds.

The nature reserve has a long and varied history which can be traced as far back as Roman times, although more recently farming and coal mining has shaped the area. Mining subsidence has caused permanent open water areas to form where the River Dearne once flowed and these are now rich in aquatic life.

NEAREST POSTCODE
S64 0JJ

GRID REFERENCE
SE 496 008

RESERVE SIZE
23.35 ha

PUBLIC TRANSPORT
Train to Conisbrough or Mexborough from Doncaster, then approximately a 30 minute walk to the nature reserve.

DIRECTIONS
Denaby Ings lies north east of Mexborough. Take the A635 towards Barnsley for 1.5 miles to Marr. Just before the village take a left onto a minor road signposted Mexborough. At the staggered crossroads turn left towards High Melton and almost immediately right downhill towards Mexborough. Bear right, over the Old Dearne and between a disused railway line and turn left into the car park.

SITE DESIGNATION
SSSI

OTHER INFORMATION
The Field Centre is open on Saturdays only.

LOCATION

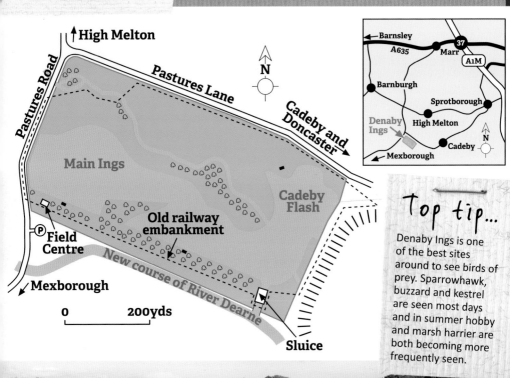

↑ **High Melton**

Pastures Road

Pastures Lane

N

Cadeby and Doncaster

Main Ings

Cadeby Flash

Old railway embankment

ℙ **Field Centre**

New course of River Dearne

↙ **Mexborough**

| 0 | 200yds |

Sluice

Inset map
← Barnsley
A635
37
Marr
A1M
Barnburgh
Sprotborough
Denaby Ings
High Melton
Cadeby
N
← Mexborough

Top tip...

Denaby Ings is one of the best sites around to see birds of prey. Sparrowhawk, buzzard and kestrel are seen most days and in summer hobby and marsh harrier are both becoming more frequently seen.

Pochard

See pochards and other diving ducks during winter

SPRING
Kingfisher
Lapwing
Waterfowl

SUMMER
Bee orchid
Pyramidal orchid
Common spotted orchid
Grass snake
Bats

AUTUMN
Common sandpiper
Green sandpiper
Wood sandpiper
Redshank
Greenshank
Black-tailed godwit

WINTER
Lesser redpoll
Siskin
Fieldfare
Goosander
Pochard

ELLERBURN BANK

A warm sunny day brings this limestone grassland to life, with colourful butterflies such as small copper and day-flying moths including six-spot burnet fluttering between vibrantly coloured meadow flowers. Skylark, with their distinctive flight and lilting song, breed in the adjacent fields.

NEAREST POSTCODE
YO18 7LU

GRID REFERENCE
SE 853 860

RESERVE SIZE
2.89 ha

PUBLIC TRANSPORT
Regular bus services into Thornton Dale. Nearest train station is in Malton.

DIRECTIONS
At the south west corner of Dalby Forest. Take the Whitby road for 1.5 miles and turn right into Dalby Forest Drive. Take one of two forest tracks into the nature reserve by foot.

SITE DESIGNATION
SSSI

This excellent example of limestone grassland has never been farmed or worked in any way and its thin, free draining soils support species such as rock-rose, cowslip and quaking grass. A few rarities can also be found here including some orchid species.

Hebridean sheep

The Trust's sheep graze on the pasture

The meadows are generally at their most picturesque in June and July, an impressive sight for such a small nature reserve. Rabbits, foxes, badgers and roe deer are frequent visitors that leave telltale signs, whilst stoats can be seen whisking through the stems during the day. Adders are seen occasionally around the drystone wall. Butterflies breeding here include small copper and small skipper. The site also attracts small birds, including skylark which breed on the adjacent arable land and flocks of finches in winter.

The field contains small amounts of hawthorn and gorse scrub and is bounded by woodland on two sides. Situated on the shoulder of Pexton Moor the nature reserve slopes down into the valley towards Dalby Beck. Along the western edge of the site is an ancient earthwork that is thought to be a late Bronze Age double bank and ditch. This is a scheduled ancient monument on which management is limited.

Winter grazing using Hebridean sheep keeps young scrub in check and the sward healthy, allowing it to flower and seed throughout the summer. The patches of scrub that do not get grazed sufficiently by the sheep are mechanically managed to prevent spread into the pasture. The northern boundary is a drystone wall and is maintained by Trust staff and contractors. Hedges are kept in good condition by 'gapping up' with mixed tree saplings that are protected by guards.

Top tip...

To see the meadow and views at their best, visit from June to July. The sward will be in its finest bloom.

P on
Dalby
Forest
Drive

Earthwork

N

0   100yds

Pickering

A169

Dalby Bank

N

Ellerburn
Bank

A170   Wilton

Thornton-
le-Dale

Pickering   Scarborough

Fly orchid

A rare species found
in the grassland

SPRING
Roe deer
Skylark
Cowslip
Adder

SUMMER
Pyramidal orchid
Salad burnet
Quaking grass
Small skipper
Small copper

FEN BOG

Surrounded by bright purple heather, with a variety of colourful sphagnum mosses underfoot, Fen Bog is a delightful moorland nature reserve.

Common butterwort

Can be found in the mire

Fen Bog is set in the stunning location of the North York Moors, situated between the summits of Tom Cross Rigg and Crag Stone Rigg and takes the form of a long curving piece of land that is bounded at both ends by moorland streams. The 19 hectare site comprises of two main sections; the main valley mire and the higher ground leading down to it from the parking area which is primarily wet heath and moorland and is separately fenced from the rest of the site.

The mire bottom has some of the most unusual species of sphagnum moss in the region, which have survived and flourished largely due to consistent management by the Trust. The land is dependent on regional rainfall and appropriate levels of drainage to keep the mire in peak condition.

Besides controlling bracken by hand, the site is grazed by sheep from neighbouring common land. This is beneficial in keeping down coarse grasses that may threaten some of the plant species

present such as heather and hard ferns. Some of the more interesting plants are round-leaved sundew, cranberry, common butterwort, marsh violet and bog asphodel which are all located within the mire. In the upper areas there is a population of chickweed wintergreen, also known as Arctic starflower, that benefits from being in one of the few areas that are ungrazed on the moor.

The site is good for butterflies with small pearl-bordered fritillary and large heath both occurring in early summer. Curlew can be heard calling from the surrounding moors and whinchat, wheatear and meadow pipit all breed. Look out for merlin passing through.

If you time your visit well you may also see a steam train pass down the Pickering railway line adjacent to the nature

Top tip...

Visit in autumn for the bright autumn colours of sphagnum mosses and the purple haze of blooming heather on the surrounding moors.

NEAREST POSTCODE
YO18 7AT

GRID REFERENCE
SE 857 982

RESERVE SIZE
18.83 ha

PUBLIC TRANSPORT
Nearest mainline railway station at Sleights. Bus services along the A169 from Pickering to Whitby. The Lyke Wake Walk crosses the nature reserve. Follow the stone track from the parking area down to the mire.

DIRECTIONS
Adjacent to the A169 between Whitby and Pickering just north of RAF Fylingdales and south of Ellerbeck bridge and the turn off to Goathland.

OTHER INFORMATION
Dogs allowed on public footpaths only.

reserve. Fen Bog was gifted to the Trust in 1964 by Air Marshal Sir John Baldwin and Major CL Baldwin in memory of their son and nephew respectively who were killed in action in World War II.

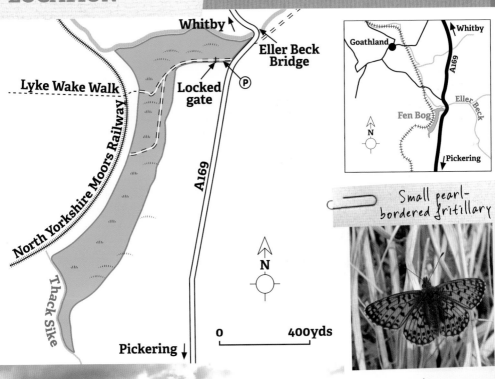

Whitby

Eller Beck
Bridge

Lyke Wake Walk

Locked
gate

North Yorkshire Moors Railway

A169

Thack Sike

N

Pickering

0   400yds

Goathland

Whitby

A169

Fen Bog

Eller Beck

N

Pickering

Small pearl-
bordered fritillary

See in early summer

SUMMER
Whinchat
Adder
Small pearl-
bordered fritillary
Large heath
Common
butterwort

SPRING
Curlew
Meadow pipit
Emperor moth

AUTUMN
Merlin
Stonechat

FEN CARR

Fen Carr is a hidden gem surrounded by a traditional farming landscape of small hedgerow bounded fields. These traditional hay meadows contain locally rare and nationally declining species and form a vital stepping stone in the landscape.

Sympathetically farmed for nearly half-a-century by a local tenant farmer, Fen Carr comprises two traditional hay meadows that form part of the pastoral working landscape.

Due to the 1825 Hatfield, Thorne and Fishlake Enclosure Award the owner of Fen Carr is required by Parliament to maintain 'forever' some of the hedgerows bordering the site. The Award also decrees that the two little brick bridges at the entrances be maintained, and goes as far as to specify the depths and widths of all the ditches.

These ditches are important, as the high water table here supports the wildlife present.

The nature reserve is of botanical importance, containing over 70 species of which many are locally rare as well as nationally declining. Sneezewort, sweet vernal grass and pepper saxifrage all grow at Fen Carr. These and others support a healthy population of butterfly and moth species including a number of browns, blues, coppers, hairstreaks, whites and occasional skippers. Of the birds and mammals that visit the nature reserve of particular interest are curlew and green woodpecker.

A late haycut occurs, after which the land is grazed, usually by cattle. The Trust works to restore the hedgerows in addition to those that were recognised as important in the 1825 Award.

NEAREST POSTCODE
DN7 5LU

GRID REFERENCE
SE 657 156

RESERVE SIZE
3.77 ha

PUBLIC TRANSPORT
Train link available to Hatfield and Stainforth railway station from Doncaster railway station. Bus services run from Doncaster town centre.

DIRECTIONS
A mile after the hamlet of Fosterhouses the road turns sharply to the right. On the bend, an unsigned dirt track leads off to the left (Carr Head Lane). Parking is on the lane but with consideration to farm machinery. The nature reserve is about 200m up the lane on the right hand side.

Small copper

See small coppers and many other butterflies

Pepper saxifrage

Provides nectar for the many butterflies

Tideworth
Hague
Gorse

Clay Dyke

Fen
Carr

Fen
Carr

Strunns Lane

N

0   200yds

Carrhead Lane

A614

Sour Lane

River Don

M18

N

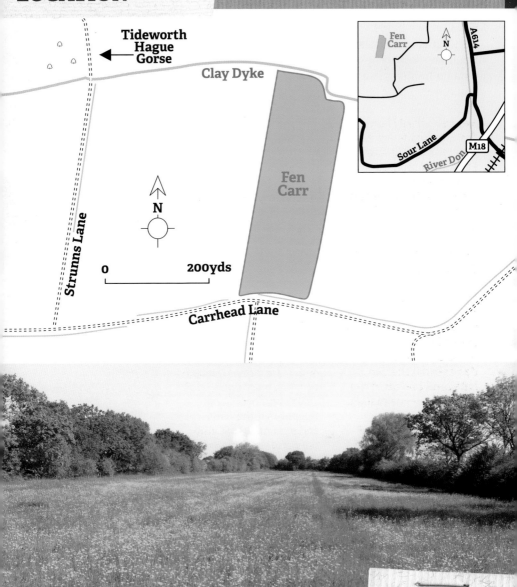

SPRING
Curlew
Green
woodpecker
Green hairstreak

SUMMER
Large skipper
Common blue
Pepper saxifrage
Sneezewort
Sweet vernal
grass

AUTUMN
Roe deer
Grassland fungi

Top tip...

With an abundance of
wildflowers, this nature
reserve provides a real
treat when visiting in late
spring or early summer.

FILEY DAMS

The last remaining freshwater marsh of any size in the area, Filey Dams is a magnet for migratory birds but is also a haven for plants, small mammals and amphibians.

NEAREST POSTCODE
YO14 0DG

GRID REFERENCE
TA 106 807

RESERVE SIZE
5.89 ha

PUBLIC TRANSPORT
Regular buses and trains serve Filey from Scarborough.

DIRECTIONS
A car park is at the end of Wharfedale, take a left turn when entering Filey on the Muston Road from York and Bridlington, 450 metres before the railway crossing.

OTHER INFORMATION
Wheelchair access to Main Hide and pond-dipping platform. Bikes to car park only.

Palmate newt

All three UK newt species are found here

This quiet gem consists of large freshwater lagoons surrounded by marsh and grassland grazed with cattle. Soft rush dominates, joined in the shallow water by toad rush, bottle sedge and branched bur-reed and the distinctive yellow flag iris.

A short walk from the car park and the adjacent Main Hide takes in a small copse with nestboxes used by tree sparrows, and leads along a boardwalk to a pond-dipping platform at the edge of a quiet pool. Here dragonflies skim the water settling on the mat

of amphibious bistort; the fortunate might see a water vole but are more likely to hear them crunching their way through the soft stalks of water forget-me-not. All three British species of newt occur here – smooth, palmate and great crested, the latter species in nationally-important numbers.

Walk further along the boardwalk and arrive at the East Pool Hide where close views can be had of water birds such as little grebe and migratory waders such as greenshank, green and wood sandpipers in the autumn. Across the pool the barn owl box may be occupied, the male often sitting nearby when displaced by his family.

The nature reserve is leased from Scarborough Borough Council and is managed in conjunction with Filey Brigg Ornithological Group, who record the species of the area and carry out routine maintenance.

Little grebe

Listen for their high pitched trilling call

Top tip...

Try a dawn or dusk trip for a good chance of seeing a roe deer, fox or hunting barn owl.

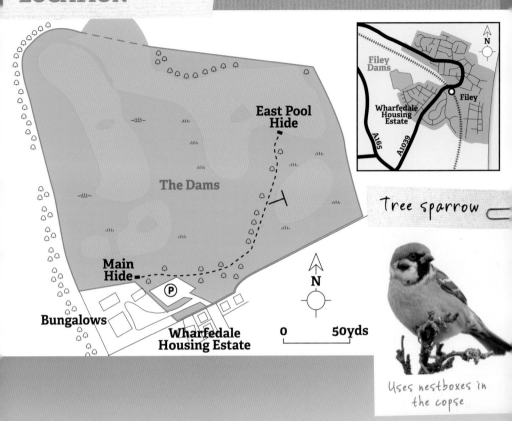

East Pool Hide

The Dams

Main Hide

Bungalows

Ⓟ

Wharfedale Housing Estate

N

0   50yds

Filey Dams

Wharfedale Housing Estate

Filey

A165

A1039

N

Tree sparrow

Uses nestboxes in the copse.

SPRING
Fox
Willow warbler
Tree sparrow
Broad-bodied chaser
Cuckooflower

SUMMER
Greenshank
Wood sandpiper
Great crested newt
Ruddy darter
Amphibious bistort

AUTUMN
Teal
Ruff
Little stint
Redwing
Common darter

WINTER
Little grebe
Wigeon
Sparrowhawk
Barn owl

FLAMBOROUGH CLIFFS

Flamborough Head has one of the most important seabird colonies in Europe. In summer the cliffs are packed with tens of thousands of breeding auks, gannets and gulls creating a memorable experience. The chalk grassland, especially in Holmes Gut, is rich in flowers attracting butterflies and a number of uncommon moths.

Guillemots

Throng the cliffs in early summer

Flamborough Cliffs nature reserve consists of three sections, Breil, Holmes and Thornwick, each with their own character but all important for the seabird colonies nesting on the 100-foot high sheer chalk cliffs.

For a brief period in the summer the cliffs host internationally important numbers of breeding seabirds including fulmars, herring gulls, kittiwakes, guillemots, razorbills and puffins. A small number of shags also breed while gannets, nesting nearby at Bempton Cliffs, can be seen flying past in straggly lines. Landward of the cliff top footpath are grassland fields which host nesting skylark and meadow pipit whose numbers have increased as grazing has improved the habitat.

Razorbill

Shag

Can be seen fishing offshore

Top tip...

A visit to view the breeding seabirds between mid May to mid July for the sheer number of birds, for the sights, sounds and smells is a must. Catch up with puffins, seen easier here than at any other site in Yorkshire.

Puffin

Return to the cliffs to breed every summer

SPRING
Migrant birds
Seabirds

SUMMER
Peregrine
Seabirds
Wildflowers
Butterflies
Harbour
porpoise

AUTUMN
Shearwaters
Skuas
Short-eared owl
Migrant birds

WINTER
Lapland bunting
Snow bunting
Peregrine

FLAMBOROUGH CLIFFS

Common starfish

In Holmes there is an area of gorse scrub which attracts breeding linnet and yellowhammer. At Thornwick the two reed beds, though small, host reed warbler, sedge warbler and reed bunting.

Both the base of the steps into Holmes and near Thornwick cottages are fantastic spots for wildflowers. Growing here in the chalk grassland is bird's-foot trefoil, common spotted and pyramidal orchids. Along the cliff edge there is a beautiful show of delicate pink thrift and occasionally Northern marsh orchid can bloom in profusion.

A number of butterflies are attracted to these flowers including small skipper and

Lightbulb sea squirt

Seen all year round in rockpools at North Landing

Spotted at North Landing

ringlet. The nature reserve is also home to the scarce burnet companion moth.

In autumn birdwatching interest switches to migration. Out at sea, all four skuas may be seen plus large numbers of common seabirds, divers, grebes and wildfowl. Clifftop fields attract migrant short-eared owl, wheatear and whinchat, whilst the berry-laden scrub and wooded areas in Holmes Gut attracts hordes of migrant thrushes, warblers and finches. Scarce migrants are also frequently seen, including yellow-browed warbler. Throughout the year North Landing provides endless opportunities for rock pooling with starfish, crabs, fish and an array of marine molluscs to be found as well as a rich and varied carpet of seaweeds. Just be careful to watch the tides!

NEAREST POSTCODE
YO15 1BJ

GRID REFERENCE
TA 239 720

RESERVE SIZE
36.23 ha

PUBLIC TRANSPORT
Regular bus service from Bridlington; closest train station is at Bridlington.

DIRECTIONS
From Flamborough village follow the B1265 signposted for North Landing. The road terminates above North Landing with a car park on the left.

SITE DESIGNATION
SSSI, SAC, SPA, Flamborough Head Heritage Coast

OTHER INFORMATION
Yorkshire Wildlife Trust's Living Seas Centre at South Landing (page 26) has information and education facilities.

Sea thrift

Grows on the cliffs

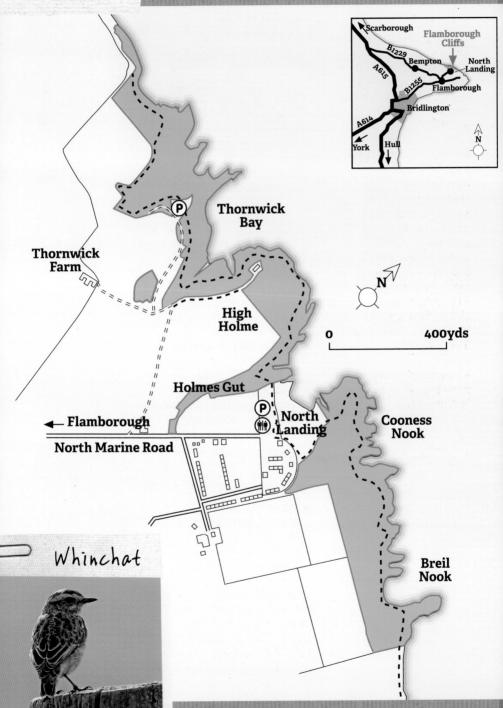

Scarborough
B1229
Bempton
A615
B1255
Flamborough
Bridlington
A614
York Hull
Flamborough Cliffs
North Landing
N

Thornwick Bay

Thornwick Farm

High Holme

Holmes Gut

Flamborough

North Marine Road

North Landing

Cooness Nook

Breil Nook

N

0   400yds

Whinchat

Puffin
Fratercula arctica

☑ SPRING
☑ SUMMER
☐ AUTUMN
☐ WINTER

☐ GRASSLAND
☑ BY THE COAST
☐ WETLAND
☐ FARMLAND

See puffins in spring

One of the most well-known and charismatic birds, puffins return each spring to nest in burrows dug into the boulder clay on top of the great chalk cliffs of Flamborough Head. Flamborough is the most southerly of their east coast breeding sites and is also one of the easiest to visit, with excellent access.

For most of the year, puffins live far out at sea. They are highly adapted to this pelagic lifestyle, feeding on small fish caught below the surface. Puffins, like penguins, use their wings to 'fly' underwater. They can be surprisingly quick and agile, catching fast-swimming fish such as greater sand eel. For a few months each year, puffins visit Yorkshire to breed. This gives us a wonderful opportunity to watch this seabird. Puffins pair for life; and this can be a long life, puffins as old as 38 have been identified through research. They may live even longer than this.

The brightly-coloured beak which is used for display, is only seen in the spring and summer. The colourful outer cover is shed after the breeding season. Puffins can be quite vocal at breeding sites, but otherwise remain silent. They are smaller than the two other auk species that nest at Flamborough Cliffs, guillemots and razorbills, and can be told at a distance by their bright orange feet, more compact shape and their habit of flying high above the sea surface.

Puffins can be seen at Flamborough Cliffs from mid-March onwards, though the best time is April to July. Birds can be seen flying to and from their clifftop breeding sites, resting on the water around the headland or perched on the cliffs. The best way to see them is by taking a boat trip from North Landing. By August most birds have headed back out to sea with their fledged young.

Water vole
Arvicola amphibius

☑ SPRING
☑ SUMMER
☑ AUTUMN
☑ WINTER

☐ WOODLAND
☐ PASTURELAND
☑ WETLAND
☐ FARMLAND

Man-made water vole habitat

The UK has seen a dramatic fall in numbers of the endearing water vole in recent times. The decline is generally believed to be a result of a combination of land use intensification and increased predation by a growing population of the non-native American mink.

A number of Yorkshire populations managed to hang on during this time and, whilst they are by no means thriving yet, they can now be regularly sighted (if you are patient and know where to look!) in much of Yorkshire including parts of the Yorkshire Wolds, Humberhead Levels, Vale of York and River Aire.

Water voles are adapted to live in most wetland habitats and can be found on rivers, streams, canals, lakes and ponds as long as there is cover from predation and a good food source (they eat mainly grasses and other vegetation, although common reed is a particular favourite).

Yorkshire Wildlife Trust has a successful track history of working with landowners and other organisations to create and restore the habitats needed, and the connections between them, to help this species become a common sight across the whole county once again. This includes education work as water voles are similar in appearance to the brown rat and can therefore suffer misplaced persecution. They are relatively easy to distinguish however, with their rounder nose and face, small ears (sometimes completely hidden) and significantly shorter tails. They are also much better swimmers than rats.

Perched high on a hillside overlooking the Rivelin Valley is one of Sheffield Wildlife Trust's newly extended nature reserves.

Redstart

Named after their fiery tail, which they quiver

THE Wildlife TRUSTS

Sheffield & Rotherham

NEAREST POSTCODE
S10 4LW

GRID REFERENCE
SK 288 865

RESERVE SIZE
23 ha

PUBLIC TRANSPORT
Buses run from Sheffield to Bakewell and Castleton. Alight on Rivelin Valley Road and walk 0.8 miles to the nature reserve.

DIRECTIONS
From Sheffield city centre take the Manchester Road (A57) out of the city. At Rivelin take Lodge Lane. Parking is available on Lodge Lane or at Rivelin Dams.

SITE DESIGNATION
LNR

The site is notable for its peaceful atmosphere and spectacular views over the Rivelin Dams and the woods of Wyming Brook further up the valley. Fox Hagg's own varied and dramatic scenery is as stunning as the view, with its patchwork of bilberry and heather moorland, silver birch woodland and scrubby areas.

This range of upland habitats attract a wide variety of birds including both resident meadow pipits and summer-visiting tree pipits. Both species perform aerobatic parachuting songflights in spring, with the dive made by a tree pipit leading to the top of a tree or bush, unlike the similar meadow pipit, which habitually alights on the ground. A flash of red in the trees could indicate the presence of the fiery-tailed redstart, one of the most attractive of the summer migrant birds. Less visually attractive but with beautiful songs are the range of warblers that can be heard singing from the scrub and woodland, including willow and wood warblers, blackcap and whitethroat. Linnets can be seen all year round feeding on heather and other seeds.

Once managed as a holly hagg, when the soft spikeless upper leaves of holly were cut for winter fodder for sheep and cattle, Fox Hagg is now managed for its wildlife. Small areas of scrub are cut on a five year cycle, and bracken is controlled to allow heather to grow. Remnants of holly can still be seen in the gulley around the stream known as Allen Syke and along the north edge of the nature reserve.

Holly blue

See their caterpillars feeding on holly

Top tip...
Visit after a rain shower in the summer when scents of the moorland flowers are strongest.

LOCATION

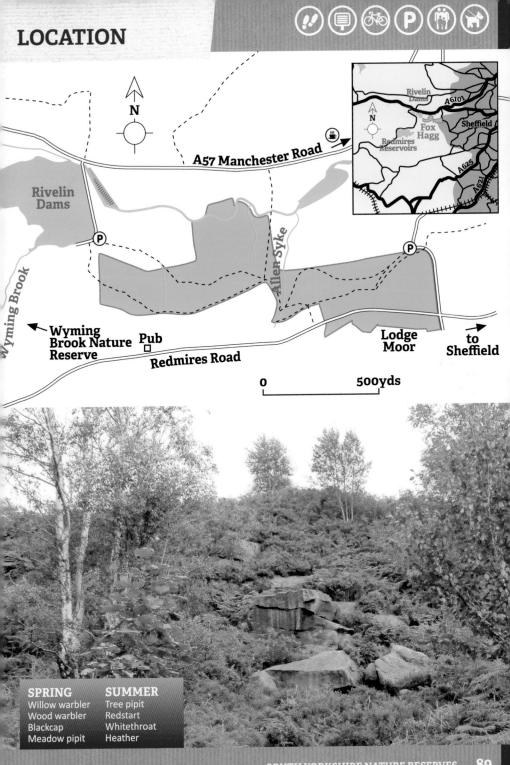

N

A57 Manchester Road

Rivelin Dams

Rivelin Dams

A6101

Sheffield

Fox Hagg

Redmires Reservoirs

A625

A621

Allen Syke

P

P

Wyming Brook

← Wyming Brook Nature Reserve

Pub

Redmires Road

Lodge Moor

to Sheffield →

0   500yds

SPRING	SUMMER
Willow warbler	Tree pipit
Wood warbler	Redstart
Blackcap	Whitethroat
Meadow pipit	Heather

GARBUTT WOOD

The dramatic Whitestone Cliff that towers above the wood shines out from the southern end of the Hambleton Hills to be seen for miles across the Vale of Mowbray to the Dales. A walk around the wood at anytime of year gives you fantastic views as well as a variety of habitats to explore.

Interesting for both its biological and geological features, this impressive nature reserve with various habitats is home to good numbers of breeding birds, beautiful flowering plants, and oak and birch woodland.

From 305m above sea level on the cliff top, the nature reserve tumbles 150m to its western boundary just above Lake Gormire. The Whitestone Cliff itself has a sheer face of around 15 – 21m. The last major rock fall was in 1775, an event recorded in the diary of Methodist John Wesley who was preaching in the area.

Above the cliff you will find bilberry and heather moor, whereas below the boulder-strewn scree many micro-habitats have established ideal for lichens, mosses and ferns. Here you will also find evidence of man's activity as the sandstone from the cliff was quarried until 1840 and shaped into square sleepers for use on the railways. The main area of woodland is acidic consisting mainly of birch, oak and holly, but pockets of other tree species occur including aspen, ash, sweet chestnut and sycamore. The more open areas of the nature reserve are covered with bracken and scrub. In the north west corner of the site where springs have made it too wet for the bracken, remnants of the plants that once existed survive. Common fleabane, ragged robin and common spotted orchid are amongst the flowers that flourish.

Established as a nature reserve in 1966, the wood forms part of Gormire SSSI and is part of a network of woodland and forestry plantations that stretches for some distance along the Hambleton Hills. The earliest reference to the woodland is from Tudor times.

Currently Yorkshire Wildlife Trust leases the land from the Forestry Commission; the Trust's main management focus is the control of sycamore. Bracken is also controlled in some areas by pulling, bashing or tree planting.

NEAREST POSTCODE
YO7 2EH

GRID REFERENCE
SE 506 835

RESERVE SIZE
23.96 ha

PUBLIC TRANSPORT
Moors Bus from Thirsk to Sutton Bank National Park Centre.

DIRECTIONS
Take the A170 Thirsk-Scarborough road to Sutton Bank. From Sutton Bank National Park Centre take the Cleveland Way north before taking the nature trail down the slope in to the nature reserve.

SITE DESIGNATION
SSSI

OTHER INFORMATION
Facilities available and a nature trail guide can be purchased at Sutton Bank National Park Centre.

Wood sorrel

Leaves that taste of lemon

LOCATION

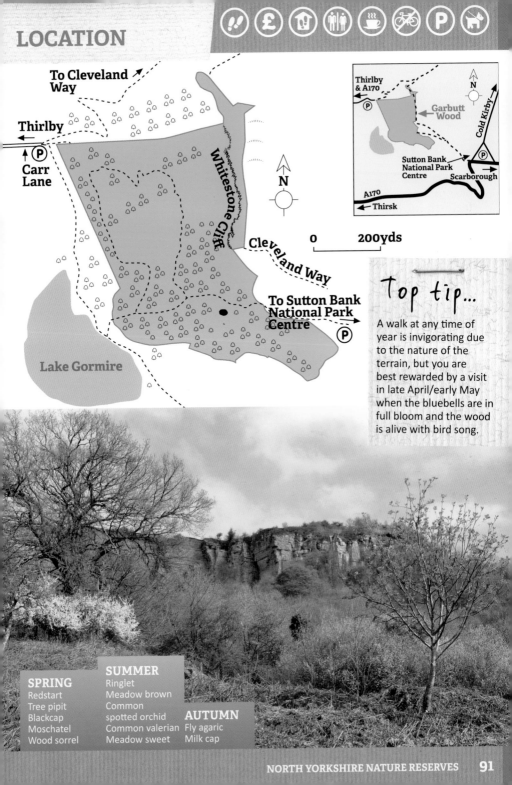

To Cleveland Way

Thirlby

Carr Lane

Whitestone Cliff

Cleveland Way

To Sutton Bank National Park Centre

Lake Gormire

N

0   200yds

Inset map:
Thirlby & A170

Garbutt Wood

Cold Kirby

Sutton Bank National Park Centre

Scarborough

A170

Thirsk

N

Top tip...

A walk at any time of year is invigorating due to the nature of the terrain, but you are best rewarded by a visit in late April/early May when the bluebells are in full bloom and the wood is alive with bird song.

SPRING
Redstart
Tree pipit
Blackcap
Moschatel
Wood sorrel

SUMMER
Ringlet
Meadow brown
Common spotted orchid
Common valerian
Meadow sweet

AUTUMN
Fly agaric
Milk cap

GLOBE FLOWER WOOD

Situated towards the edge of the Malham Tarn basin, Globe Flower Wood in late spring is a bright spot in a generally bleak and heavily grazed upland landscape.

NEAREST POSTCODE
BD24 9PR

GRID REFERENCE
SD 873 667

RESERVE SIZE
0.08 ha

PUBLIC TRANSPORT
The nearest train station is at Settle, with occasional buses to Malham.

DIRECTIONS
From Settle take the B6479 to Langcliffe. Turn right onto New Street in Langcliffe village. Stay on this road as it becomes Henside Road. The nature reserve is about four miles from Langcliffe and a mile west of Malham Tarn.

OTHER INFORMATION
There is no access to the nature reserve but it can be viewed from the wall.

Water avens

A typical flower of damp woodlands

tall herbs. The yellow of the globe flowers creates a wonderful display, blooming alongside wood cranesbill and melancholy thistle. There are some large sycamores in the drier eastern corner of the nature reserve, whilst willow scrub with some hazel, alder and birch has developed in the wet area.

One of the Trust's smallest nature reserves, Globe Flower Wood is also one of the Trust's oldest, having been acquired in 1963. The farmer at the time had kept the area ungrazed because he liked the globe flowers and upon selling the farm, he wanted the flowers to be protected. The nature reserve is a triangular limestone walled enclosure largely composed of ungrazed, damp meadow fringed by various small willows. Due to its small size

Despite its small size, Globe Flower Wood is of great interest due to the high concentration of globe flowers and other

Globe flower

Collectively form a wonderful yellow display

and wet nature, the nature reserve is a fragile site and while there is a step stile in the wall, there is no public access. Fortunately, the entire site can be viewed easily by looking over the wall.

Management is essentially to help this small area remain frozen in time, ready for the opportunity for the flowers to spread back into the surrounding area. Walls are kept stock proof, the willows are kept in check and invasive species such as nettle and rosebay willowherb are removed.

Top tip...
Visit at the end of May or in early June, when the globe flowers are at their best.

LOCATION

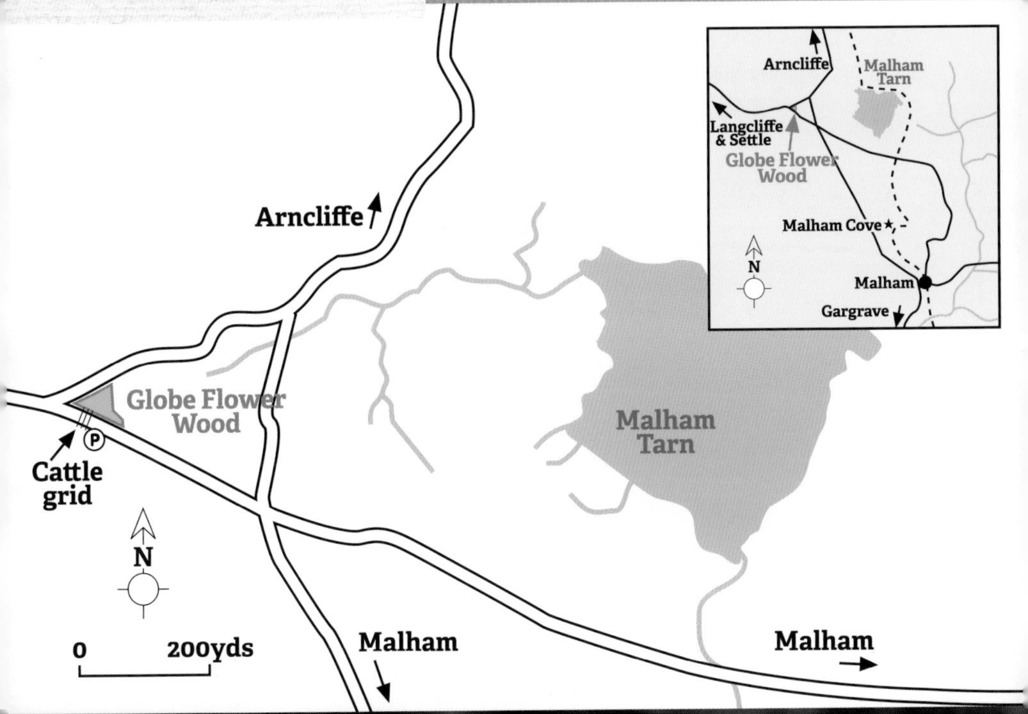
Arncliffe
Malham Tarn
Langcliffe & Settle
Globe Flower Wood
Malham Cove
N
Malham
Gargrave
Arncliffe
Globe Flower Wood
Malham Tarn
P
Cattle grid
N
0
200yds
Malham
Malham

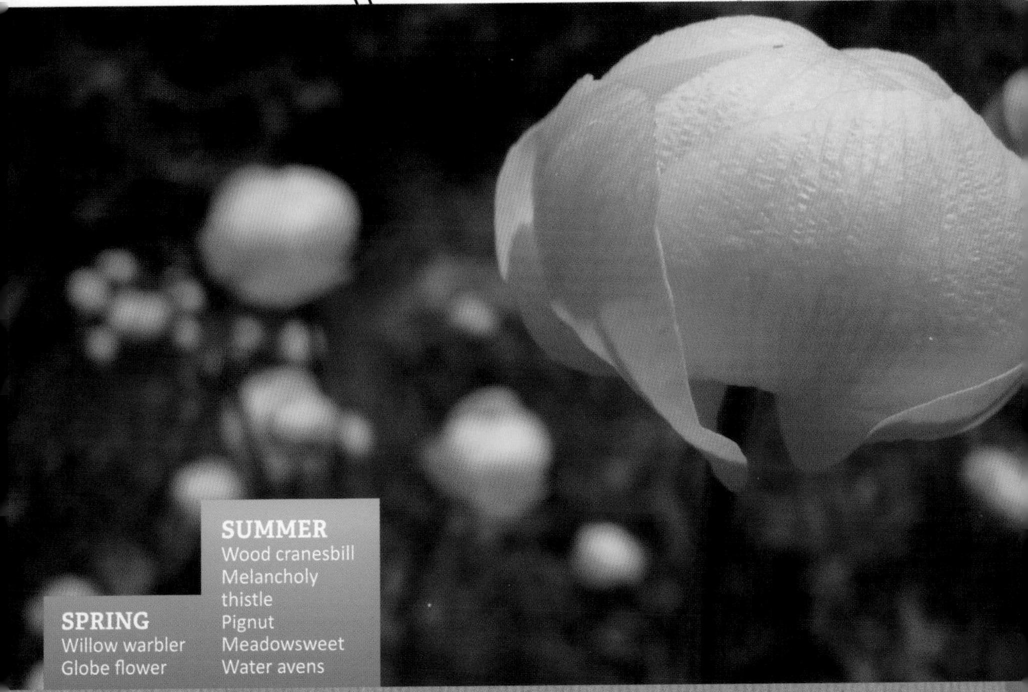

SPRING
Willow warbler
Globe flower

SUMMER
Wood cranesbill
Melancholy thistle
Pignut
Meadowsweet
Water avens

GRASS WOOD

At 78 ha, Grass Wood is one of the largest areas of broadleaved woodland in the Dales. It is a wildlife-rich ash woodland occupying an area of carboniferous limestone on the north side of Wharfedale.

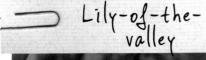

Lily-of-the-valley

A perennial plant that spreads with underground rhizomes

Grass Wood's importance lies mainly in its extremely rich and varied plant life. It is located on a series of limestone terraces, with much exposed rock and, therefore, open areas. This habitat contributes greatly to a varied flora which includes characteristic plants such as lily-of-the-valley and rock-rose. Other plants found here are indicators of ancient woodland. Alongside the many interesting and attractive plants are a whole range of other, sometimes nationally uncommon, fungi, insects and other wildlife. Resident birds include tawny owl, the familiar chaffinch and the exotic looking green woodpecker. Grass Wood is also the home base for a

Common puffball

One of many types of fungi that can be found

Treecreeper

Climbs up tree trunks searching for insects

SPRING
Pied flycatcher
Spotted flycatcher
Bluebell
Primrose
Lily-of-the-valley

SUMMER
Northern brown argus
Dropwort
Bloody cranesbill

AUTUMN
Roe deer
Common puffball
Milkcap
Brittlegills
Clouded funnel cap

WINTER
Tawny owl
Nuthatch
Treecreeper

GRASS WOOD

Wood warbler

Stinking hellebore

Gives off a pungent odour

A long distance migrant returning in May

number of returning migratory birds such as pied and spotted flycatchers, willow and wood warblers.

The continued existence of the diverse wildlife on the site relies on the persistence of the light and airy conditions found underneath upland ash. Underplanting with conifers and the removal of native trees in the middle of last century was detrimental to the site, and current management aims to extend the area of mature ash woodland by addressing these issues.

The Trust originally became involved in managing the wood when, in the 1960s, it leased a small portion from the Forestry Commission. Over the years it became more involved, finally completing purchase of the whole wood in 1983, since which date it has gradually increased active management, ably supported by an enthusiastic team of volunteers.

Pied flycatcher

Readily uses nestboxes in the wood

NEAREST POSTCODE
BD23 5NE

GRID REFERENCE
SD 985 655

RESERVE SIZE
78.25 ha

PUBLIC TRANSPORT
The nearest bus service goes to Grassington, approximately a 1 mile walk, with the nearest rail station at Skipton.

DIRECTIONS
From the B6265 in Grassington take Wood Lane on your right and travel north. Follow this for one mile, the nature reserve lies alongside the Grassington to Conistone minor road.

SITE DESIGNATION
SSSI

Top tip...

Grass Wood looks splendid in late spring when the richness of the site is at its most obvious. The extraction track into the wood from the gate furthest from Grassington gives superb views up Wharfedale.

LOCATION

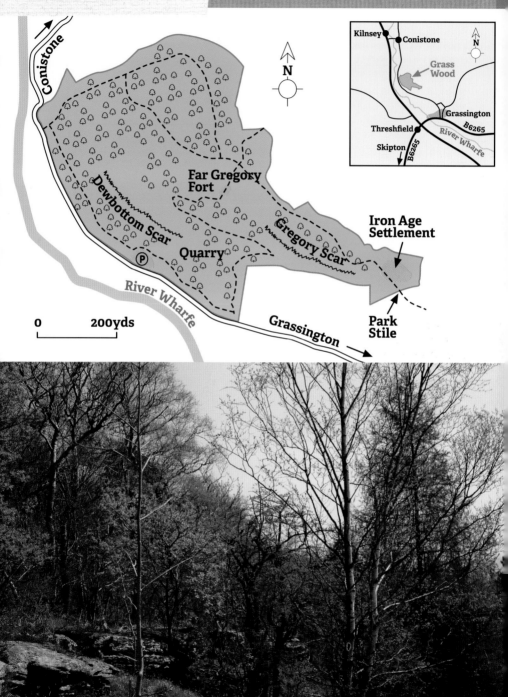

Conistone

N

Kilnsey
Conistone
Grass Wood
Grassington
B6265
Threshfield
River Wharfe
Skipton
B6265
N

Far Gregory Fort

Dewbottom Scar

Quarry

(P)

Gregory Scar

Iron Age Settlement

Park Stile

River Wharfe

Grassington

0   200yds

GRENO WOODS

Covering an area of 169 ha, Greno Woods is a beautiful ancient woodland with its existence recorded as far back as the Middle Ages.

Below the canopy of 30 tree species a wide range of characteristic wildflowers can be found including carpets of bluebells in May, followed later by more unusual species such as common cow-wheat and goldilocks buttercup. Heather and bilberry grow in open patches, where the influence of the sandstone creates more acidic conditions. This diverse plantlife in turn attracts many insects; the moth fauna is particularly notable, with species including dusky brocade. There is also an important population of the rare shining guest ant.

Over 60 species of birds have been recorded including breeding spotted flycatcher, exquisite wood warblers and

Crossbill

Flocks of crossbills can be heard flying overhead, calling 'chip'

all three woodpeckers with the diminutive lesser spotted having been seen recently. In the heathland areas nightjars breed and the evocative churring of these birds can be heard from the end of May on warm, still evenings. Visitors may see woodcock roding along the edge of clearings, flying at tree-top height. This unusual wader nests in the woods and males defend their

Common cow-wheat

An indicator species of ancient woodland

Peacock

Can be seen feeding on thistle flowers in open areas

GRENO WOODS

territories by flying around the boundaries at dawn and dusk, uttering a sharp squeak and peculiar grunting sounds. At other times, particularly during winter, woodcock are sometimes flushed from underfoot in damp wooded areas, where they fly up rapidly on arched, rufous wings, twisting away through the trees. Greno and the surrounding woodlands were managed as coppices from at least as early as medieval times until the late 19th Century with larger standard trees in 20 to 30 year cycles. Timber from the standards was used as a building material projects and the underwood for charcoal, clog soles, brush heads and baskets. Two soaking ponds survive today from these activities.

The purchase of the woods by Sheffield Wildlife Trust in 2012 means that in the future sustainable management techniques will be employed including timely thinning, removal of some of the non-native conifers, track maintenance and footpath creation.

Sheffield & Rotherham

NEAREST POSTCODE
S35 7DS

GRID REFERENCE
SK 328 954

RESERVE SIZE
169 ha

PUBLIC TRANSPORT
Buses from Sheffield to Rotherham calling at Hillsborough, Grenoside, High Green, Chapeltown, Thorpe Hesley and Rotherham.

DIRECTIONS
From Sheffield city centre take the A625 until Hanover Way. Follow the A61 across three roundabouts. Turn left at Salt Box Lane, then right at Main Street. Continue onto Woodhead Road. The Forestry Commission car park is opposite Greno Woods on the left hand side of Woodhead Road.

SITE DESIGNATION
LNR

Woodcock

keep a watchful eye for this well-camouflaged bird

Wood ant

Predatory colonies feed on insects including this lacewing

Top tip...

Visit on a summer evening to watch roding woodcocks, bats and dusk flying moths such as the northern spinach.

LOCATION

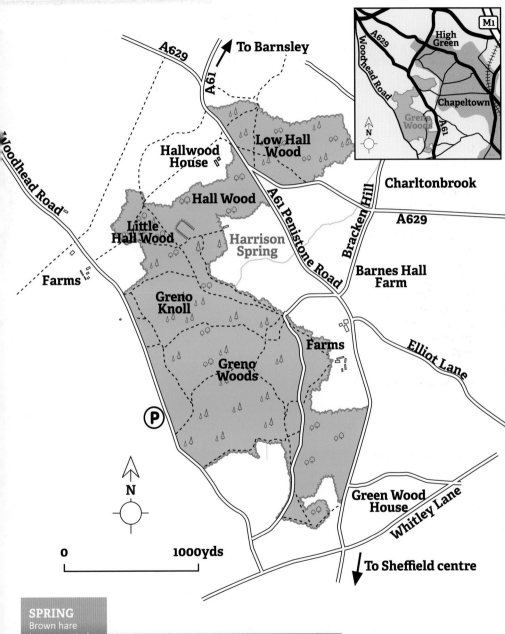

To Barnsley

A629

A61

Hallwood House

Low Hall Wood

Hall Wood

Little Hall Wood

Harrison Spring

Greno Knoll

Farms

Greno Woods

Farms

Woodhead Road

Charltonbrook

A629

Bracken Hill

A61 Penistone Road

Barnes Hall Farm

Elliot Lane

Green Wood House

Whitley Lane

To Sheffield centre

P

N

0   1000yds

Inset map labels:
M1
High Green
Woodhead Road
A629
Chapeltown
A61
Greno Woods
N

SPRING
Brown hare
Lesser spotted woodpecker
Adder
Bluebell
Wood anemone

SUMMER
Grass snake
Common cow-wheat

AUTUMN
Willow tit
Nuthatch
Fungi

WINTER
Roe deer
Woodcock
Bullfinch

HAMMOND'S FIELD

One of the few remaining areas of unimproved farmland around the moorland fringes, Hammond's Field forms a small part of the South Pennine Moors Special Protected Area (SPA). Rich in wildlife, this semi-improved wet pasture has an interesting mosaic of habitats enclosed by traditional drystone walls.

Hammond's Field is generally very wet in winter as evidenced by large areas of soft rush and smaller clumps of sphagnum moss. Field wood-rush and grasses such as Yorkshire fog, common bent and marsh foxtail are very much in evidence. Other common species include creeping buttercup, cuckooflower, heath bedstraw and tormentil.

The field is important for wading birds such as curlew, snipe, redshank and lapwing, both in the breeding and wintering seasons. A scrape has been excavated for their use. A large number of common toads and smooth newts have been found hibernating in the old dry-stone wall on the southern boundary. It is thought they spawn in the adjacent drainage ditch along with breeding invertebrates including common hawker dragonfly.

Management is focused around the control of soft rush, with work mostly taking place where grazing with cattle occurs during autumn when there is least disturbance to breeding birds and ground flora. In the past the site has been drained and the Trust is now working to reverse this.

There is no access to the field itself, but a viewing area has been created at the south west corner at the end of the approach track.

NEAREST POSTCODE
S10 4QZ

GRID REFERENCE
SK 263 859

RESERVE SIZE
4.20 ha

PUBLIC TRANSPORT
A bus service runs to nearby Lodge Moor. The nearest train station is in Sheffield.

DIRECTIONS
On the western outskirts of Sheffield, adjacent to the Redmires Reservoirs, 1.5 miles to the west of Lodge Moor. From Sheffield, take the A57 Manchester road, turning left at Crosspool. Alternatively at Rivelin Mill Bridge take Lodge Lane uphill to Lodge Moor, turning right to Redmires Reservoirs. Access is along the conduit path opposite the Upper Reservoir. The car park is 200m beyond the conduit path at the corner of the reservoir. There is a small layby for vehicles with disabled passengers.

SITE DESIGNATION
SPA, SSSI

Common toad

Hibernates in the dry stone wall

Redshank

Redshank and other waders are present all year round

LOCATION

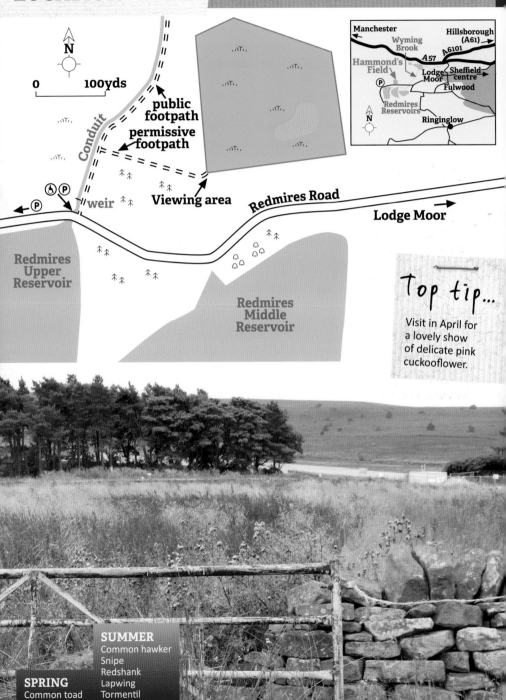

N

0 100yds

Conduit

public footpath

permissive footpath

Viewing area

weir

P

P

Redmires Road

Lodge Moor

Redmires Upper Reservoir

Redmires Middle Reservoir

Manchester
Hillsborough (A61)
Wyming Brook
A6101
A57
Hammond's Field
Lodge Moor
Sheffield centre
Fulwood
P
Redmires Reservoirs
Ringinglow
N

Top tip...

Visit in April for a lovely show of delicate pink cuckooflower.

SPRING
Common toad

SUMMER
Common hawker
Snipe
Redshank
Lapwing
Tormentil

HARLAND MOUNT

Set on a steep hill ascending out of Scarborough, this rough acid pasture and scrub woodland nature reserve offers beautiful views across the town and over the sea.

NEAREST POSTCODE
YO12 5NL

GRID REFERENCE
TA 021 871

RESERVE SIZE
7.77 ha

PUBLIC TRANSPORT
Regular bus and train services into Scarborough.

DIRECTIONS
The nature reserve is situated just off the A170 out of Scarborough, next to Jacob's Mount Caravan Park.

OTHER INFORMATION
There is space for three cars in the lay-by off the A170. Nearest facilities are in Scarborough town centre.

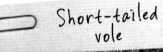

Short-tailed vole

Common in the grassland

in the magnificent views afforded here.

The steeply sloping woodland bisects the meadows and is primarily a dense mix of ash, oak, elder and hawthorn. Yorkshire Wildlife Trust currently thins out the woodland to allow ferns and other flora to colonise more of the ground making the most of the newly created lighter conditions. Bluebell, primrose and dog violet grow on the banks below the woodland.

The fields here are grazed in spring and autumn to ensure a healthy sward and to allow flowering plants to seed. Weeds are managed by selectively spot-spraying thistles, nettles and docks.

There is a small dew-pond in the upper field that has long been dry and offers potential for restoration in the future.

In the past this acid grassland has seen some improvement but now the pasture at Harland Mount Nature Reserve is managed by traditional methods to restore it to the species rich grassland it once would have been.

There are currently few rarities on site, but interesting and attractive species including ox-eye daisy and common knapweed flourish. The nature reserve is worth a visit simply for its unspoilt nature, as well as to take

Ox-eye daisy

Fill up the new open areas

Top tip...
To see the meadow and views at their best visit from late May to early July. With flowers in bloom, the sward is buzzing with the sight and sound of bees, grasshoppers and many other insects.

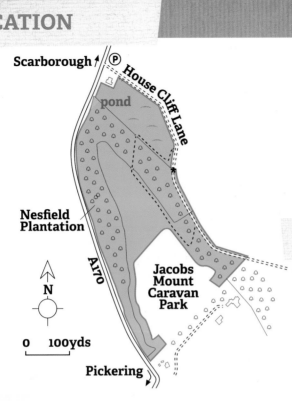

Scarborough
House Cliff Lane
pond
Nesfield Plantation
A170
N
0   100yds
Jacobs Mount Caravan Park
Pickering

Scalby
A165
A171
North Sea
Scarborough
Harland Mount
A170
East Ayton
B1261
Eastfield
N

Dog violet

See these delicate flowers in spring

SPRING	SUMMER	AUTUMN	WINTER
Bluebell	Grasshoppers	Fungi	Roe deer
Primrose	Dog violet		
	Yarrow		
	Ox-eye daisy		

HETCHELL WOOD

A mix of woodland, species rich grassland and wet flushes, Hetchell Wood provides a tranquil retreat on the edge of the conurbation of Leeds. The variety of habitats provide refuge for rare species which were once widespread in the local landscape. The path network allows visitors to explore each of the habitats in turn along with other significant features such as the imposing rocky crags.

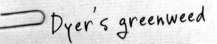

Dyer's greenweed

Once used to colour wool

When visiting Hetchell Wood for the first time you soon become enthralled by its beauty and awakened to a landscape which appears locked in times gone by. Walking through the woodland, evidence of historical coppicing for fire wood is all around. The multi-stemmed hazel stools grow back with vigour and the recent re-establishment of this ancient practice lets in valuable light to the woodland floor, igniting wildflowers from the soil's depths and promoting regeneration of the trees themselves.

Toothwort

This unusual plant is a parasite on hazel and alder roots

Hoary plantain

An edible plant reputed for its medicinal effects

SPRING
Wood barley
Dog's mercury
Wood anemone
Greater
stitchwort
Toothwort

SUMMER
Thistle
broomrape
Dyer's
greenweed
Fragrant orchid
Frog orchid
Hoary plantain

AUTUMN
Treecreeper
Jay
Fungi

WINTER
Roe deer
Tawny owl
Nuthatch

HETCHELL WOOD

The grassland which lies at the centre of the nature reserve sits like a jewel in the crown, showcasing a once more widespread snapshot of how pastures used to look before intensive farming became commonplace. A host of wildflower species are found here providing a valuable nectar source for a variety of insects and food for some of the Trust's Hebridean sheep.

Picture perfect images are created year-round with the stream at the bottom, which meanders slowly amongst the trees and the rocky outcrops alongside the bridleway. The beech plantation provides dappled light and some magnificent mature trees which add further interest to an afternoon walk.

Jay

Listen out for their raucous calls

Common twayblade

The distinctive paired leaves can be seen in spring and summer

NEAREST POSTCODE
LS23 6NA

GRID REFERENCE
SE 380 422

RESERVE SIZE
11.74 ha

PUBLIC TRANSPORT
A bus runs via Bardsey, alight here and walk approximately 1 mile to the nature reserve.

DIRECTIONS
The nature reserve is seven miles north east of Leeds. If approaching from Wetherby via the A58 Leeds-Wetherby road, to reach the main entrance on Milner Lane take the left turn signposted Thorner at the Bracken Fox pub crossroads at Scarcroft. Keep left at a triangular intersection and the nature reserve entrance is on the left, 0.5 miles further on. There is also a public footpath (parking for a few cars) from the side of the A58 at Bardsey.

SITE DESIGNATION
LNR

Top tip...

Hetchell Wood provides contrasting views throughout the seasons. In spring the site comes alive, summer brings the flowering meadow, autumn the spectrum of colour and winter the chance to spot wildlife hiding in the undergrowth.

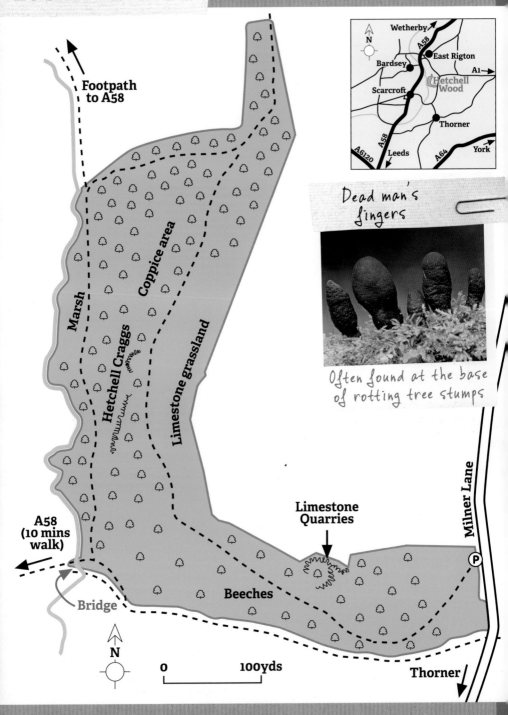

Footpath to A58

Wetherby

A58

East Rigton

Bardsey

A1

Scarcroft

Hetchell Wood

Thorner

A6120

A58

Leeds

A64

York

N

Dead man's fingers

Often found at the base of rotting tree stumps

Marsh

Coppice area

Hetchell Craggs

Limestone grassland

Limestone Quarries

Milner Lane

A58 (10 mins walk)

P

Bridge

Beeches

N

0   100yds

Thorner

HODGSON'S FIELDS

Vivid cerise marsh orchid spikes grow within grassy glades surrounded by hawthorn scrub. Large pastured fields that attract whimbrel in autumn are surrounded by mature hedgerows, home to farmland birds and butterflies.

Hodgson's Fields is an oasis of rough grassland and scrub within the mainly arable landscape of South Holderness. This extensive patch of habitat is rare in the area. Although farmed it was not intensive, which is unusual in the locality. As a result the site is a haven for wildlife.

Ringlet

Seen from mid-June to August

The 45 hectare nature reserve supports grassland in which plants including yarrow, wild angelica, self-heal and meadow vetchling thrive. An impressive display of Southern and Northern marsh orchids bloom during June and July. Tussocky grassland is ideal for small mammals, and barn owls and kestrels can regularly be seen hunting for them throughout the year. Whimbrel also frequently drop into feed in the fields on their autumn migration.

Some areas support scattered bushy-scrub of varying age range and structure. This, along with mature hedgerows of hawthorn, rose, blackthorn and bramble are excellent sources of food and shelter for many birds. Farmland birds such as linnet, yellowhammer and tree sparrow are commonly seen and heard here. Scrub also provides shelter for insects and butterflies such as large skipper, meadow brown, ringlet and small heath. A small farm pond provides hunting ground for migrant hawker dragonflies. The site is a great spot for mammals including brown hare, harvest mouse and short-tailed vole — look out for the white rumps of roe deer bobbing along the hedgerow as you walk along. A visit at dusk may well reward you with the sight of several species of bat feeding in the sheltered flight lines between scrub patches and hedgerows.

Management here focuses on rotational hedgerow management, maintenance of scrub of different ages, as well as traditional meadow management and grazing by rare breed cattle to keep areas of grassland open.

NEAREST POSTCODE
HU19 0UU

GRID REFERENCE
TA 377 206

RESERVE SIZE
45.09 ha

PUBLIC TRANSPORT
A bus service passes by Skeffling on the way to Easington. Closest train station is in Hull.

DIRECTIONS
From Hull take the A1033 Withernsea road. In Patrington take the B1445 Easington Road. At the eastern end of Skeffling village turn left down Out Newton Road. After almost a mile the road dissects the nature reserve.

OTHER INFORMATION
Dogs allowed on leads on the public right of way in western part of nature reserve. Café, toilets and information centre are located nearby at Spurn. Paths are unsurfaced.

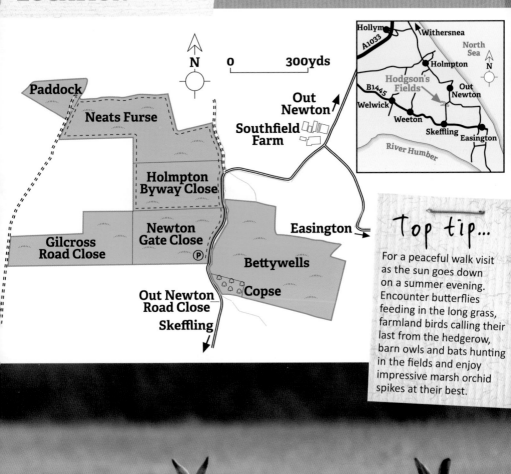

N

0 — 300yds

Paddock

Neats Furse

Holmpton Byway Close

Gilcross Road Close

Newton Gate Close (P)

Out Newton Road Close

Skeffling

Out Newton

Southfield Farm

Easington

Bettywells

Copse

Inset map: Hollym, A1033, Withersnea, North Sea, Holmpton, Out Newton, B1445, Hodgson's Fields, Welwick, Weeton, Skeffling, Easington, River Humber, N

Top tip...

For a peaceful walk visit as the sun goes down on a summer evening. Encounter butterflies feeding in the long grass, farmland birds calling their last from the hedgerow, barn owls and bats hunting in the fields and enjoy impressive marsh orchid spikes at their best.

SPRING	SUMMER	AUTUMN	WINTER
Whitethroat	Large skipper	Barn owl	Roe deer
Grasshopper warbler	Ringlet	Yellowhammer	Redwing
Brown hare	Small tortoiseshell	Linnet	Fieldfare
	Marsh orchids	Whimbrel	

HOPYARD HAY MEADOW

Hopyard Hay Meadow is home to a mix of wildflowers surrounded by ancient hedgerows.

The hedgerows surrounding this small meadow are mentioned in the Hatfield, Thorne and Fishlake Enclosure Award of 1825 which shows that this site has been grassland for hundreds of years.

There is a list of over 70 plant species, including sweet vernal-grass, pignut, great burnet, pepper-saxifrage and four species of buttercup including goldilocks. The ratio of meadow foxtail to great burnet suggests a flood meadow of a rare grassland type. Butterfly and moth species recorded include the chimney sweeper moth, a good indicator species for old grassland, good numbers of blues, coppers, whites, skippers and recent records of purple hairstreak. Birds recorded include green woodpecker, little owl and large numbers of wintering finches, some of which breed. The Trust is in the process of trying to enhance the floristic diversity of the site through native seed translocation and by carrying out annual hay cuts in late summer. Also, there are plans to replant wild service tree saplings, a species which until recently grew in the hedgerows here.

NEAREST POSTCODE
DN7 6QE

GRID REFERENCE
SE 663 109

RESERVE SIZE
1.73 ha

PUBLIC TRANSPORT
Train link available to Hatfield and Stainforth from Doncaster Railway station. Bus services available from Doncaster town centre.

DIRECTIONS
In Hatfield village (north east of Doncaster) turn north past the church and continue past the school and Victoira Avenue onto a dirt track (Cuckoo Lane) for about 0.5 miles. About 20 yards prior to the Pumping Station turn left into Guile Carr Lane. The nature reserve is on the right where the lane bends.

Snake's head fritillary

Flowers in April

Nearby site
OWSTON MEADOWS

GRID REFERENCE
SE 552 112

Eight miles west of Hopyard is Owston (Old Glebe) Meadows, a SSSI and a truly stunning example of a traditional hay meadow. This nature reserve has no public access to prevent trampling of the fragile plant species, but the Trust runs guided walks during the flowering season to allow the public to enjoy this rare gem. The fields have traditionally been managed for hay with autumn grazing resulting in a rich assemblage of plants with over 90 species recorded. Species of more limited distribution in South Yorkshire include snake's head fritillary, common twayblade and adder's-tongue fern.

LOCATION

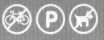

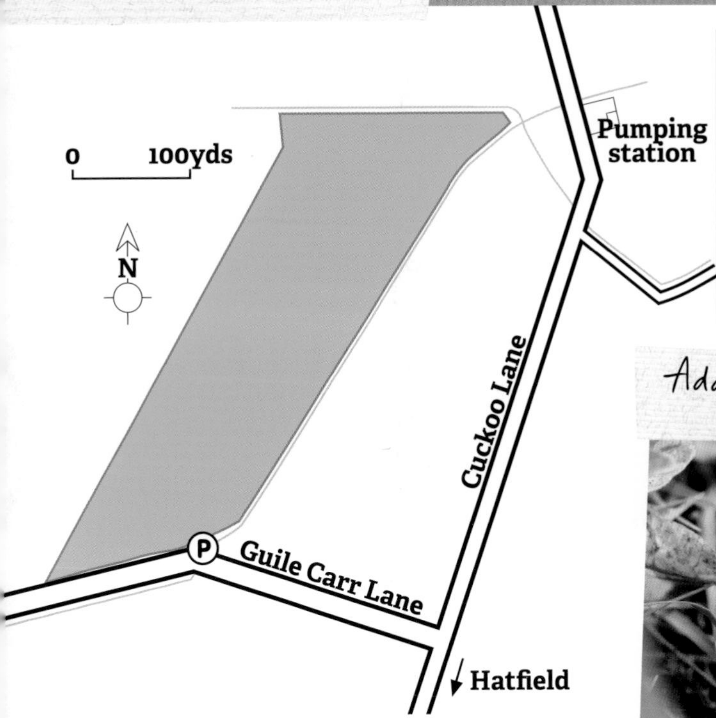
0 100yds
N
Pumping station
Cuckoo Lane
P
Guile Carr Lane
Hatfield

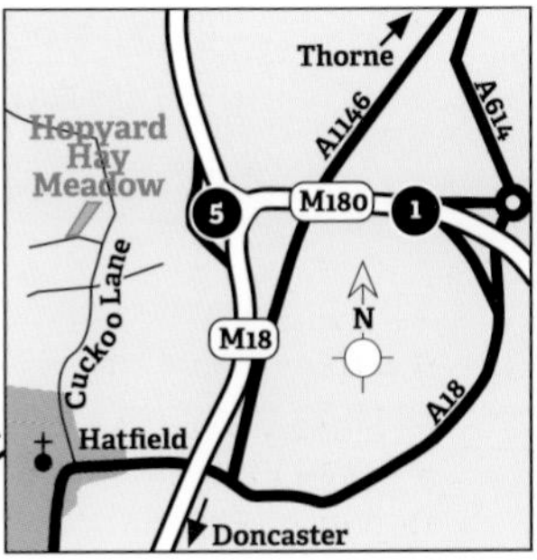
Thorne
A1146
A614
Hopyard Hay Meadow
5
M180
1
Cuckoo Lane
N
M18
A18
Hatfield
Doncaster

Adder's tongue fern

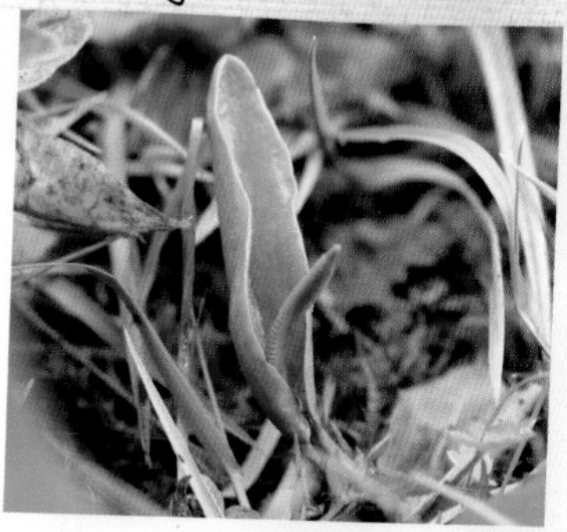

The spore-bearing stalk resembles a snake's tongue

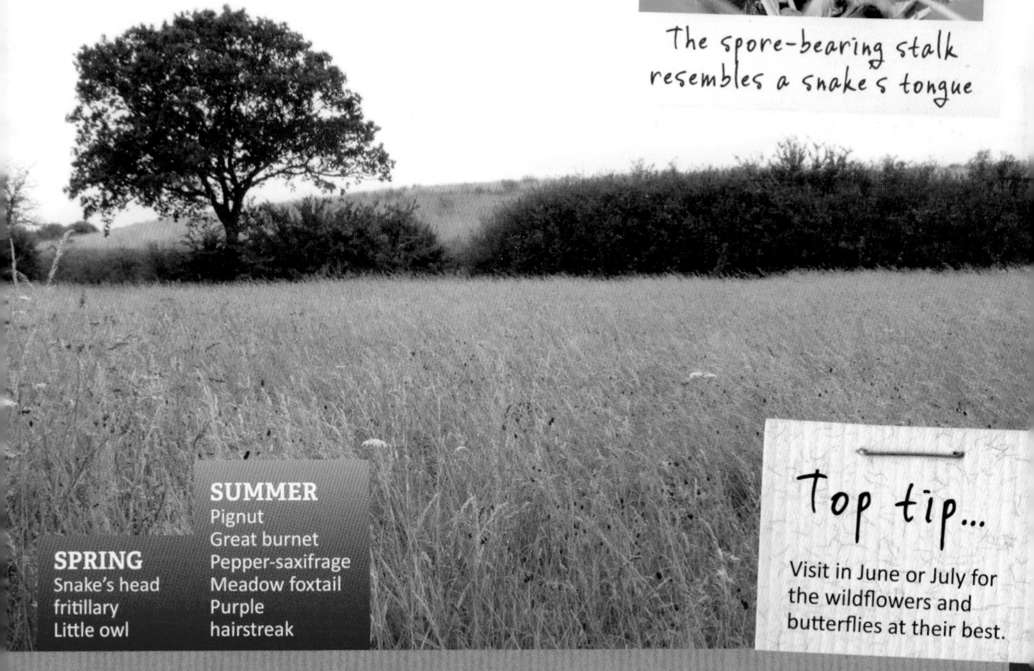

SPRING
Snake's head fritillary
Little owl

SUMMER
Pignut
Great burnet
Pepper-saxifrage
Meadow foxtail
Purple hairstreak

Top tip...

Visit in June or July for the wildflowers and butterflies at their best.

JEFFRY BOG (& KIRKHAM WOOD)

Jeffry Bog lies in the tranquil setting of Kirkham Gorge and offers a range of habitats, with an impressive range of wildflowers, including early purple orchid, bogbean and betony.

Standing on the banks of the River Derwent, Jeffry Bog is a relic wet pasture with an important lowland marsh that is embraced by the Howardian Hills Area of Outstanding Natural Beauty. Despite its small size, the range of different habitats make this an interesting place to visit, particularly during the spring and summer. In spring the grasslands are yellow with the flowers of cowslip and primrose, whilst in the wetter areas the large glossy heads of marsh marigolds can be seen. Other notable plants early in the season include early purple orchid. Adjacent to the nature reserve, areas of wet woodland known as alder carr will be coming into leaf.

By summer the cocoons of spiders and moths can be found among the tall grasses. The grasslands thrive with betony, great and salad burnet, and common spotted orchid. In the marsh, blunt-flowered rush, oval and brown sedges, and marsh arrowgrass can be found among the cream sprays of meadowsweet, cerise ragged robin and prominent yellow flag iris. At ground level, some spiders can be seen carrying parcels of young whilst others guard territories. Damselflies and day-flying moths can be seen in abundance on warm, sunny days.

Visitors should keep an eye overhead as buzzards are a regular sight. Look along the riverbank as signs of otter presence are frequent, though this shy mammal is only rarely seen. Barn owls can be seen at any time of the year hunting for voles, though are most active when feeding young in summer. Kingfishers are a regular sight along the river, joined in summer by an occasional common tern and in winter by goosanders. There is historical evidence of farming on site, with remnants of ridge and furrow to be seen in the grassland. Today, Yorkshire Wildlife Trust grazes the nature reserve with cattle to help encourage wildflowers.

The Trust also owns nearby Kirkham Wood (0.25 ha; Grid Ref. SE 734 656).

NEAREST POSTCODE
YO60 7NJ

GRID REFERENCE
SE 762 666

RESERVE SIZE
2.97 ha

PUBLIC TRANSPORT
Malton buses stop in Westow.

DIRECTIONS
Six miles south west of Malton, two miles east of Kirkham Abbey and about one mile north of Westow. Park cars at the roadside opposite the entrance to church farm being careful not to obstruct either of the farm tracks. Walk down the farm track opposite the farm to the nature reserve. The Centenary Way footpath along the river passes through the site.

Marsh valerian

A great nectar source for insects

River Derwent

Centenery Way

Ant hills

Ridge and furrow

Ditch

Jeffry Bog Plantation

N

0   100yds

Limited parking (take care not to block farm tracks)

P

River Derwent

Jeffry Bog

Malton

A64 & Kirkham

Church Farm

Westow

N

Buzzard

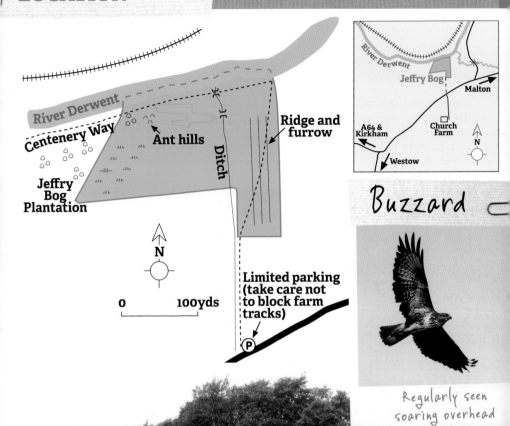

Regularly seen soaring overhead

SPRING
Early purple orchid
Cowslip
Primrose
Marsh marigold

SUMMER
Barn owl
Banded demoiselle
Yellow meadow ant
Marsh valerian
Betony

AUTUMN
Buzzard

WINTER
Goosander

KELDMARSH

Step back in time with a visit to Keldmarsh, a remnant of the kind of habitat that would have once covered this area. Clear chalk springs bubble up in pools and flow through this secluded wet woodland. Impressive willow trunks scatter the site and wrens sing their clear song from fringing blackthorn thickets.

Keldmarsh is derived from the Scandinavian word for spring *Kelda*. This aptly describes the nature reserve, which in wet years sees several springs emerging, forming pools and streams of clear water. This water is fed by underground streams that run through the chalk bedrock. Where the chalk meets a layer of impermeable clay, water is forced upwards and emerges at the ground surface. Sadly in some years these springs can run dry, probably due to changes in surrounding land use and water extraction over the last few decades.

The site is covered by woodland which, due to changing ground conditions, appears to be making a transition itself. Crack willow and alder, trees fond of getting their roots wet, are giving way to young ash which survive better in the drier conditions. Some venerable ancient willows lie fallen, but their twisted trunks and stems still provide homes for wildlife in their nooks and crannies. Elderberry, hawthorn and blackthorn provide scrubby areas of cover and birds breeding on site include chiffchaff, blackcap and dunnock.

Some of the rarest species found at Keldmarsh are slime moulds. These strange 'growths' look like lichen or fungi, but are actually colonies of very tiny, primitive creatures, that act as one organism. Often found on wet, dead timber they can be seen to move if observed over several days. Wetland plants such as fool's water-cress, yellow flag iris and marsh marigold are found in and around the wet pools and common frogs are a regular sight.

NEAREST POSTCODE
HU17 8UL

GRID REFERENCE
TA 034386

RESERVE SIZE
0.35 ha

PUBLIC TRANSPORT
The nearest train station is Beverley, from which it is a 20 minute walk to the nature reserve.

DIRECTIONS
On the southern outskirts of Beverley. Turn off Keldgate onto the A164 at the double mini roundabout, signposted Cottingham and Humber Bridge. At the next roundabout turn left onto Woodmansey Mile, then right on to Lincoln Way. Park in the lay-by on the left where the road bends round. Walk across a paved path and the grass to the nature reserve.

OTHER INFORMATION
Unsurfaced tracks.

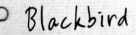

Blackbird

Foraging for berries

Orange-tip

LOCATION

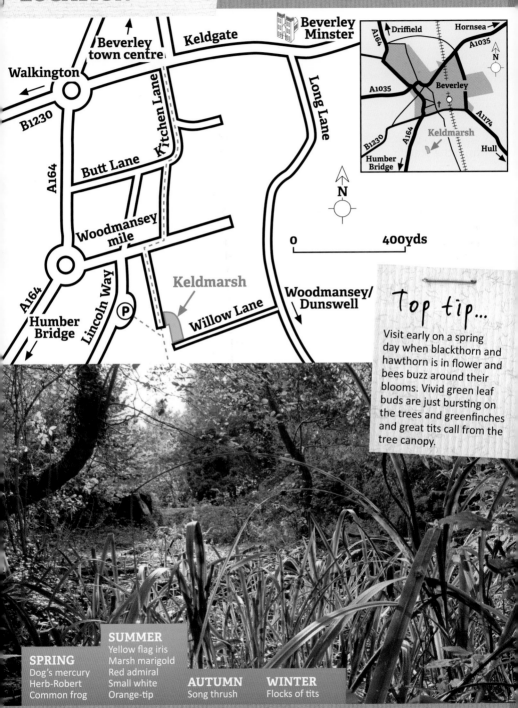

Walkington

B1230

A164

Butt Lane

Kitchen Lane

Beverley town centre

Keldgate

Beverley Minster

Woodmansey mile

Lincoln Way

A164

Humber Bridge

Long Lane

Keldmarsh

Willow Lane

Woodmansey/ Dunswell

P

N

0   400yds

Driffield   Hornsea

A164   A1035

A1035   Beverley   N

B1230   A164   A1174

Humber Bridge   Keldmarsh   Hull

Top tip...

Visit early on a spring day when blackthorn and hawthorn is in flower and bees buzz around their blooms. Vivid green leaf buds are just bursting on the trees and greenfinches and great tits call from the tree canopy.

SPRING
Dog's mercury
Herb-Robert
Common frog

SUMMER
Yellow flag iris
Marsh marigold
Red admiral
Small white
Orange-tip

AUTUMN
Song thrush

WINTER
Flocks of tits

KILNSEA WETLANDS

Intensively farmed until 2011, this area of land has been developed to create new habitat for wading birds. It is managed in partnership with the Environment Agency.

This new nature reserve has been created to compensate for habitat being lost nearby on the eroding Holderness coastline. Kilnsea Wetlands is intended to provide refuge for passage and wintering roosting waders that leave the adjacent Humber mudflats at high tide to roost. Golden and grey plovers, knot, dunlin, sanderling and bar-tailed godwit should all benefit from this safe refuge. A variety of habitats will provide the conditions needed to support these birds, but this will take a number of years to reach its full potential. Freshwater and saline pools with islands and spits and wet grassland with seasonal scrapes will provide this site with roosting and feeding locations, but also hopefully the right conditions in the spring for breeding oystercatcher, ringed plover and lapwing.

Engineering is only the start of this process – the nature reserve is to be managed in a sustainable manner using local livestock. This location is one of the driest parts of the UK, and without the ability to bring water on to the site from surrounding areas, functionality of the habitat will rely very much on rainfall and groundwater levels.

Farmland birds including corn bunting and tree sparrow may well use the nature reserve as it develops.

In time the grassland on the site should become established and we hope this will provide some botanical value and interest, in turn supporting a host of insects including dragonflies.

Salt-tolerant plant species such as spiral tassel weed may well find a home here too.

A hide, viewing screen, and off road parking, along with a footpath route through the nature reserve leading to Yorkshire Wildlife Trust's Blue Bell Café in Kilnsea mean this site is ideal for a visit.

NEAREST POSTCODE
HU12 0UD

GRID REFERENCE
TA 405 167

RESERVE SIZE
35 ha

PUBLIC TRANSPORT
The Spurn Ranger bus from Hull stops in Kilnsea.

DIRECTIONS
Approach Kilnsea on Easington Road. The car park is on your left just after you go over the left hand bend which rises over Long Bank and before you reach Kilnsea village.

OTHER INFORMATION
There is a dipping platform available for arranged visits. Please do not walk along Long Bank to the north of the nature reserve to avoid flushing the birds. Paths are unsurfaced. Toilets are located in Kilnsea.

Dunlin

Seeking shelter at Kilnsea

Top tip...

A visit in autumn or winter will give you a chance to see large numbers of roosting waders which this site has been specifically designed for. Check the tides to coincide your visit with high tide and you're likely to see greater numbers.

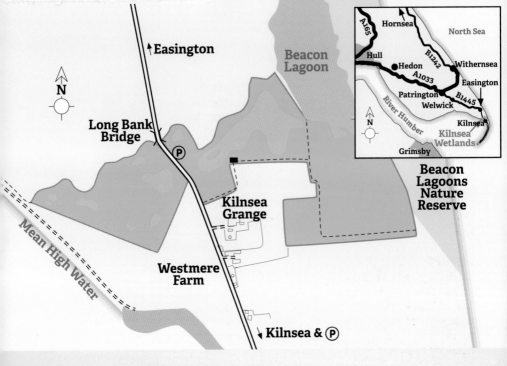

↑Easington

Beacon
Lagoon

N

Long Bank
Bridge

Ⓟ

Kilnsea
Grange

Mean High Water

Westmere
Farm

↓Kilnsea & Ⓟ

Hornsea

North Sea

A165

Hull

B1242

Withernsea

Hedon

A1033

Easington

Patrington

B1445

Welwick

River Humber

Kilnsea

N

Kilnsea
Wetlands

Grimsby

Beacon
Lagoons
Nature
Reserve

SPRING
Avocet
Little ringed
plover
Oystercatcher
Tree sparrow

SUMMER
Flowering plants
Butterflies
Dragonflies

AUTUMN
Greenshank
Grey plover
Green sandpiper
Yellow wagtail

WINTER
Brent goose
Golden plover
Lapwing
Dunlin
Merlin

KIPLINGCOTES CHALK PIT

A wander through Kiplingcotes Chalk Pit in high summer will reveal a riot of colour in the species rich grassland, with butterflies busy on the flowers in some of the sheltered spots and farmland birds such as yellowhammers calling from the scrub. A walk to the top of this old quarry will give lovely views back along the valley.

Nestled in a narrow Wolds valley Kiplingotes Chalk Pit provides a haven for chalk-loving plant and animal species. As vegetation colonises the bare chalk, different wildlife communities spring up as succession takes place over time. The first 'pioneer' species of lichens and moss colonise the quarry face and short-turfed grassland develops on the thin soils of the quarry floor supporting wild pansy, wild thyme and mouse-ear hawkweed. More established grassland on the quarry top supports common and greater knapweed, field scabious and burnet saxifrage.

Ant hills built by yellow meadow ants are scattered across the nature reserve and are characterised by being covered by springy beds of wild thyme – very fragrant when crushed. Some of these ant hills can be decades old and in the wider countryside are only found in areas that are not damaged by ploughing or mechanical cutting.

The nationally scarce red hemp-nettle is found here, as is a large population of basil thyme, which has undergone a huge decline in the UK. Butterflies typical of chalky soils occur in good numbers on the nature reserve including marbled white. Blackcap, bullfinch and linnet can be found in the scrub, whereas in winter migrant birds pass through feeding on berries.

Quarried until 1902 the site was used to supply chalk during the building of the embankment of the Beverley to Market Weighton railway line, which opened in 1865. Nature then took over and the Trust has managed the site since 1965. Management has concentrated on keeping the grassland in good condition, with autumn and winter grazing by Hebridean sheep and Exmoor ponies helping keep some of the rough competitive grasses in check, allowing finer grasses and flowering plants to thrive. Scrub and

NEAREST POSTCODE
YO43 3NA

GRID REFERENCE
SE 913 433

RESERVE SIZE
4.06 ha

PUBLIC TRANSPORT
Nearest train station is Beverley, approximately nine miles east.

DIRECTIONS
The nature reserve is 2.5 miles north east of Market Weighton. From Market Weighton take the road signposted Kiplingcotes. Use the car park on the old railway line and walk 300m north east along the line – the nature reserve is entered through a kissing gate on your left. There is limited parking on the roadside and access is down some steep steps.

SITE DESIGNATION
SSSI

OTHER INFORMATION
Unsurfaced paths. Steps to upper part of nature reserve.

weed control is carried out and cutting and laying takes place to manage the hedgerow on the northern boundary.

Basil thyme

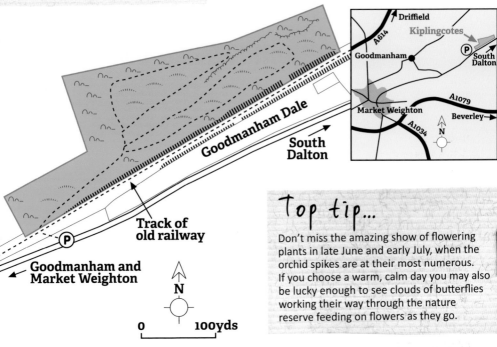

Track of old railway

Goodmanham and Market Weighton

N

0 — 100yds

Top tip...

Don't miss the amazing show of flowering plants in late June and early July, when the orchid spikes are at their most numerous. If you choose a warm, calm day you may also be lucky enough to see clouds of butterflies working their way through the nature reserve feeding on flowers as they go.

SPRING
Willow warbler
Robin
Yellowhammer
Dingy skipper
Cowslip

SUMMER
Pyramidal orchid
Common spotted orchid
Common twayblade
Wall butterfly
Marbled white

AUTUMN
Autumn gentian
Redwing
Fieldfare

WINTER
Buzzard
Red kite
Grey partridge
Badger

Large skipper

Commonly seen in summer

KIRKSTALL VALLEY

Only two miles from Leeds's bustling city centre and surrounded by both residential and commercial development, Kirkstall Valley Nature Reserve is a surprisingly green, quiet and relatively undisturbed mix of wetland, meadow and young woodland copse with great views of the River Aire.

NEAREST POSTCODE
LS4 2AW

GRID REFERENCE
SE 270 346

RESERVE SIZE
9.94 ha

PUBLIC TRANSPORT
There are regular buses along Kirkstall Road from Leeds City Centre with a bus stop at the end of Redcote Lane. Burley Park Railway Station is about 1.5 miles away or a 30 minute walk.

DIRECTIONS
The entrance to the nature reserve is towards the end of Redcote Lane (just off Kirkstall Road), past Fitness First and City Golf and just before the railway bridge on the right. There is parking here on the road near the entrance. It is about two miles from the centre of Leeds.

OTHER INFORMATION
Wheelchair access limited. There is a bar at the City Golf club house and toilets used with their permission.

Common frog

Look for frog spawn from March

Situated on the site of former Kirkstall Power Station, Kirkstall Valley Nature Reserve now supports large areas of wildflower meadow and wetland areas of pond, bog and reedbed. A large tree planting exercise also saw 15,000 trees planted to complement the existing oak, birch and willow on site with an understory of fruiting shrubs such as guelder rose, blackthorn and sea buckthorn. The area, once noted for orchards in medieval times, also supports a number of fruit trees including medlar, quince and five apple varieties.

Over 180 plant species have been recorded on site along with 65 species of birds including grey partridge and a number of mammals such as fox, badger, as well as pipistrelle, noctule and Daubenton's bats. Otters can be seen by the old ford, which is generally impassable for most of the year. There are also some large mature oak trees with spring bluebells on the island and a pond and wader scrape that has been used by little ringed plovers. Sixteen butterfly species have been recorded including comma and small copper and also six species of dragonfly.

Much of the site is raised above the floor of the Aire Valley as it rests on a plateau formed by the deposition of fly ash from the power station which was demolished in the late 1970s. The area was then used for landfill. Capped in the early 1990s the area was seeded with native wildflower mixes which are the basis of the meadows today.

Yorkshire Wildlife Trust manages the meadows through cutting and raking in late summer. The woodland is lightly coppiced and thinned in the winter.

LOCATION

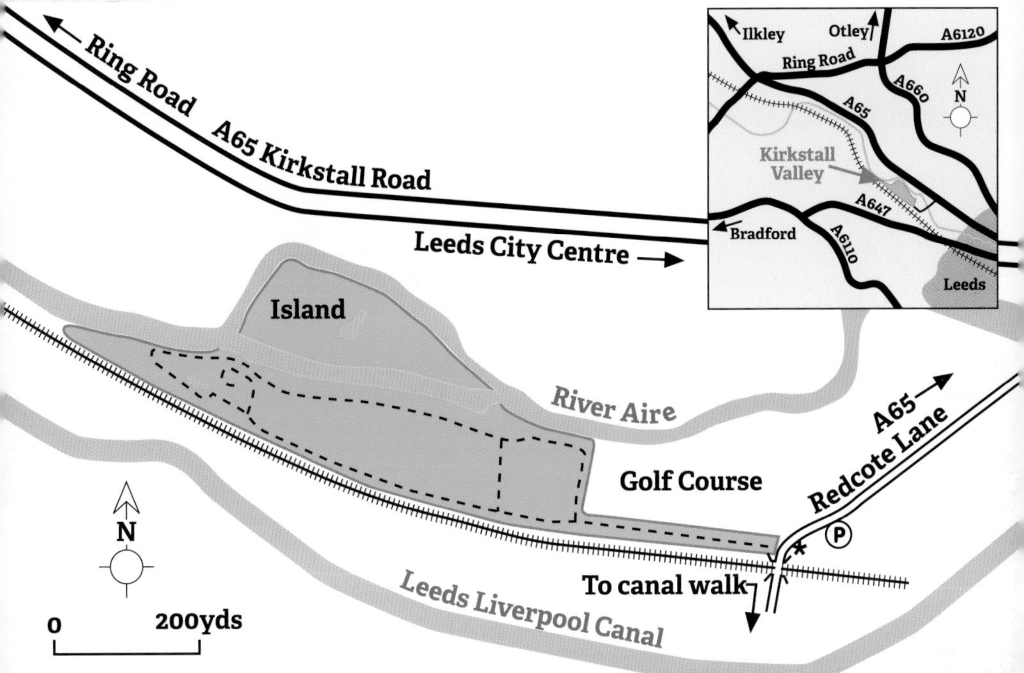

Ring Road
A65 Kirkstall Road
Leeds City Centre
Island
River Aire
Golf Course
A65
Redcote Lane
P
To canal walk
Leeds Liverpool Canal
N
0
200yds
Ilkley
Otley
A6120
Ring Road
A660
A65
N
Kirkstall Valley
A647
Bradford
A6110
Leeds

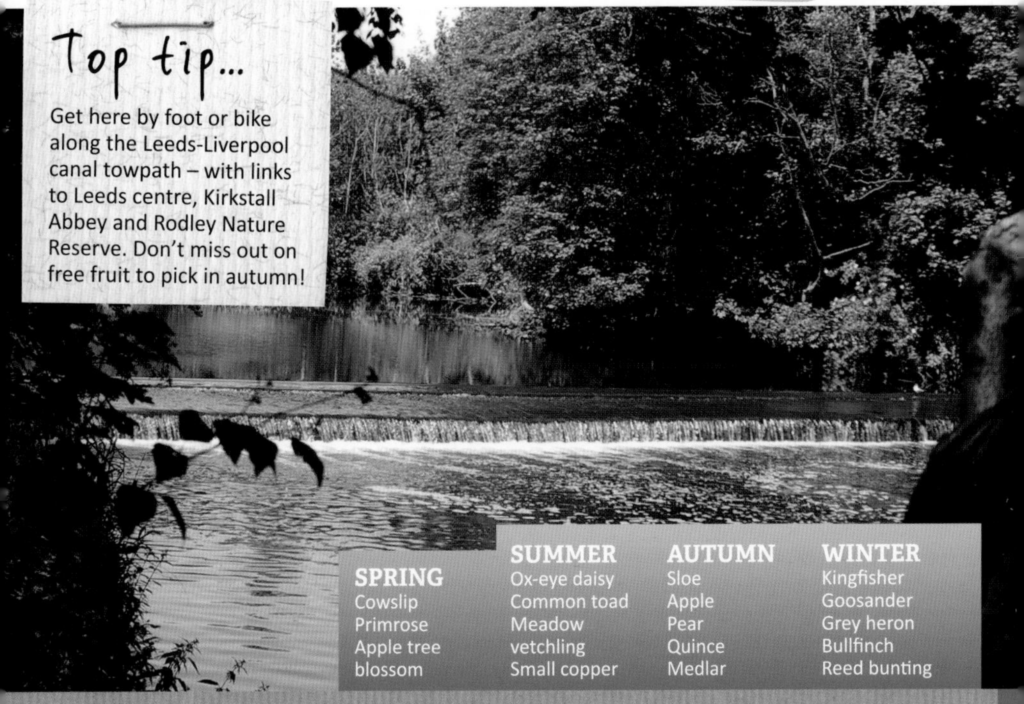

Top tip...

Get here by foot or bike along the Leeds-Liverpool canal towpath – with links to Leeds centre, Kirkstall Abbey and Rodley Nature Reserve. Don't miss out on free fruit to pick in autumn!

SPRING	SUMMER	AUTUMN	WINTER
Cowslip	Ox-eye daisy	Sloe	Kingfisher
Primrose	Common toad	Apple	Goosander
Apple tree blossom	Meadow vetchling	Pear	Grey heron
	Small copper	Quince	Bullfinch
		Medlar	Reed bunting

LEYBURN OLD GLEBE

Leyburn Old Glebe is a rare jewel in an area where so many fields are regularly fertilized and cut for silage. This small wildflower meadow is situated on a gently sloping bank above the River Ure in the lower reaches of Wensleydale, with fine views across the dale to Penhill and to the ridge above Coverdale which rises towards Great Whernside. To the north is the wooded limestone scar of Leyburn Shawl.

A traditional hay meadow, Leyburn Old Glebe is the richest remaining fragment of Ellershaw, a district well-known to naturalists since the 19th Century. The site is a fine example of the type of species rich flower meadow that would once have been common in the Yorkshire Dales before agricultural intensification resulted in the improvement of grasslands.

Over 80 plants have been recorded in recent surveys, many of which are typical of calcareous grassland. They thrive on the thin soil of the south facing slope of the nature reserve. 11 species of grass, including common bent, heath grass and quaking grass grow here. The herb flora includes abundant salad burnet and wild thyme as well as a range of other species such as cowslip, fairy flax, eyebright and orchids, including the spectacular burnt-tip.

Once belonging to the local church, the field was never ploughed or reseeded, which has allowed it to retain its integrity. Yorkshire Wildlife Trust acquired the site in 1983 and has continued to manage it as a traditional hay meadow. The wildflowers are left to grow and set seed before being cut for hay in July. The field is then usually grazed with a few sheep over winter.

You will enter the nature reserve through a field gate, which was erected in memory of Cherrill Ingram, a former Honorary Secretary to Yorkshire Wildlife Trust.

The nature reserve is a small fragile site susceptible to damage through trampling of the sward and flower picking, so please take care when visiting.

NEAREST POSTCODE
DL8 4HU

GRID REFERENCE
SE 101 895

RESERVE SIZE
2.68 ha

PUBLIC TRANSPORT
Buses and seasonal trains to Leyburn then public footpaths.

DIRECTIONS
From Hawes take the A6108 to Wensley, then turn onto Low Lane. The nature reserve is on this road.

SITE DESIGNATION
SSSI

Top tip...
Visit in May or June for the best display of wildflowers or tie in a trip with a visit to the local pub, Three Horseshoes in Wensley, for a hearty fire and pint of ale!

Cowslip and burnt-tip orchid

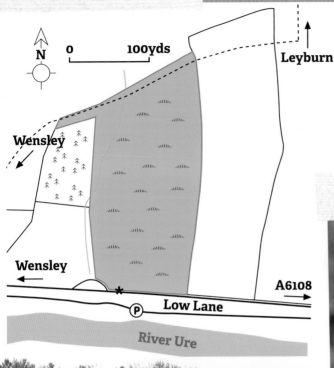

N

0   100yds

Leyburn

Wensley

Wensley

A6108

Low Lane

P

River Ure

N

Leyburn
Old Glebe

A684

Leyburn

Wensley

River Ure

A1

Hawes

A6108

Middleham

Ripon

Eyebright

Tiny white flowers growing low down in the grassland

SPRING
Cowslip
Salad burnet
Burnt-tip orchid

SUMMER
Small skipper
Common blue
Eyebright
Fairy flax

LITTLE BECK WOOD

Little Beck Wood is a glorious mix of oak, ash, alder and cherry under the canopies of which lives a wealth of plants, mammals and insects.

Primarily broadleaved woodland with a small pasture at the southern end, the site avoids the worst of the North York Moors weather being situated in a secluded position at the bottom of the valley.

The nature reserve is split into two as the small river of Little Beck dissects it. Whilst the majority of tree species here are oak, ash, alder and cherry there is also an under-storey of hazel, holly and rowan. Both sections are rich in ground flora which sustains the healthy mammal population.

In the spring and early summer wood anemone, bluebell, primrose and early purple orchid are in full flower, whilst ferns dominate the shadier areas. Badger scrapes may be discovered around dense areas of bluebells, whilst deer tracks might be seen in the damp sections of the path and rodent holes in the banks around the site. Sightings of birds are commonplace, including the secretive treecreeper and dipper. Dead wood provides an important food source for insects, several of which are listed in the Red Data Book as being rare; these in turn support the population of birds and animals higher up the food chain.

Yorkshire Wildlife Trust has worked to maintain the woodland since taking over the lease in 1970 from the Forestry Commission and then later purchasing it in 1986. Bird boxes provide vital breeding spaces for nuthatch, tits and owls. Tree health is also a primary concern, with any diseased or damaged trees made safe with regards to the public and left as dead wood where possible. The understory is also managed to retain tree health, with the thinning of holly and coppicing of hazel. The pasture is cut for hay and grazed by a neighbouring farmer's livestock.

The site was formerly an important alum works, being on top of Jurassic shale, evidence of which can be seen by the presence of a shallow cave on the east side where care should be taken.

NEAREST POSTCODE
YO22 5HA

GRID REFERENCE
NZ 879 049

RESERVE SIZE
26.38 ha

PUBLIC TRANSPORT
The nearest train station is in Ruswarp.

DIRECTIONS
Take either the A169 from Pickering or the B1416 from Scarborough. Turn off to the village of Littlebeck where the woodland is situated immediately south of the ford.

OTHER INFORMATION
Parking available at Littlebeck Village Hall.

SITE DESIGNATION
SSSI

Early purple orchid

Flowers in the woodland in spring

Weasel

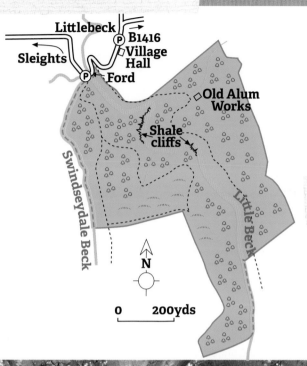

Coal tit

One of several tit species present

Top tip...

Visit in April when the spring flowers are blooming and the trees have not yet cast complete shade.

SPRING
Bluebell
Wood anemone
Primrose
Early purple orchid
Dog violet

SUMMER
Moschatel
Opposite-leaved golden-saxifrage
Green woodpecker

AUTUMN
Fungi

WINTER
Badger
Treecreeper

LOW WOOD

Low Wood is an attractive, secluded woodland which is notable for its beautiful spring displays of bluebell and foxglove, coupled with occasional sightings of badger and roe deer.

Beside the canal, Low Wood provides a pleasant oasis away from the noise of the Keighley urban area. Beautifully carpeted with bluebells in spring, this broadleaved woodland is also home to a wide range of fungi (over 36 species), together with the usual range of birds and plants.

Some of the birds that you might be lucky to encounter on a visit to the woodland include blackcap, great spotted woodpecker, tawny owl, treecreeper and nuthatch. Three species of bat also make this nature reserve their home.

The woodland is steeply sloping with evidence of glacial melt water erosion of the millstone grit series forming cliffs towards the top. There is a footpath encircling the wood but the upper parts are steep and require care and energy. The views from the top are excellent.

The woodland is managed through the hard work of volunteers and over the last seven years self-seeded sycamore have been removed from the wood to favour the indigenous species such as oak, birch and rowan in the canopy, with holly, hawthorn and hazel in the understory. Glades have been created within the woodland and these help to encourage butterflies such as speckled wood; management of the dense carpet of bracken has allowed successful re-establishment of ground flora. The small pond within the site is used by amphibians, including common frogs which congregate in numbers in early spring.

NEAREST POSTCODE
BD20 5QN

GRID REFERENCE
SE 056 439

RESERVE SIZE
2.83 ha

PUBLIC TRANSPORT
The bus service from Bradford to Keighley stops at Grange Road, Riddlesden. The nearest train station is located in Keighley. Cycle and footpath access is gained by following the towpath of the Leeds – Liverpool canal going northwards to Booth's Bridge.

DIRECTIONS
The nature reserve is located alongside the Leeds-Liverpool canal just below the Riddlesden Golf Course. This is reached by continuing along the unmade track from the end of Scott Lane West as far as the golf course club house (about 0.75 miles) then turning down by the canal where there is a small area for parking at the site entrance. Access is gained by a small gate, which is signed a Scout Activity Area; carry along the track past the Scout site.

Blackcap

Males can be identified by their black cap

Top tip...

If you want to get away from the noise of the town then this is a secluded woodland retreat. The bluebells are not to be missed, badger viewing is a thrill and there is the experience of listening to the wood going to sleep at night in any season.

LOCATION

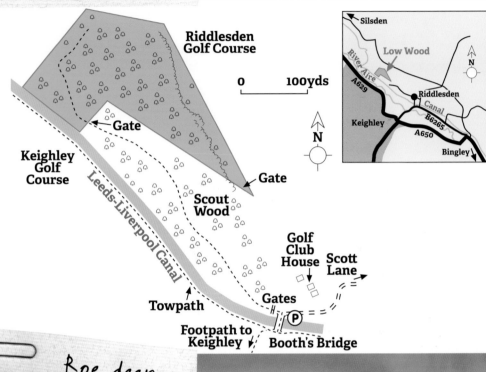

Riddlesden Golf Course

0   100yds

N

Gate

Keighley Golf Course

Leeds-Liverpool Canal

Gate

Scout Wood

Golf Club House

Scott Lane

Towpath

Gates

P

Footpath to Keighley

Booth's Bridge

Silsden

Low Wood

River Aire

A629

Riddlesden

Canal

Keighley

B6265

A650

Bingley

N

Roe deer

SPRING	SUMMER	AUTUMN	WINTER
Bluebell	Foxglove	Fungi	Roe deer
Nuthatch	Woodland birds		
Treecreeper	Badger		
	Speckled wood		
	Bats		

MALTBY LOW COMMON

A mosaic of grassland communities rich in wildflowers and grasses, including grass of Parnassus. Changing geology allows visitors to revel in the change of vegetation from one part of the site to another.

Thimble morel

Cap hangs from the stem like a thimble on a pencil

Maltby Low Common has a wide variety of soil types, giving rise to dry grassland and fen meadow which provides an excellent home for both wildflowers and insects. The south part of the site has typical limestone grassland species including grass of Parnassus, field scabious and small scabious. The flat area below the bank includes species more typical of fen meadow.

Other plants to be found include marsh valerian, mat grass, tufted hair-grass, heather, pepper saxifrage, meadow thistle, sneezewort, lousewort

and aspen. Sedges include glaucous, oval and carnation. Beautiful common spotted orchids flower in abundance from early June. The site is rich in insects, well over 400 species have been recorded to date. Many species of butterfly and moth can be seen including brimstone, orange-tip, small copper, wall, heath, cinnabar and silver Y. Birds to be seen include buzzard, kestrel, turtle dove, cuckoo, barn owl, whitethroat and garden warbler. In the winter, parties of foraging tits and thrushes can be seen.

The nature reserve is leased from the Earl of Scarborough and is part of a much wider site which is managed by the Sandbeck Estate. It was opened as a nature reserve in 1971 and management has focused on improving the habitats for wildlife since then.

Recent management has included laying some of the hedges that bound the site to improve the habitat for nesting birds and reduce shading of the grassland.

NEAREST POSTCODE
S66 7JX

GRID REFERENCE
SK 543 914

RESERVE SIZE
6.5 ha

PUBLIC TRANSPORT
Buses run from Doncaster to Maltby. From Maltby the nature reserve is a 20 minute walk.

DIRECTIONS
Approximately one mile south east of Maltby. From the M18 Junction 1 take the A631 to Maltby. Then take the right fork, the A634 Blyth road. After passing Maltby Craggs School, turn left at the next signpost, then right after 100 metres. Pass the Sports Ground and park cars near the corner where the road turns left into the Birks Holt housing estate. Proceed on foot over the railway bridge, along the unsurfaced track and descend to the Low Common.

SITE DESIGNATION
SSSI, LNR

Columbine

These purple flowers grow well in the dry grasslane

LOCATION

Top tip...

Anyone wanting to compare the floristic diversity of calcarious, acid and neutral grassland should certainly pay Maltby Low Common a visit. With all three grassland types in close proximity, this site provides a unique opportunity.

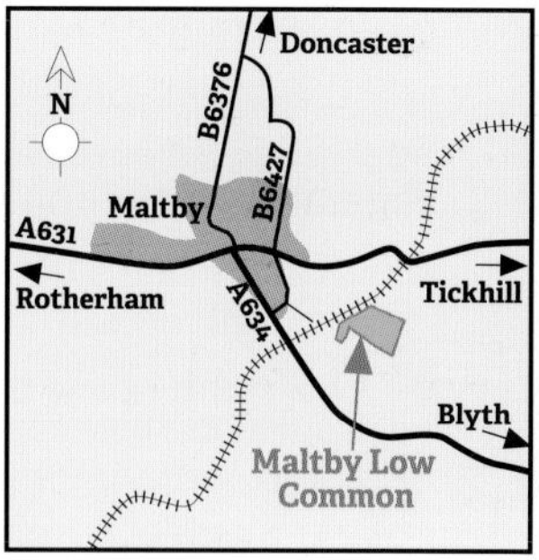

N

0   100yds

Birk Holt Housing Estate

Sports Ground

B6427 Ⓟ

✕

N

B6376
B6427
Doncaster
Maltby
A631
Rotherham
A634
Tickhill
Blyth
Maltby Low Common

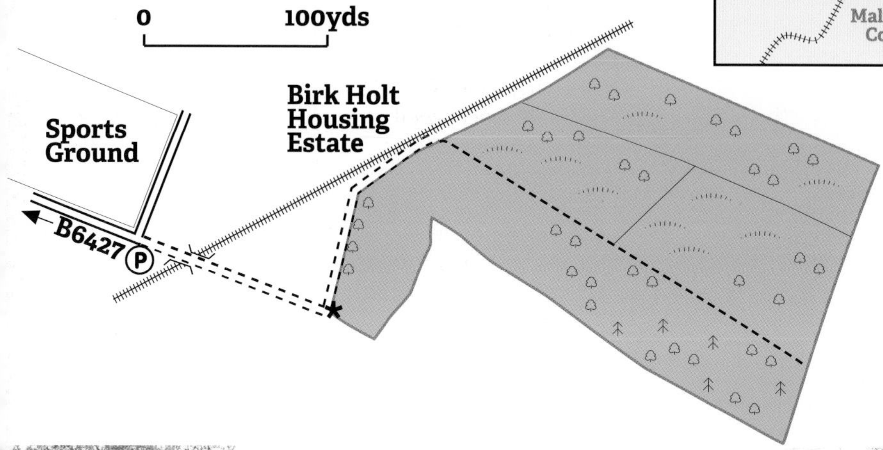

SUMMER
Grass of Parnassus
Tufted hair-grass
Pepper saxifrage
Meadow thistle
Sneezewort

SPRING
Whitethroat
Orange-tip

AUTUMN
Flocks of tits
Fungi

MOORLANDS

This small woodland is part of the ancient Forest of Galtres and is ablaze with colour in spring. Snowdrop, primrose, daffodil and bluebell form a backdrop to a succession of mature rhododendrons, azaleas and maple.

Moorlands is a beautiful small woodland with the additional attraction of a spectacular collection of rhododendrons and azaleas, some of which are very old, large and unusual. These provide a succession of flowers from March to the end of June accompanied by a carpet of snowdrop, bluebell, primrose and wood sorrel.

The wealth of trees and flowering plants in turn attract many species of bird and mammal. A number of bat boxes have been erected and these have been successfully used by common pipistrelle and brown long-eared bats, with soprano pipistrelle, Brandt's and Daubenton's bats having also been recorded within the nature reserve.

From the tree house a great variety of woodland birds, including great spotted woodpecker, nuthatch and a variety of tits can be observed as they visit the feeders. Woodcock are occasionally seen during autumn, which is also an ideal time to find amazing fungi during a stroll through the leaf litter.

The trees are a source of great pleasure with some mature native species growing alongside the more unusual snakebark maple, magnolias and two dawn redwoods. There are two small ponds, the first of which has a large dipping platform

Rhododendrons

The nature reserve has a spectacular display of rare and mature azaleas and rhododendrons

Many were planted in 1909 in the Victorian woodland style

SPRING	SUMMER	AUTUMN	WINTER
Primrose	Bats	Maple	Woodcock
Cuckooflower	Foxglove	Fungi	Great spotted
Marsh marigold	Woodland ferns	Nuthatch	woodpecker
Rhododendron	Common blue		
Azalea	damselfly		
	Speckled wood		

MOORLANDS

Nuthatch

Regularly seen on the feeders from the tree house

NEAREST POSTCODE
YO32 2RE

GRID REFERENCE
SE 579 587

RESERVE SIZE
6.98 ha

PUBLIC TRANSPORT
Buses using the A19 stop in Skelton.

DIRECTIONS
About 5½ miles north of York. From York, take the A19 Thirsk Road for about 3½ miles to Skelton. Turn right off the A19, continue through the village and the nature reserve is another 2 miles further on, on the left of the road. Parking is allowed on the verge near the entrance gate.

to provide much interest to anyone with a net. A third secluded pond helps to feed the other ponds via a dyke.

Mr Edward Grosvenor Tew bought Moorlands House and estate in 1909 and planted many of the rhododendrons and azaleas. The estate was then acquired by the Retreat in York for use as a hospital in 1940, before selling 17 acres to become Yorkshire Wildlife Trust's second nature reserve in 1955. Management of the site aims to both preserve the special character of the Edwardian woodland garden and to encourage native wildlife within the nature reserve.

Stinkhorn

One of the many species of fungi that can be found

Top tip...

This is a great site for all age groups, with a level path and seating at regular intervals.

LOCATION

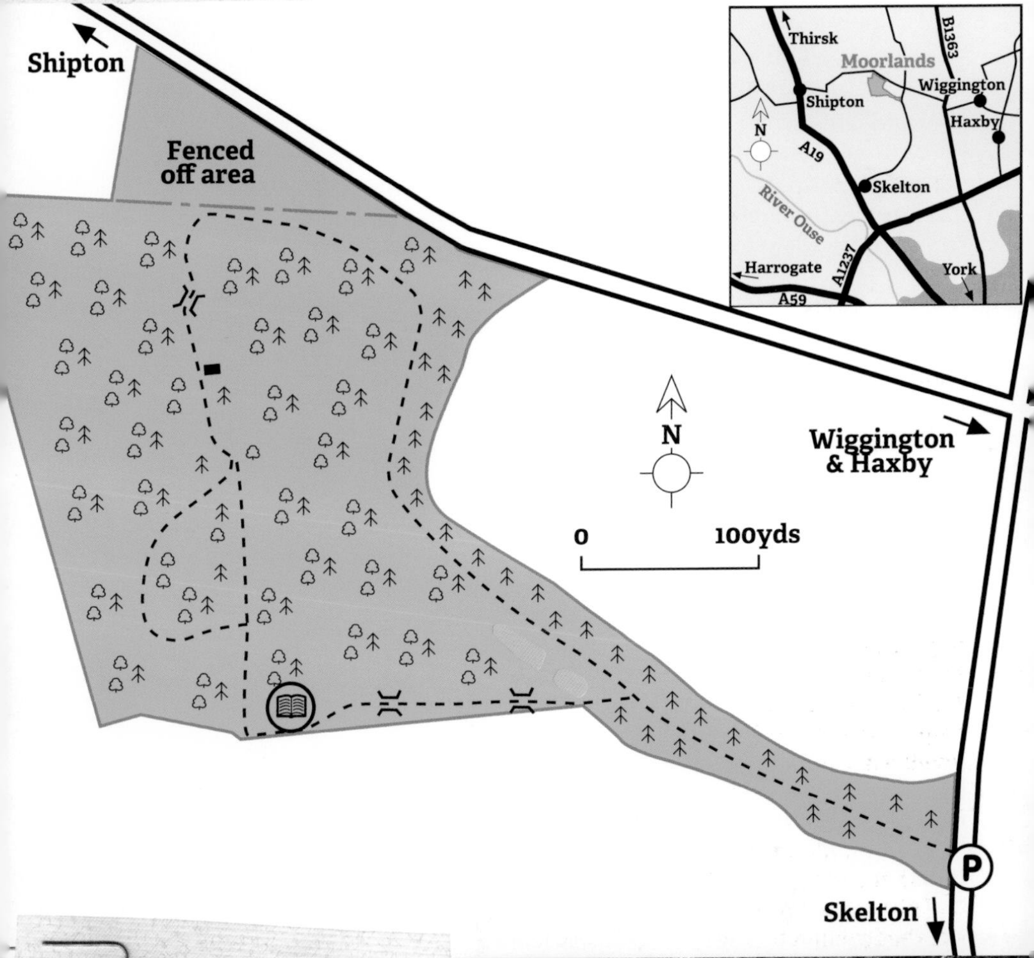

Shipton

Fenced off area

N

0   100yds

Wiggington & Haxby

Skelton ↓

P

Thirsk
Moorlands
Shipton
Wiggington
Haxby
A19
River Ouse
Skelton
Harrogate
A1237
A59
York
N
B1363

View of the pond

MOSS VALLEY

Moss Valley is a wonderful, quiet and peaceful woodland complex, including Coal Pit Wood with oaks, occasional horse chestnuts and sycamores, and Newfield Spring Wood which attracts many different types of animals and insects. Nearby at Long Wood, oaks and beech dominate while Bridle Road Wood has been extensively coppiced to provide sheltered sunny spots, ideal for feeding butterflies.

Sheffield & Rotherham

NEAREST POSTCODE
S8 8BG

GRID REFERENCE
SK 376 805

RESERVE SIZE
26.3 ha

PUBLIC TRANSPORT
Buses to Bochum Parkway and from Sheffield city centre. Walk to Lightwood Lane.

DIRECTIONS
By car, follow the Sheffield Ring Road (A6102) and at the Norton roundabout turn on to Hazelhurst Lane, continue for about 1 mile. Park in layby or on surrounding streets.

SITE DESIGNATION
LNR

Wildflowers like bluebell, yellow pimpernel, St John's-wort, wood speedwell and sweet including the tiny white-letter hairstreak around the remnant elms.

Slow worm

Often mistaken for a snake, this is actually a type of lizard!

Brown trout and the extremely rare native white-clawed crayfish have been found in the two streams which run through the nature reserve. Increasingly scarce birds such as linnet, song thrush and bullfinch are frequently found in the woods and open areas; grey wagtails and kingfishers by the streams; and tawny owls and sparrowhawks hunt small birds and mammals. Adders, slow worms and great crested newts have all been spotted, as have larger animals like badgers, brown hares and roe deer.

woodruff all indicate areas of ancient woodland. Thanks to its south-facing aspect, unimproved soils and wide variety of plants and habitats, the grasslands on site are teeming with invertebrates. Many species of moth and butterfly can be found

Top tip...

A visit in May is essential to see one of the best displays of bluebells in South Yorkshire.

Linnet

Flocks plunder weed seeds in the open area

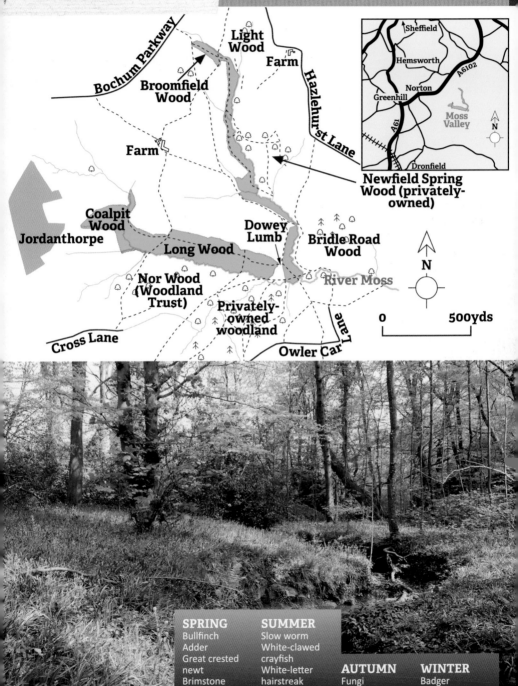

Newfield Spring Wood (privately-owned)

Light Wood

Farm

Broomfield Wood

Bochum Parkway

Hazlehurst Lane

Farm

Coalpit Wood

Jordanthorpe

Long Wood

Dowey Lumb

Bridle Road Wood

River Moss

Nor Wood (Woodland Trust)

Privately-owned woodland

Cross Lane

Owler Car Lane

N

0   500yds

Sheffield

Hemsworth

Norton

Greenhill

Dronfield

Moss Valley

A6102

A61

N

SPRING	SUMMER		
Bullfinch	Slow worm		
Adder	White-clawed		
Great crested	crayfish		
newt	White-letter	**AUTUMN**	**WINTER**
Brimstone	hairstreak	Fungi	Badger
Bluebell	Yellow pimpernell	Roe deer	Tawny owl

NORTH CAVE WETLANDS

North Cave Wetlands is a true example of a 21st century nature reserve, developed in the footprint of a large sand and gravel quarry. A day spent here any time of the year will reward visitors with close up views of a range of wetland wildlife. And the good news is it's still a work in progress, so will continue to get better for wildlife and people!

Little ringed plover

One of the first birds to colonise when quarrying ceases

North Cave Wetlands, although a former sand and gravel quarry, is now an oasis of thriving wildlife. A mixture of shallow and deep water lakes and reedbeds provide outstanding habitat for passage, breeding and wintering wildfowl, waders, terns and gulls. A 2km perimeter path gives access around the established nature reserve and four large hides are positioned to give excellent viewing over key areas for birdwatchers and photographers alike.

Shallow gravel islands have been created in three lakes to provide breeding grounds for little ringed and ringed plovers, avocet, oystercatcher, lapwing and common tern. There is a resident population of tufted duck, gadwall, great crested and little grebe

Avocet

These elegant birds return in March from their wintering grounds on the Humber Estuary

Black-tailed skimmer

Can be seen resting on paths and roads, or flying low over the water

SPRING
Little ringed plover
Avocet
Sand martin
Warblers
Wheatear

SUMMER
Shelduck
Common tern
Butterflies
Dragonflies
Damselflies

AUTUMN
Water vole
Migrant waders
Tree sparrow

WINTER
Water rail
Snipe
Teal
Tufted duck
Peregrine

and sometimes shoveler. In spring and autumn small numbers of migrant wading birds pass through. Reed and sedge warblers and reed buntings are common in and around the reedbed and north side of the nature reserve.

Butterflies, dragonflies and damselflies thrive on the grassy banks beside the perimeter path; watch out for emperor dragonfly and sometimes water vole. There is a small colony of brown argus butterflies in the meadow between Main and Carp Lakes, access to which is opened in summer months.

The original 40 hectare nature reserve was acquired in 2001. In the following three years 250,000 tonnes of material was moved in, out or around the site to create a suitable open wetland habitat, with established trees confined to the boundaries and to the western end. Six large lakes provide both deep and shallow water with wide margins and islands, connected underground to give control over winter and summer water levels. Starting in 2008 and finishing 12 to 15 years thereafter an additional 100 ha of land to the immediate south and west is being quarried. This will be progressively restored with wildlife in mind before being gifted to Yorkshire Wildlife Trust. Currently some 500 pairs of sand martins breed in the neighbouring quarries and feed over the site. During 2012 Dryham Ings, 20 ha of flood meadow, was completed; the remainder will comprise more lakes, flood meadow and reedbeds.

NEAREST POSTCODE
HU15 2LY

GRID REFERENCE
SE 886 328

RESERVE SIZE
38.98 ha

PUBLIC TRANSPORT
Nearest bus stop is in North Cave village 0.5 miles away.

DIRECTIONS
Come off at Junction 38 of the M62/A63 and take the B1230 east to North Cave. At the first crossroads in the village, turn left onto Townend Lane and follow the brown reserve signs. If approaching north on the A1079 Market Weighton bypass take the minor road south through North Cliffe to North Cave then follow signs. The nature reserve is 15 miles west of Hull, off Cliffe Road on Dryham Lane.

OTHER INFORMATION
Dogs are allowed only on Dryham Lane (on leads please).

Sand martin

One of the first summer visitors to arrive

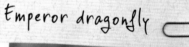

Emperor dragonfly

LOCATION

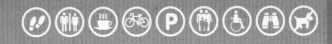

Hobby

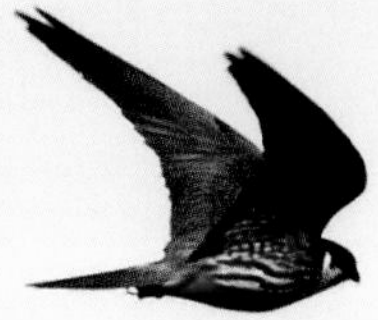

Consume dragonflies on the wing

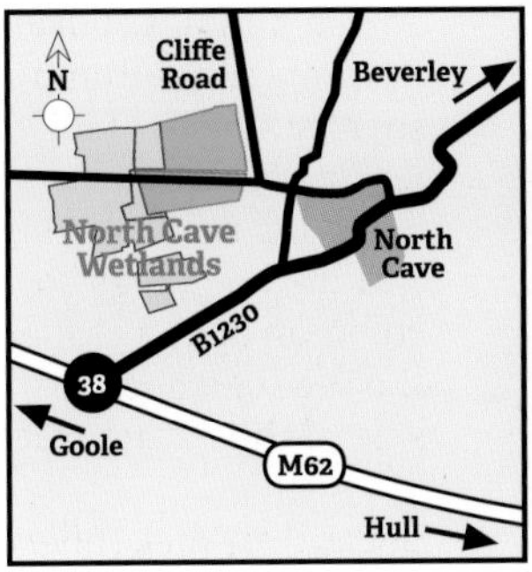
N
Cliffe Road
Beverley
North Cave Wetlands
North Cave
B1230
38
Goole
M62
Hull

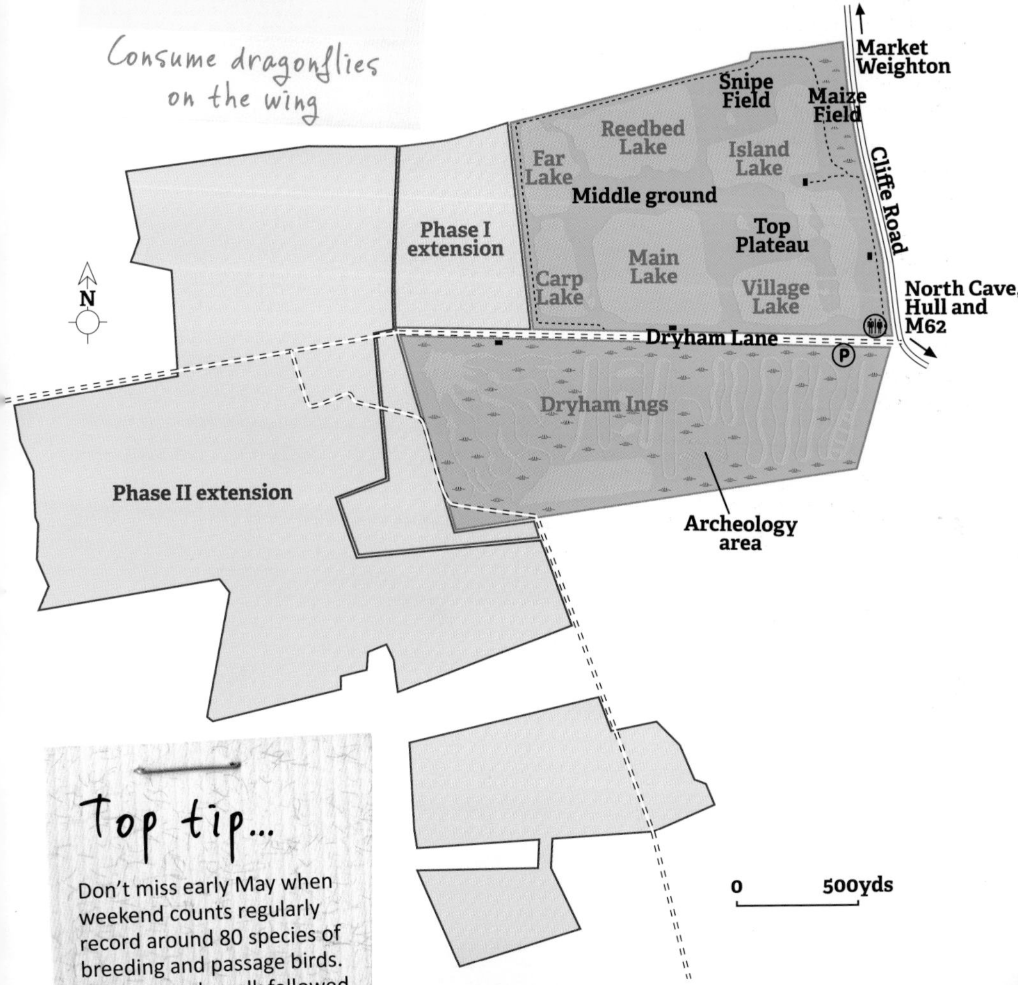
Market Weighton
Snipe Field
Maize Field
Reedbed Lake
Island Lake
Far Lake
Middle ground
Cliffe Road
Phase I extension
Top Plateau
Main Lake
Carp Lake
Village Lake
North Cave, Hull and M62
N
Dryham Lane
Dryham Ings
Phase II extension
Archeology area
0
500yds

Top tip...

Don't miss early May when weekend counts regularly record around 80 species of breeding and passage birds. Enjoy an early walk followed by breakfast at Angie's Wild Bird Café by the entrance.

NORTH CLIFFE WOOD

A lovely woodland nature reserve rich in wildlife. In spring, a lilac haze of bluebells stretches out beneath the vibrant green leaves of birch, while the songs of a host of warblers can be heard all around.

North Cliffe Wood is a woodland nature reserve lying on sandy soils. In spring a carpet of bluebells and other woodland flowers provide a beautiful sight, while in the woodland canopy, migrant warblers, including willow and garden, plus chiffchaff and blackcap, add their songs to the resident species, such as treecreeper, great spotted and green woodpeckers. In recent years, woodlark has colonised, adding their rich and evocative song to the chorus.

North Cliffe Wood was drained in the late 19th Century and the mature trees clear-felled in 1921. Bracken and rabbits were then able to fully exploit the sandy soils and prevent the regeneration of trees until myxomatosis destroyed the rabbit population in 1954. Conditions were thus set for the rapid spread of birch and mountain ash, the seeds of which are readily distributed by wind and birds respectively. These two species are still the most common trees in the wood today, although over 20 species have been recorded.

The site is quite varied, with the lower lying western areas flooding in most winters, providing suitable conditions for willow scrub. To the south of the main entrance there is an area of high oak forest, with a clump of multi-stemmed alders nearby, being evidence of coppicing activity that took place in the original forested landscape. In the south west corner there is a substantial clearing of lowland heathland that supports typical species including ling heather, heath rush and common cotton grass. Several pools within the woodland and heathland areas provide homes for damselflies and dragonflies and grassy clearings within the wood are a hive of activity for summer butterflies. Grass snakes can regularly be seen basking in the sun along paths and in open areas.

NEAREST POSTCODE
YO43 4XE

GRID REFERENCE
SE 860 374

RESERVE SIZE
33.35 ha

PUBLIC TRANSPORT
Irregular bus service from Market Weighton to North Cliffe village.

DIRECTIONS
From A1079 Market Weighton head south down Cliffe Road. Then turn right after four miles down Sand Lane. Park on the left by the wood.

Brimstone

On the wing as early as March

Willow warbler

This species nests on the ground

LOCATION

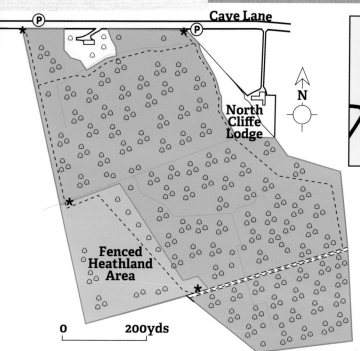

Cave Lane

P   **P**

North
Cliffe
Lodge

N

Fenced
Heathland
Area

0   200yds

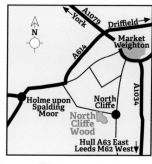

North
Cliffe
Wood

Top tip...

If you go before the trees are fully in leaf you'll get good views of great spotted woodpecker chasing through the trees and may be lucky enough to hear woodlarks singing from the heathland clearings.

SPRING	SUMMER	AUTUMN	WINTER
Blackcap	Garden warbler	Siskin	Treecreeper
Chiffchaff	Grass snake	Black darter	Green
Brimstone	Speckled wood	Common hawker	woodpecker
Bluebell	Cotton grass	Fungi	Great spotted
Primrose	Purple		woodpecker
	loosestrife		Redwing

EAST YORKSHIRE NATURE RESERVES **143**

NORTH NEWBALD BECKSIES

In spring a visual feast of marsh flowers can be enjoyed at this spring-fed Yorkshire Wolds nature reserve, whilst later in summer marsh orchids abound.

North Newbald Becksies is fed by several clear chalk springs which are almost never known to dry up. The water remains at a remarkably constant temperature of 9°C throughout the year and can be seen steaming on cold winter mornings. The terrain of the nature reserve is fairly undulating and in most areas extremely wet – wellies are a must; though there is a drier section at the north east corner.

By far the most interesting sections of the site are the open marshy areas which contain a good range of marsh plants including abundant marsh orchids, said to be a hybrid swarm of mainly *Dactylorhiza praetermissa*, though other species do occur. Another special plant is bog bean – a rarity in this part of Yorkshire. Grass of Parnassus was recorded as recently as the mid 1990s and may still be present. Moorhen and snipe occur in the wetter areas. Water shrews are present and there have been sightings of water voles.

The Trust looks after the nature reserve by removing scrub which encroaches on to the marsh and also reduce the abundance of greater willowherb and meadowsweet to allow other plants to prosper. The marsh was originally used for pasturing cattle from the village while they were waiting to be milked and as such is classed as common land. Today, a small number of cattle are used to assist with site management through summer grazing.

NEAREST POSTCODE
YO43 4SQ

GRID REFERENCE
SE 917 371

RESERVE SIZE
1.81 ha

PUBLIC TRANSPORT
Irregular bus service from Market Weighton to North Newbald village.

DIRECTIONS
Just east of North Newbald village on the south side of the Beverley road, five miles south of Market Weighton. Park considerately in the village (or arrive by bus), and then walk the short distance to the site.

OTHER INFORMATION
A very wet site, wellies are advised.

Crosswort

Has unstalked leaves and small yellow flowers

Moorhen

Watch for their flicking white tail

Top tip...

Visit in spring to witness the greatest variety and colour of marsh flowers. The marsh orchids flower later.

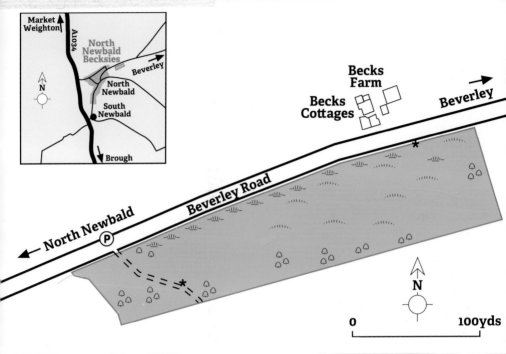

Market Weighton
A1034
North Newbald Becksies
Beverley
North Newbald
South Newbald
Brough
N

Becks Farm
Becks Cottages
Beverley
Beverley Road
North Newbald
P

N

0   100yds

SPRING
Marsh marigold
Cuckooflower
Water avens
Bog bean
Orange-tip

SUMMER
Marsh orchids
Lady's mantle
Water cress
Fool's water-cress
Meadowsweet

AUTUMN
Devil's-bit scabious

WINTER
Snipe

European otter

Lutra lutra

Expert fishers

- ☐ GRASSLAND
- ☑ BY THE COAST
- ☑ WETLAND
- ☐ FARMLAND

- ☑ SPRING
- ☑ SUMMER
- ☑ AUTUMN
- ☑ WINTER

Much has been documented about the fate of the otter in the UK. By the early 1980s it was evident that a massive population crash had occurred, with a real possibility that an iconic mammal could be lost from most rivers in England.

Thankfully 30 years later the otter is making a comeback and has returned to every river system. Surveys have shown a slow but steady increase in otter activity along Yorkshire waterways. Their broad, flat head and blunt muzzle, with eyes, ears and nose all on the same level looking out from the water, combined with their long streamlined body and wide rudder-like tail make this an unmistakeable encounter. They are a large animal with males sometimes measuring up to 1.5m in length and weighing well over 10kg.

In the east of the county, the River Hull is the main river catchment, where a small population hung on in the 1980s. Surveys from 2010 have shown that otters are present throughout the catchment with records even occurring on the coast and the Humber estuary. The inner Humber around Goole has a number of watercourses flowing in. It is the connected landscape of river corridors that is essential to the success of the otter. If rivers were not well managed for wildlife; with programmes to clean the water of pollutants, restoration and creation of their habitat and management of fish stocks, the otter would not be able to survive. Work has also been carried out in other parts of Yorkshire and otters have now been recorded in the Dales rivers, like the Swale and Ure, the Ouse and Foss around York and in sections of urban rivers in Leeds and Sheffield.

For the best chance to encounter an otter visit one of the nature reserves, as they are elusive and rarely venture out in the day. However, wait quietly in a hide, and you never know...

Red kite

Milvus milvus

☑ SPRING
☑ SUMMER
☑ AUTUMN
☑ WINTER

☑ GRASSLAND
☑ IN VILLAGES
☐ WETLAND
☑ FARMLAND

Five foot wingspan

Red kites are one of the conservation success stories of modern times. In the middle ages, they were abundant, especially in urban areas where they scavenged for carrion and discarded rotten food. Considered a pest by many due to their predatory nature, centuries of persecution eradicated them from virtually the whole of the UK so that by the 20th Century only a handful of pairs remained in the central valleys of Wales.

In 1989 a programme to reintroduce birds into England and Scotland began and this has been a roaring success. Ten years later, the initial project had been so successful the re-established population in the Chilterns was able to supply 68 young birds for release in Yorkshire. From the release site at the Harewood Estate near Leeds these majestic birds have spread out and can be found mainly in the Wharfe Valley and on the Yorkshire Wolds.

Red kites are a large bird with a wingspan of 1.5m (5ft), and one that can be seen relatively easily as they scavenge along roads and around villages. Adult males and females look similar but can be told from younger birds by their silvery grey heads, deeper tail fork and more contrasting colouration.

Red kites can be told from common buzzards, which have naturally re-colonised Yorkshire from the west, by their long forked tail rather than the shorter square or fanned tail characteristic of buzzards. Also, when flapping, kites' longer wings give their wing beats a more fluid, elastic style compared to the energetic flapping of buzzards. When soaring, red kites hold their wings slightly bowed, whereas buzzards hold them in a pronounced 'v' shape.

PAULL HOLME STRAYS

Paull Holme Strays lies alongside the mighty River Humber offering spectacular views across the south Holderness landscape including local historical features. Managed in partnership with the Environment Agency.

NEAREST POSTCODE
HU12 8AX

GRID REFERENCE
TA 180 247

RESERVE SIZE
104.7 ha

PUBLIC TRANSPORT
Bus service from Hull to Paull village.

DIRECTIONS
Car park entrance is off Thorngumbald road, Paull. The car park is signposted from the village and Thorngumbald road.

SITE DESIGNATION
Adjacent to the Humber Estuary Special Protection Area (SPA), Ramsar Site and Special Area of Conservation (SAC).

To see Paull Holme Strays at its spectacular best a visit during the winter months is a must. Thousands of wintering waders use the site to feed and roost and this large gathering entices predators including peregrine and merlin. Many an hour can be passed watching the shimmering flocks of knot and golden plover swirling around. Other waders at this time include black and bar-tailed godwits, redshank, dunlin, lapwing and curlew. The surrounding ditches, grassland and farmland provides winter hunting grounds for short-eared owl, hen and marsh harriers along with regular sightings of roe deer, brown hare and stoat.

The summer is a quieter time for the site but still produces some great wildlife encounters. Water voles are present in the freshwater habitats along with a variety of dragon and damselfies, including common darter, broad-bodied and four-spotted chasers, migrant hawker and small red-eyed damselfly. The song of skylark is ever present along with little egret feeding on the fringes and the striking yellow wagtail along the banks.

Paull Holme Strays was the first major managed realignment scheme on the River Humber and was breached by the Environment Agency in 2003. The site provides approximately 80 ha of inter-tidal habitat to compensate for the loss of saltmarsh and mudflats in the area, and is fronted by the extensive Paull Holme Sands.

Bar-tailed godwit

See this winter visitor looking for worms

Merlin

Top tip...

Check tide times. If you visit in the winter a couple of hours before a large incoming tide then the wader spectacle can be simply stunning.

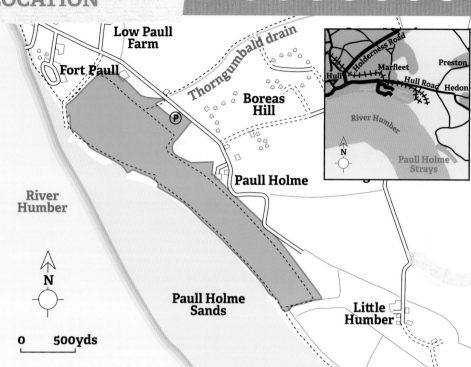

Low Paull Farm

Fort Paull

Thorngumbald drain

Boreas Hill

Paull Holme

River Humber

Paull Holme Sands

Little Humber

N

0   500yds

Holderness Road

Hull

Marfleet

Preston

Hull Road

Hedon

River Humber

Paull Holme Strays

N

SPRING	SUMMER	AUTUMN	WINTER
Cuckoo	Marsh harrier	Avocet	Merlin
Yellow wagtail	Spotted redshank	Green sandpiper	Dunlin
Sedge warbler	Little stint	Common	Redshank
Reed warbler	Curlew	sandpiper	Bar-tailed godwit
	Dragonflies	Whimbrel	Golden plover

POTTERIC CARR

Famed for its wetland birds including bitterns, Potteric Carr has a network of paths enabling visitors to explore the mosaic of habitats and enjoy the stunning vistas found at this large nature reserve. With excellent facilities including café, shop, toilets and hides it really is a great place to visit.

Colt's foot

An early flowering species of disturbed ground

Potteric Carr is an area of low-lying land to the south east of Doncaster which forms the flood plain of the River Torne. The site is fabulous for birdwatching with marsh and water birds being particularly numerous. Over 230 species of birds have been recorded and 102 species have bred, with over 65 species breeding each year. A recent major extension to the site was designed to enhance this and has already resulted in booming bitterns. Spring and autumn are exciting times as a wide range of migrant birds can arrive at any time.

Potteric Carr's marshes support a wide range of plants providing a spectacle of colour throughout the summer. Plants include greater and lesser spearwort, water soldier, water violet and Southern marsh

Black-necked grebe

This handsome species has nested in recent years

orchid. The disused railway embankments, constructed from magnesian limestone, encourage plants such as common spotted and bee orchids and old man's beard, Britain's only wild clematis. Great crested and palmate newts are present in some of the pools and toads are common. Mammals include water shrew, harvest mouse and roe deer. The nature reserve is excellent for insects and other invertebrates too, with impressive lists of moths, spiders, beetles, bugs and hoverflies. Purple hairstreak and brown argus are among the 28 species

SPRING	SUMMER	AUTUMN	WINTER
Black-necked grebe	Green sandpiper	Roe deer	Bittern
Marsh harrier	Southern marsh orchid	Little egret	Lapwing
Little ringed plover	Banded demoiselle	Teal	Golden plover
Avocet	Emperor dragonfly	Gadwall	Lesser redpoll
Colt's-foot	Brown argus	Willow tit	Siskin

POTTERIC CARR

This page is sponsored by Phoenix Mechanical Services Ltd

of butterfly to have been seen, with 21 species of dragonfly noted.

The mosaic of habitats we see today is largely due to recent management work by the Trust's staff and its hardworking volunteers. In the 16th Century the area was a small part of the Hatfield Royal Deer Chase but it eventually fell out of favour due to being continuously flooded. Over a period of 150 years various attempts were made at draining the area, the final successful attempt being in the 1760s. In the 1950s coal seams

from Rossington Colliery penetrated under the area. Over the next 15 years, as subsidence occurred, the former fen conditions returned together with the associated wildlife. In 1968, a small area (13 ha) was declared a nature reserve by Yorkshire Wildlife Trust. Over time the area of the site was gradually increased by purchase or lease and, in 2005, was extended to 200 ha when a further 75 ha of former farmland was purchased and major developments took place to improve habitats and visitor facilities and create a new extensive marsh.

NEAREST POSTCODE
DN4 8DB

GRID REFERENCE
SE 589 007

RESERVE SIZE
200 ha

PUBLIC TRANSPORT
From Frenchgate Interchange take one of the regular buses to Lakeside. Alight at the B&Q on Woodfield Way and cross the White Rose Way, then walk down Mallard Way. Nearest train station is in Doncaster.

DIRECTIONS
From the A1 take the M18 east bound, taking the first junction left to Doncaster on the White Rose Way, and then turn right at the roundabout.

OTHER INFORMATION
The reception is located within Sedum House. There is a picnic area.

SITE DESIGNATION
SSSI

Banded demoiselle

Top tip...

A late afternoon visit in winter can provide a great chance to see a bittern. Ask for latest sightings at reception. Wrap up warm and wait quietly and patiently!

A beautiful species found among bankside vegetation

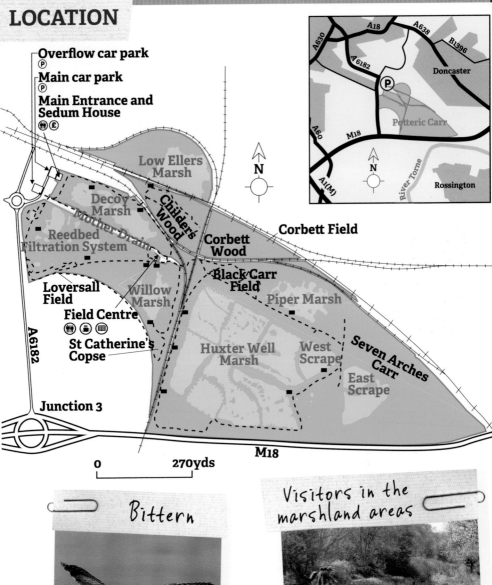

LOCATION

- Overflow car park Ⓟ
- Main car park Ⓟ
- Main Entrance and Sedum House ♿ £

Low Ellers Marsh

Decoy Marsh

Childers Wood

Mother Drain

Reedbed Filtration System

Corbett Field

Corbett Wood

Black Carr Field

Piper Marsh

Loversall Field

Willow Marsh

Field Centre 🚻 ♿ 🏛

St Catherine's Copse

Huxter Well Marsh

West Scrape

East Scrape

Seven Arches Carr

Junction 3

A6182

M18

N

A630 · A18 · A638 · B1396
A6182 · Doncaster
Ⓟ
Potteric Carr
A60 · M18
A1(M) · River Torne · Rossington
N

0 ———— 270yds

Bittern

Potteric's winter speciality, best looked for at dusk

Visitors in the marshland areas

PULFIN BOG

Pulfin Bog is a remnant of the extensive fens that once occupied the valley of the River Hull and probably owes its survival to the springs that emerge as pools on the surface.

The name Pulfin is believed to be a corruption of "pool fen" the name given to the site in a 14th Century document. The nature reserve is bounded on three sides by the River Hull and on the fourth side is an old flood bank. When the site was acquired by the Trust a ditch was clearly visible bisecting the site into northern and southern sections. The northern half, dominated by reed sweet-grass, was grazed until 1955. The southern half, in which the springs emerge, is dominated by common reed.

Pulfin is very rich in plantlife. Fenland plants such as common meadow-rue, common valerian and marsh woundwort can be found during the summer along with yellow and purple loosestrifes and the rare marsh pea. Patches of scrub occur, most of them dominated by grey willow, but bay willow is also present.

The opening of one of the springs has been greatly enlarged to form a pool providing habitat for aquatic plants including water soldier and marsh fern. Both sedge and reed warblers regularly breed around the margins and water rail, kingfisher and reed bunting can be found throughout the year. There have been 16 species of dragonfly seen, with large red damselfly and hairy dragonfly two of the first species to emerge in spring. Otters are present on the river and roe deer use the site regularly.

The Trust has now re-established grazing on part of the northern section and on adjacent grassland. Recent droughts are thought to have had a negative effect on some of the plant communities, particularly the common reed and

NEAREST POSTCODE
HU17 7NR

GRID REFERENCE
TA 050 441

RESERVE SIZE
14.58 ha

PUBLIC TRANSPORT
Buses from Beverley stop in Tickton.

DIRECTIONS
Pulfin Bog lies about two miles north east of Beverley. The nearest parking is at Hull Bridge, on the old part of the A1035. From Beverley take the A1035 eastwards and after crossing the River Hull, turn right for Tickton, then right again immediately afterwards. Park on the roadside near the footbridge over the river. Walk north along the public footpath on the east bank of the river for about one-and-a-half miles until a large lake is reached. Turn left along the bank between the lake and the river, then right on reaching a row of trees. The nature reserve starts where the trees end.

SITE DESIGNATION
SSSI

the Trust is carrying out extensive monitoring on the site to get a better understanding of this.

Large red damselflies

Top tip...

Keep an eye on the sky as hobbies regularly hunt dragonflies during the summer.

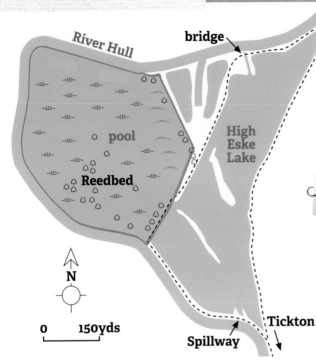

River Hull

bridge

pool

Reedbed

High Eske Lake

N

0   150yds

Spillway

Tickton

Pulfin Bog

River Hull

N

Hull Bridge

Hornsea →

A1035

Tickton

Beverley

P

Highland cow

Well suited to the wet boggy conditions

SPRING
Sedge warbler
Hairy dragonfly
Large red damselfly

SUMMER
Brown hawker
Yellow flag iris
Yellow loosestrife
Marsh pea
Water soldier

AUTUMN
Snipe
Reed bunting
Common darter
Migrant hawker

WINTER
Roe deer
Kingfisher
Water rail

RIFLE BUTTS QUARRY

The nature reserve is a small jewel of grassland that hums and buzzes with life in high summer.

Clustered bellflower

Flowers in late summer

Rifle Butts Quarry was created to provide stone for the construction of the railway line adjacent to the nature reserve. The site was then used as a rifle range from the 1890s to the First World War.

Of particular interest at this small nature reserve is the geological feature exposed on the quarry face. The exposure, of national importance, shows a Cretaceous unconformity, where sediments from the Jurassic and Lower Cretaceous periods were eroded away. In the late Cretaceous period the sea once again covered the area depositing red and then white chalk. Compared to other areas in North Yorkshire some 1000 metres of sedimentary rock is missing from the Rifle Butts sequence. A shelter has been constructed to protect the quarry face from erosion.

Over 150 plants have been recorded on this site, which still displays some characteristic chalk species including cowslip, marjoram, field scabious and wild basil. The old target marker pit has been filled in with topsoil and as a result winter aconite, comfrey, giant bellflower, sweet cicely and leopard's-bane were introduced to the site. Breeding birds include willow warbler and yellowhammer. Ringlet and common blue butterflies breed.

The Trust works to protect the rock exposure and the chalk grassland. Hawthorn and elder scrub is removed from the most important grassland areas and the grassland is maintained by mowing. The Trust also plans to graze the site with sheep.

NEAREST POSTCODE
YO43 3JA

GRID REFERENCE
SE 897 427

RESERVE SIZE
0.27 ha

PUBLIC TRANSPORT
Market Weighton is served by buses from York and Goole via Holme-on-Spalding-Moor. The Hudson Way cycle route runs on a disused railway line between Market Weighton and Beverley.

DIRECTIONS
After passing Market Weighton Secondary School continue straight on at the next junction. A mile further on take a sharp turn left, go between the embankments where a bridge once took the Market Weighton – Beverley railway line over the road. The site is on the right hand side at the end of the first field and parking is on the wide grass verge in front of the nature reserve. Please don't block the gate into the field next to the site.

SITE DESIGNATION
SSSI

Giant bellflower

Bloody cranesbill

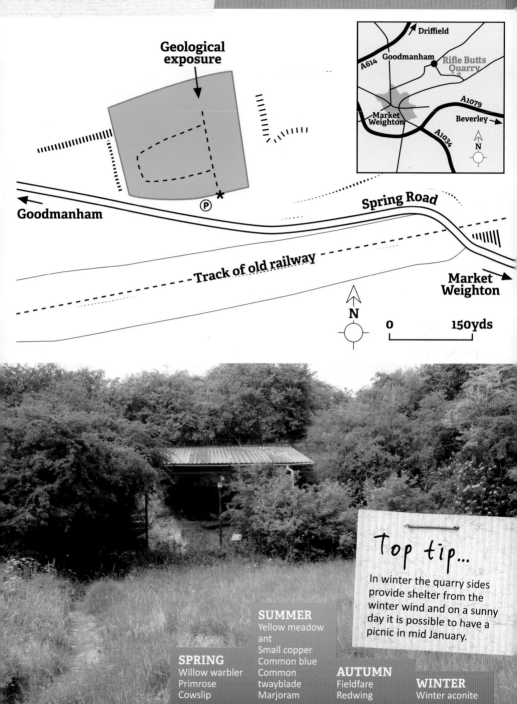

Geological exposure

Driffield

Goodmanham

A614

Rifle Butts Quarry

A1079

Beverley →

Market Weighton

A1034

N

← Goodmanham

P

Spring Road

Track of old railway

Market Weighton →

N

0   150yds

SUMMER
Yellow meadow ant
Small copper
Common blue
Common twayblade
Marjoram

SPRING
Willow warbler
Primrose
Cowslip

AUTUMN
Fieldfare
Redwing

WINTER
Winter aconite

Top tip...

In winter the quarry sides provide shelter from the winter wind and on a sunny day it is possible to have a picnic in mid January.

RIPON LOOP

A dynamic nature reserve lying within the largest meander of the River Ure and featuring rarities such as thistle broomrape and otters.

On summer days the Ure loops tranquilly around the grassland and wet woods of Ripon Loop, whilst in times of flood the river changes course and cuts directly across the site creating an oxbow lake as it recedes. This water, held in pools and ditches, provides natural flood protection for areas downstream. Ripon Loop is a 41 hectare nature reserve forming part of the Ripon Parks Site of Special Scientific Interest.

Kingfishers dart past and in winter large fish-eating goosander are frequently seen. Numbers increase if cold weather freezes over lakes and gravel pits in the area, forcing them to use the open water of the river. In summer, sand martin feed on insects overhead, breeding nearby in the soft river banks. They are one of the earliest summer migrant birds to arrive and their buzzing calls can be heard from early March. The site is rich in plantlife with marsh cinquefoil and narrow buckler fern in the wetlands, and bluebell, primrose and the nationally scarce yellow-star-of-Bethlehem in the woodlands. Thistle broomrape is a very rare plant that only grows in Yorkshire. Though the plant flourishes here the population is variable; in some years there are hundreds of the cream-coloured flower spikes growing from the base of thistles, in other years, there are hardly any. Ponds within the grassland, which are formed by subsidence, are home to smooth and great crested newts. Dragonflies are common with banded demoiselles abundant along the river.

The wildflower-rich grassland is maintained by grazing with sheep and cattle. Thistles are cut to prevent them becoming dominant, but some are left to maintain the colony of thistle broomrape.

NEAREST POSTCODE
HG4 3HJ

GRID REFERENCE
SE 317 737

RESERVE SIZE
41.36 ha

PUBLIC TRANSPORT
Ripon to Masham buses stop on the A6108 at Ripon City Golf Club.

DIRECTIONS
0.75 miles north of Ripon on the A6108, turn right at Ripon City Golf Club. Drive past the tennis club and driving range, past a right turn to a farm and take the next right (just after a no unauthorised entry sign) and drive to the end. A small parking area is available on the left before the gate. A surfaced track leads towards the river but access to the riverbank and meadows during the summer is difficult due to the tall vegetation.

SITE DESIGNATION
SSSI

Thistle broomrape

Top tip...
Visit in late June or July for your best chance of seeing the colony of thistle broomrape.

Check the bases of thist for this unusual plant

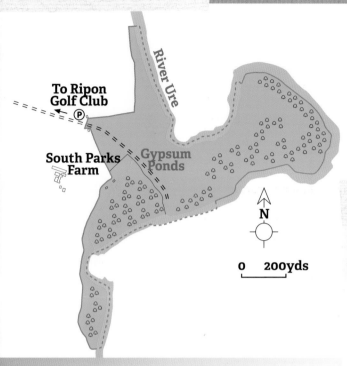

To Ripon
Golf Club

South Parks Farm

Gypsum Ponds

River Ure

N

0   200yds

South Parks Farm

Nunwick

Ripon Loop

Hutton Convers

Leyburn

A6108

A61

Thirsk

Ripon

Sharow

Meadow vetchling

Grows alongside the main track

SPRING
Sand martin
Bluebell

SUMMER
Banded demoiselle
Thistle broomrape
Meadow vetchling
Common figwort

AUTUMN
Kingfisher
Southern hawker

WINTER
Goosander
Green woodpecker
Bullfinch

SALMON PASTURES

Next to the River Don, amongst the industry of Attercliffe tucked alongside the Five Weirs Walk, this tiny but important wildlife haven has a variety of habitats in a very small area attracting many birds and insects. It is a great place to sit back and watch the many species of beautiful butterflies flitting between the flowers and warming themselves in the sun.

THE wildlife TRUSTS
Sheffield & Rotherham

NEAREST POSTCODE
S4 7WT

GRID REFERENCE
SK 371 881

RESERVE SIZE
0.5 ha

PUBLIC TRANSPORT
Nearest train station is Sheffield. Frequent buses run to the city centre.

DIRECTIONS
From Sheffield city centre take Saville Street (A6109) from the A61. Take a right turn onto Attercliffe Road (A6178); there is limited street parking on the road.

SITE DESIGNATION
LNR

The locally rare hoverfly *Cheilosa mutablis* is amongst the 22 species of hoverfly that have been recorded at the nature reserve and there are also many dragonflies, moths and butterflies, including gatekeeper and orange-tip. Birds such as mistle thrush, bullfinch, goldfinch and long-tailed tit nest and feed in the woods, while kingfisher, little grebe, moorhen and mallard all live nearby and can be seen from the banks of the River Don. Due to its closeness to the city centre and its unique mix of habitats that support myriads of birds and invertebrates, this nature reserve plays a vital role in Sheffield's green corridor.

Top tip...

Due to its easy access for pushchairs this is a great nature reserve for a visit with young children to introduce them to the wonders of nature.

Bullfinch

A shy species with a quiet, piping call

Long-tailed tit

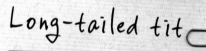

LOCATION

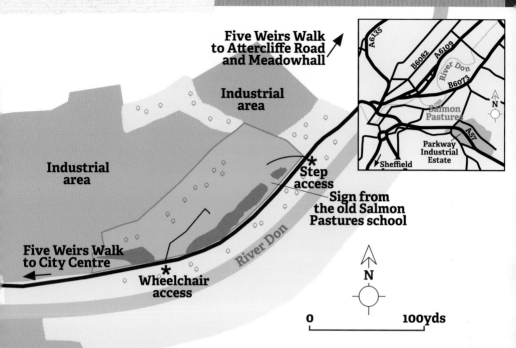

Five Weirs Walk
to Attercliffe Road
and Meadowhall

Industrial
area

Industrial
area

Step
access

Sign from
the old Salmon
Pastures school

Five Weirs Walk
to City Centre

Wheelchair
access

River Don

Inset map: A6135 · B6082 · A6109 · River Don · B6073 · Salmon Pastures · A57 · Parkway Industrial Estate · Sheffield · N

N

0   100yds

SPRING
Little grebe
Kingfisher
Mistle thrush
Orange-tip

SUMMER
Gatekeeper
Dragonflies
Damselflies

AUTUMN
Long-tailed tit

WINTER
Bullfinch
Goldfinch

SALTMARSHE DELPH

There are a remarkable number of habitats to be discovered at this small nature reserve, including open water, reedbeds and an old willow garth, which are all home to a fantastic array of wildlife. Come to enjoy peace and quiet; a moment away from it all whilst appreciating the rich variety of wildlife.

The mosaic of habitats at Saltmarshe Delph are well worth a visit. Open water and reedbeds contain lesser reedmace and attract marsh harrier and water rail, whereas in the woodland fringe mature willow, oak and ash grow. Birds of prey often frequent the site so make sure you take the occasional look up during your visit.

The site is divided neatly into two compartments by the Hull to Doncaster railway, known as the Delph and Willow Garth. In the north east corner is an area of wet willow carr, a habitat which is full of song in spring with resident willow tit joined by reed warbler, blackcap and chiffchaff. In high summer, dragon and damselflies aplenty make themselves at home, with 19 species recorded. Other insects including the lesser stag beetle and ringed china-mark moth can also be found. This rich insect life in turn attracts bats including Daubenton's. Winter is a great time to see hundreds of ducks of several species on the water.

The Delph was excavated in 1864 to provide spoil for the approach to the railway bridge close by. The Willow Garth to the west of the railway was commercially worked until 1956, providing materials to make agricultural baskets. In 1972 the site became a nature reserve. Yorkshire Wildlife Trust works to keep the ponds and reedbeds in their present condition and to control willow encroachment.

NEAREST POSTCODE
DN14 7RX

GRID REFERENCE
SE 775 248

RESERVE SIZE
5.43 ha

PUBLIC TRANSPORT
The nearest train station is at Saltmarshe, which is 2.1 miles from the nature reserve. A Trans-Pennine footpath passes the site.

DIRECTIONS
The nature reserve is 2.5 miles south east of Howden. Turn off the A614 roundabout signed Kilpin and Laxton. Take the Skelton road and proceed through the village, then turn left away from the River Ouse before the railway swing bridge. The nature reserve is 400m along the road to Saltmarshe.

Water rail

Broad-bodied chaser

A stocky dragonfly found in early summer

Top tip...
Visit in late spring for willow tits, marsh harriers and water rails. Or come late summer and be on the look out for dragonflies.

LOCATION

Mute swans

Howden

Skelton

River Ouse

A pair with cygnets

Inset map: Howden, A63, A614, M62, B1230, Kilpin, 37, N, Skelton, Klaxton, Saltmarshe, Saltmarshe Delph

N

0   200yds

The Delph

Willow Garth

Railway

Laxton and Saltmarshe

SUMMER
Emperor
dragonfly
Ruddy darter
Small red-eyed
damselfly
Broad-bodied
chaser
Southern hawker

SPRING
Mute swan
Marsh harrier
Cuckoo
Sand martin
Sedge warbler

AUTUMN
Gadwall
Teal
Wigeon

WINTER
Common buzzard
Hen harrier
Merlin
Peregrine
Wildfowl

SEATA QUARRY (& SALT LAKE QUARRY & ASHES PASTURE)

From May until late autumn there will always be an abundance of flowers, at this very flower-rich site. Shelter from the west wind encourages butterflies and allows the sweet scent of cowslips to hang in the air.

Blue moor-grass is the most abundant grass and its metallic blue flowers are impressive in April. Both meadow and hairy oat-grasses are found along with quaking grass but the star of the grasses is the rare spikey fescue, a native of the Pyrenees. Two other Pyrenean plants occur, round-leaved St John's-wort can be seen on a ledge and fairy foxglove is abundant on the quarry walls. The thin soils have more typical calcareous grassland species with abundant bird's-foot trefoil, fairy flax, harebell and especially small scabious. In a damp autumn the autumn gentian can reach 20cms high. Where soil is exceptionally thin field madder, parsley piert and biting stonecrop join the fairy foxglove. Four species of orchids occur. In mid-summer six-spot burnet moth, common blue and ringlet enjoy the flower-rich habitat. Curlew and grey partridge have nested here and sometimes brown hares are seen.

Sheep grazing within the nature reserve is limited to the winter months to allow over 100 plant species to flower. In autumn the deeper soils support a dense growth which is removed by strimming, raking and burning. Seata Quarry is leased from Township of Aysgarth and was once used to supply stone to the local area. Some local properties retain the right to take stone, but practical difficulties fortunately prevent uptake.

Fragrant orchid

The flowers are often pollinated by moths

NEAREST POSTCODE
DL8 3AL

GRID REFERENCE
SD 988 881

RESERVE SIZE
41.36 ha

PUBLIC TRANSPORT
Buses from Leyburn and Hawes.

DIRECTIONS
The Quarry lies north of the Aysgarth to Thornton Rust road in Wensleydale. A green lane leaves this road 0.5 miles from the junction with the A684 in Aysgarth. After two right-angled bends the lane ends at the quarry entrance. Footpaths also link the quarry to the A684 and back to Aysgarth.

SITE DESIGNATION
Common Land

Top tip...

Although an alien species amongst wonderful natives the fairy foxgloves' ability to colonise the narrowest of hairline cracks is really impressive.

The Trust also manages Salt Lake Quarry (Grid ref. SD 773784) and Ashes Pasture (Grid ref. SD 775 784).

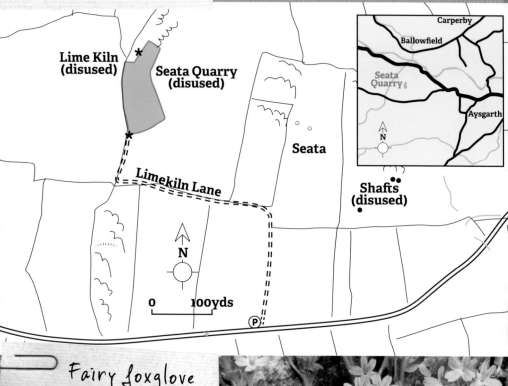

Lime Kiln (disused)

Seata Quarry (disused)

Limekiln Lane

Seata

N

0   100yds

Shafts (disused)

Carperby

Ballowfield

Seata Quarry

Aysgarth

N

Fairy foxglove

SPRING
Blue moor-grass
Cowslip
Early purple
orchid
Fairy foxglove

SUMMER
Spikey fescue
Round-leaved
St. John's-wort
Small scabious
Fragrant orchid
Butterflies

AUTUMN
Autumn gentian

SEMER WATER

From the air Semer Water resembles a pearl lying in the heart of Raydale. Ducks and waders wheel over the nature reserve with the calls of curlew, oystercatcher and snipe filling the air.

Semer Water is the largest of only three natural water bodies in Yorkshire; a glacial lake which was formed at the end of the last Ice Age when huge amounts of glacial till blocked the outflow.

Crooks Beck takes the water from three feeder dales upstream through the nature reserve. There is a full range of habitats from open water with swamp species like yellow water lily, through to fen, marsh and willow carr to developing ash woodland on the driest part. The sandy shore supports a fine growth of needle spike-rush and mudwort but elsewhere rushes and an abundance of sedge species dominate and it is here that the waders feed. The willow species are challenging with many hybrids but bay willow dominates.

Once the ground-nesting birds have fledged the nature reserve is grazed with cattle and sheep and excess rush is cut in late summer when possible.

NEAREST POSTCODE
DL8 3DJ

GRID REFERENCE
SD 918 866

RESERVE SIZE
37.09 ha

PUBLIC TRANSPORT
Bus service to Bainbridge then walk up the River Bain footpath to the lake and on to the site.

DIRECTIONS
Take the A684 Leyburn-Hawes road and exit at Bainbridge. Follow signs for Semer Water. Park at Low Blean Farm for a small charge and take the footpath opposite the farm across the fields to the nature reserve. There is also limited free parking in Stalling Busk.

SITE DESIGNATION
SSSI

SPRING
Lapwing
Curlew
Redshank
Tufted duck
Great crested grebe

SUMMER
Reed bunting
Sand martin
Willow warbler
Devil's-bit scabious

AUTUMN
Roe deer

WINTER
Wigeon
Teal
Mallard

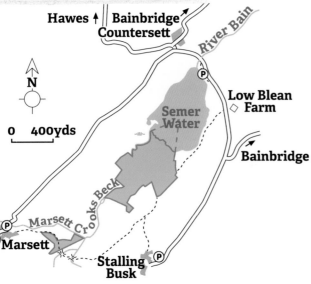

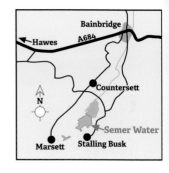

Top tip...

Visit when the ice breaks up, its music echoes around the dale.

Recently a belt of mixed ash wood has been planted on the eastern boundary as part of a project to slow rainwater run off into the lake. Much of the site is an old lake bed which still floods regularly and Yorkshire Wildlife Trust also control a wedge of the lake to a central buoy. The level of the lake was lowered by 3ft in 1937 and the old shore line is still visible.

Nearby site
NEWBIGGIN PASTURES

Recently acquired by Yorkshire Wildlife Trust, Newbiggin Pastures Nature Reserve is a mix of many different habitats, from flower rich meadows characteristic of the region, to the upland rough grassland of the high moors. Stretching from the valley bottom of Bishopdale up to the edge of Wassett Fell, visitors are afforded with spectacular views across the stunning landscape.

A work in progress, the Trust manages parts of the site as a traditional hay meadow with grazing by sheep in the autumn and a hay cut following the seeding of the wildflowers. The rough grassland at the upper end of the site is managed to provide a variety of habitats suitable for upland bird species including lapwing and curlew. As part of the working agricultural landscape of the Yorkshire Dales and managed by a local tenant, we ask visitors to keep to field edges and not to disturb the livestock. Dogs are not permitted on site.

NEAREST POSTCODE
DL8 3TF

GRID REFERENCE
SD 987 850

RESERVE SIZE
27.81 ha

Meadow pipit

SHERBURN WILLOWS

Enjoy colourful pasture where butterflies feed on the pink starbursts of greater knapweed flower heads, birds sing from the scrub edge on the bank top, and white park cattle regard you with curiosity as they graze.

A small nature reserve straddling flower-filled magnesian limestone grassland which runs steeply down a slope to a wet area of fen and willow carr woodland. In spring and summer the grassland is a carpet of colour, changing with the months; cowslip, ox-eye daisy, hairy violet and common knapweed all bloom. Good shows of common spotted orchid, bee orchid and common twayblade bring colour in midsummer. Other species of note as rare locally, include purple milk vetch, sainfoin and pale St John's-wort. The wildflowers attract many butterflies, moths and other insects.

NEAREST POSTCODE
LS25 6AN

GRID REFERENCE
SE 487 326

RESERVE SIZE
2.6 ha

Reed warbler, reed bunting and chiffchaff all breed on site. The grassland is being restored by removing scrub and grazing with rare breed white park cattle. In the areas of wet woodland Yorkshire Wildlife Trust coppices the willow to keep it rich in wildlife.

LEDSHAM BANK

A botanist's dream come midsummer, Ledsham Bank is alive with colour from the fantastic displays of wildflowers.

Situated in a north-south-running valley on the magnesian limestone, the nature reserve supports vivid spikes of pyramidal, common spotted and fragrant orchids which are scattered around the site

creating an amazing show in June and July. Other typical limestone loving plants here include hoary plantain, yellow-wort, and impressive stands of the bright yellow dyer's greenweed – rare in Yorkshire. In spring there is a good show of cowslip across the site. Later in summer field scabious and common knapweed give showy purple and pink flowers. A mature hedgerow runs down the west side of the nature reserve, providing food and shelter for winter

NEAREST POSTCODE
LS25 5LL

GRID REFERENCE
SE 461 300

finches and thrushes. A surprising number of butterflies have also been recorded here including small and large skippers, common and holly blues and commas.

The nature reserve is managed to enhance the limestone grassland by controlling invasive scrub and weed species such as ragwort, hogweed and burdock. Grazing cattle and sheep help with this management through the winter months.

BOLTON PERCY STATION

Nature has taken hold of this old station yard – bramble scrambles over the old platform, flower-filled grassland grows where once there were rail tracks and scrub growth provides sheltered scallops filled with fluttering butterflies and moths in the summer months.

Once a railway goods platform and still lying next to the Leeds-York railway line, this nature reserve covers the old platform and bridge embankments. Areas of the ground are cindery, while in other places you can see the remains of dumped rail-track ballast. The plant life here suggests a limestone influence, with primrose growing on the neighbouring railway banks.

Wildflowers in the grassland areas include bird's-foot trefoil,

NEAREST POSTCODE
YO23 7AW

GRID REFERENCE
SE 527 416

dove's-foot cranesbill and selfheal. There is also a small lower lying damp fen area. The edges of hawthorn scrub on the boundaries are scalloped, providing sheltered areas where you can get good views of butterflies and moths including common blue, two species of burnet moth and latticed heath. Hedge bottom plants such as garlic mustard and red campion, along with longer areas of tussocky grass provide homes for gatekeeper, wall and small heath. Peacock and red admiral butterflies can be seen basking on the south east facing wall of the old platform, and bramble is controlled creating sheltered sun traps. Four amphibian species have been recorded here including great crested newt.

LOCATION

Top tip...

Enjoy a warm June day with a visit to these three special sites for best views of a range of orchids and butterflies.

SOUTHERSCALES

Perched high on the side of Ingleborough this impressive nature reserve has large areas of prime limestone pavement with its associated rich plant life but also high quality limestone grassland and blanket bog.

The outstanding feature of Southerscales is a huge area of open limestone pavement which is a truly awe-inspiring sight with a fascinating pattern of runnels on its surface and deep grykes which provide shelter for many interesting plants including baneberry and rigid buckler fern. In the shallower, grassy grykes, plants such as meadow rue, fragrant orchid, Northern and limestone bedstraw and field garlic grow. In the wetter places you may find the stunning bird's-eye primrose.

The limestone grassland is covered with thousands of early purple orchids in spring followed by a succession of beautiful flowers such as small scabious, harebell, eyebright and carline thistle over the summer. The acid grassland holds a different range of species typical of its condition, including round-leaved sundew, cross-leaved heath, ling heather and bog asphodel. There are a wide range of grasses and sedges here too.

You may find palmate newt in the two small ponds on site, along with common frog. On warm days, many butterflies can be seen including the fast-flying dark green fritillary, common blue, small heath and meadow brown. Britain's largest moth, the emperor can be seen in spring.

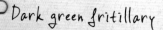

Dark green fritillary

Fragrant orchid

Can be seen around
Southerscales on warm days

Have a light scent
similar to cloves

SPRING
Emperor moth
Wheatear
Rue-leaved
saxifrage
Early purple
orchid
Primrose

SUMMER
Mouse-ear
hawkweed
Wild thyme
Fragrant orchid
Dark green
fritillary

AUTUMN
Black darter
Painted lady
Small tortoiseshell
Goldfinch

WINTER
Ferns
Mosses
Lichens

SOUTHERSCALES

At an altitude of 1,100 feet this large site is part of the Ingleborough National Nature Reserve and has been managed by the Trust since 1982. Lying on a bench of carboniferous limestone, some areas are covered with boulder clay leading to the formation of acid grassland and blanket bog.

There are a number of caves and potholes to explore, including the massive shakehole of Braithwaite Wife Hole right by the main path.

The pavement can be extremely slippery during wet weather and limestone blocks can be loose. Visitors should take special care at all times and watch out for deep grykes and potholes.

The Trust manages the grassland with grazing, employing the traditional method of cattle in summer and sheep in winter to maintain the ecological balance of the site.

Top tip...

Take the path through the nature reserve – many plants can be seen along the edges without the need to venture on to the fragile and hazardous limestone pavement.

NEAREST POSTCODE
LA6 3AR

GRID REFERENCE
SD 742 769

RESERVE SIZE
42.15 ha

PUBLIC TRANSPORT
A bus service links to Chapel le Dale on Sundays only from Darlington and Lancaster. The nearest train station is in Ribbleshead.

DIRECTIONS
The nature reserve is off the B6255 Ingleton to Hawes road. Follow path below the layby and small water company building on the B6255 through the gate. Follow the track towards Ingleborough for three fields to the nature reserve entrance. Another entrance is accessible by parking near the Old Hill Inn and walking south.

OTHER INFORMATION
Please take special care due to the hazardous terrain particularly during wet weather.

Wheatear

Present from March till September

Limestone pavement

Slippery when wet!

LOCATION

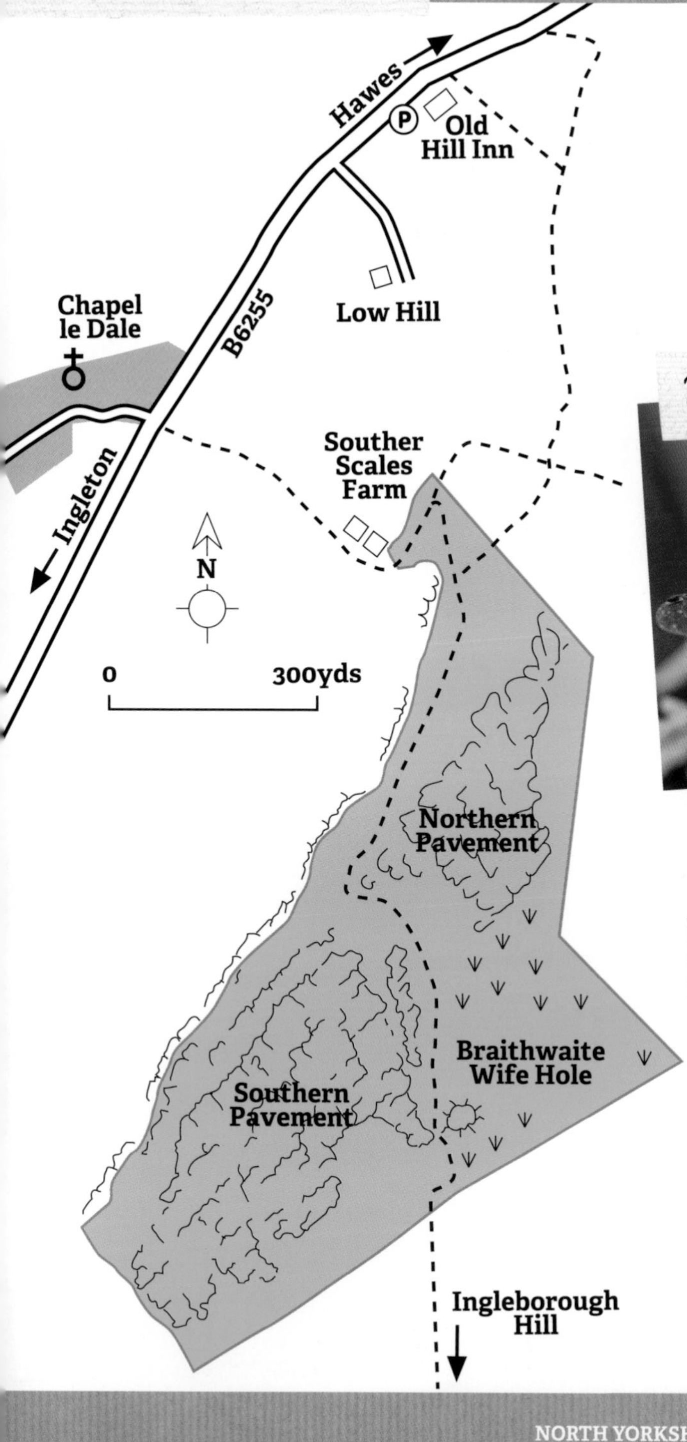

Hawes
Old Hill Inn
Low Hill
B6255
Chapel le Dale
Ingleton
Souther Scales Farm
N
0
300yds
Northern Pavement
Southern Pavement
Braithwaite Wife Hole
Ingleborough Hill

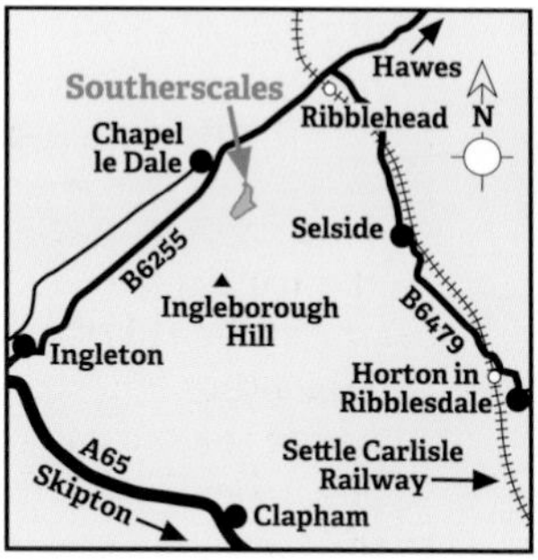

Southerscales
Hawes
N
Chapel le Dale
Ribblehead
Selside
B6255
Ingleborough Hill
B6479
Ingleton
Horton in Ribblesdale
A65
Skipton
Settle Carlisle Railway
Clapham

Black darter

Found around small boggy pools

Emperor moth

A large and distinctive species

SPROTBROUGH FLASH

Picturesque Sprotbrough Flash is one of the richest wildlife sites in South Yorkshire. A mosaic of open water, wetland, woodland and limestone grassland, the site offers a year-round treat for wildlife enthusiasts.

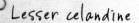

Lesser celandine

One of the earliest flowers to appear in spring

The impressive diversity of wildlife found at Sprotbrough Flash results from the range of habitats which have developed on the unusual magnesian limestone bedrock. The nature reserve is located in the Don Gorge, where the River Don cuts through the elevated limestone ridge to the west of Doncaster.

Magnesian limestone formed in a shallow tropical sea in the Permian period, some 280 million years ago. Now this rare rock type is only found in a narrow band running approximately north-south from Durham to Nottinghamshire. Due to its value as a building material and its many industrial uses, magnesian limestone (dolomite) has been widely quarried in the local area. The site protects fragments of ancient woodland on the slopes of the gorge, while wildflower-rich grassland can be found on the limestone plateau and a restored quarry

Great crested grebe

Courtship display can be seen in spring

site at the north end of the nature reserve.

The limestone woodland, protected within the nature reserve, is dominated by ash, wych elm and sycamore, with a varied shrub layer typical of this woodland type, with species such as hazel, spindle and guelder rose. There are some magnificent specimens of small-leaved lime and an avenue of mature yew, and the woodland immediately to the north west supports a nationally notable array of ancient woodland invertebrates. The wood is home to good populations of breeding woodland birds – all three species of woodpecker have been recorded here.

Small areas of limestone grassland occur on the plateau at the top of the wooded slopes, supporting a dizzying variety of specialist limestone wildflowers and insects. Over recent years the area of this valuable habitat has been significantly increased through scrub removal and its condition has been enhanced by the introduction of conservation grazing, using traditional breeds of sheep. Botanical highlights

SPRING
Great crested grebe
Early purple orchid
Sanicle
Greater stitchwort
Woodruff

SUMMER
Grassland wildflowers
Butterflies
Dragonflies
Damselflies
Bats

AUTUMN
Bittern
Osprey
Small leaved lime
Spindle

WINTER
Kingfisher
Laurel bloom
Lesser celandine

include good displays of cowslip, common spotted and pyramidal orchids, with common twayblade, bee orchid, carline thistle, quaking grass and autumn gentian among many others. Brown hares can be seen on the grassland and dashing across the adjacent arable fields, while grass snakes are also a common sight basking on the grassland in the morning sun.

Bones found locally indicate that woolly mammoth and woolly rhinocerous lived in the Sprotbrough area during the last Ice Age. When this period ended, approximately 12,000 years ago, water from the melting ice-sheets forced its way through a fault in the elevated limestone ridge, creating the Don Gorge which dominates the local landscape today. Coal mining extended underneath the Don Gorge causing subsidence and then flooding.

Little egret

This small white heron is becoming more common

Green woodpecker

Listen out for the loud yaffling call

Top tip...

Stunning displays of wildflowers can be enjoyed in spring and summer, while interesting migrant birds may drop in during autumn and winter. For a full day out, Denaby Ings nature reserve is a pleasant 3 mile walk to the west of Sprotbrough Flash along the Trans-Pennine Trail.

NEAREST POSTCODE
DN5 7NB

GRID REFERENCE
SE 530 077

RESERVE SIZE
28 ha

PUBLIC TRANSPORT
Sprotbrough village is served by bus services from Doncaster Interchange, while the nearest train station is at Conisbrough, approximately 2 miles to the west of the site. The nature reserve is located on the Trans-Pennine Trail, a long-distance walking and cycling route.

DIRECTIONS
0.5 miles to the south of Sprotbrough village, immediately adjacent to the Boat Inn. Public car parking is available next to the toll house on Nursery Lane, which is a two minute walk along the towpath from the nature reserve.

SITE DESIGNATION
SSSI

OTHER INFORMATION
Access to two wheelchair-accessible bird hides is provided along the riverside path, while visitors looking for a longer walk can climb up the side of the Don Gorge to reach ancient woodland and limestone grassland. Refreshments are available on the nature reserve's doorstep at The Boat Inn public house.

LOCATION

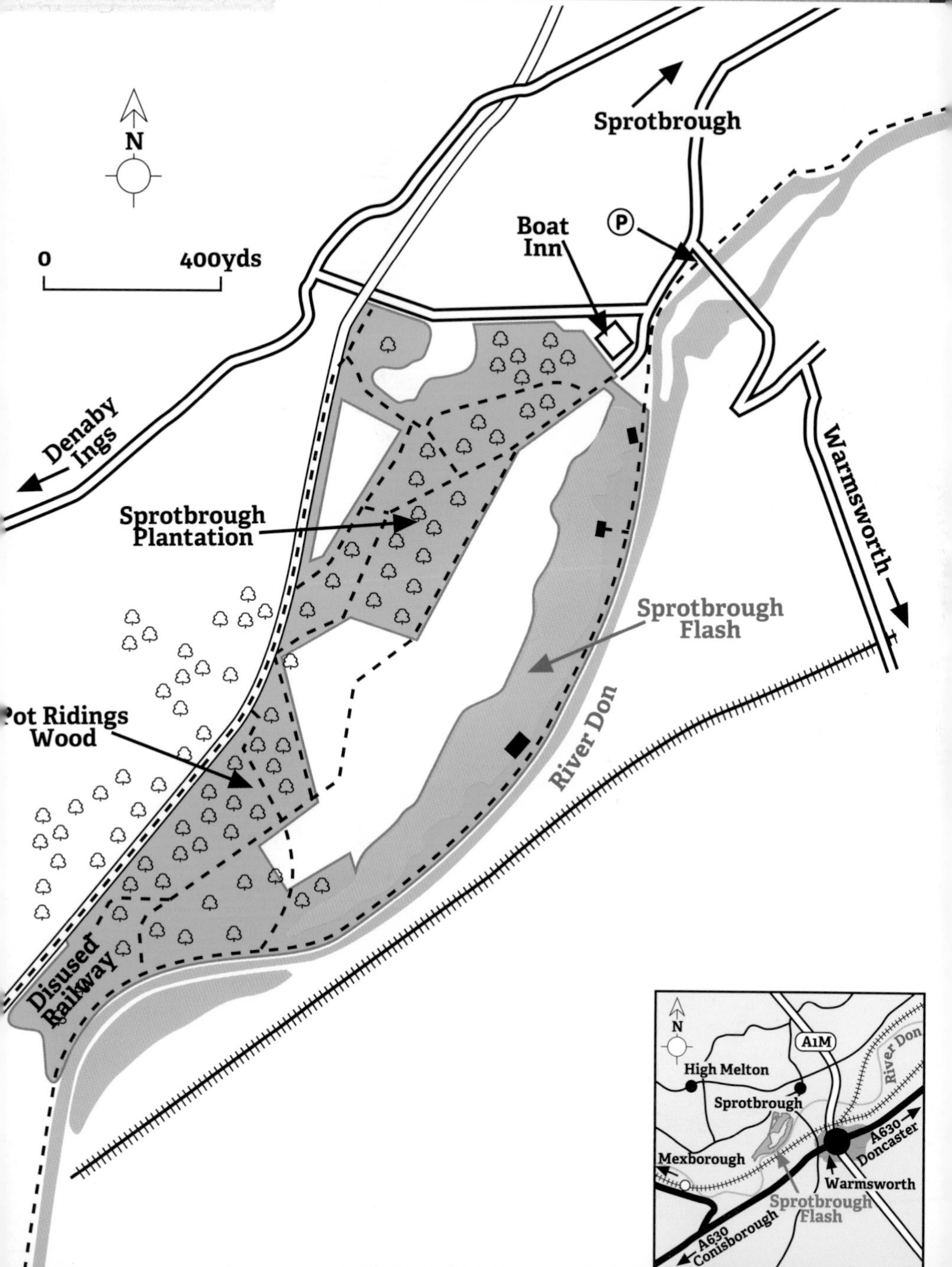

N
0
400yds
Sprotbrough
Boat Inn
P
Denaby Ings
Sprotbrough Plantation
Sprotbrough Flash
Warmsworth
Pot Ridings Wood
River Don
Disused Railway
N
A1M
High Melton
Sprotbrough
River Don
A630 Doncaster
Mexborough
Warmsworth
Sprotbrough Flash
A630 Conisborough

SPURN

Witness the breathtaking landscape of Spurn – a place of big skies and ever changing wildlife. A unique and iconic place, the nature reserve has much to offer the visitor throughout the year. A paradise for birders, Spurn is the best mainland location in the UK to witness bird migration.

Little tern

Can be seen fishing offshore

A long, narrow, crooked finger of sand reaches out from the Holderness coast across the mouth of the mighty River Humber. This is Spurn, one of Yorkshire Wildlife Trust's most iconic nature reserves. It is a wildlife-rich mosaic of beach, mudflats, saltmarsh, dunes, grassland, open water, saline lagoons and native sea buckthorn scrub.

Spurn has formed from the sediment, sand and gravels washing down the Holderness coast and by the interaction between the North Sea and the River Humber. In the past, people have tried to fortify Spurn against these dynamic natural processes, but largely these have failed. The Trust now tries to work with nature, rather than against it.

Spurn is rich in wildlife but this may not be obvious at first glance. Plants are the first feature noticed, with the marram grass-topped dunes interspersed with

Longhorn cattle

Rare-breed cattle and sheep graze to maintain the grassy areas

Sea buckthorn

Orange berries provide fuel for tired migrant birds

SPRING	SUMMER	AUTUMN	WINTER
Harbour porpoise	Little tern	Common seal	Roe deer
Wryneck	Clouded yellow	Woodcock	Brent goose
Ring ouzel	Pyramidal orchid	Arctic skua	Hen harrier
Wheatear	Sea holly	Black redstart	Short-eared owl
Scurvy grass	Sea rocket	Sea buckthorn	Wader flocks

SPURN

stunted elder and orange-berried sea buckthorn bushes. On the Humber side of Spurn, a strip of saltmarsh exists between the land and the mudflats, supporting colourful flowering plants including sea lavender, sea aster and sea rocket, along with common glasswort and eel grass. Curlew, grey plover and knot also use the saltmarsh to roost at high tide. Look out for merlin and peregrine which cause panic among the flocks of roosting waders when they start to hunt. Shelduck and brent geese are conspicuous on the mudflats during the winter.

Spring and summer sees a wide range of wildflowers appear in the grassland areas which the Trust manages by grazing with rare breed sheep and also by cutting. Magenta pyramidal orchids grow here and closer inspection of short grass around the visitor centre may reveal the rare suffocated clover. Sea holly can be seen close to the road and amongst the dunes. Roe deer are a regular sight in these grassy areas, particularly early in the morning, which is also a good time to see a fox. An hour watching the sea will not only reveal passing seabirds including locally-breeding little tern in the summer, but also harbour porpoise and for the very fortunate, a minke or even humpback whale.

Spurn is famous for migration. Birds are the most visible migrants, but impressive movements of insects, including hoverflies, ladybirds, dragonflies and butterflies can occur. Due to its prominent position, huge numbers of birds pass through Spurn during the year. The number and type of bird varies literally from week to week and are influenced by the weather conditions. The adjacent Humber Estuary is of international importance for its vast numbers of wildfowl and wading birds which can be seen on passage in spring and autumn and during the winter.

Red-veined darter

A recent colonist in the Spurn area

NEAREST POSTCODE
HU12 0UH (The Warren)

GRID REFERENCE
TA 419 149

RESERVE SIZE
327.04 ha

PUBLIC TRANSPORT
The Spurn Ranger bus service stops at Spurn and runs Easter to October, Sundays and Bank Holidays only.

DIRECTIONS
Spurn is located c. 30 miles east of Hull. From Easington follow the B1445 to Kilnsea. In Kilnsea follow the road through the village, take a sharp right bend by the Blue Bell Café before reaching the entrance. The Warren and Information Centre are 100m further in. You will be asked to show your membership card or pay admission at the barrier to drive onto the Point where there is a large car park.

OTHER INFORMATION
Footpaths open all the time. Road can be closed to vehicles – follow on site instructions. Dogs are not permitted, even in vehicles.

Top tip...

Enjoy a brisk walk on a bright winter afternoon to experience a host of birds of prey – short-eared owl, merlin, peregrine and hen harrier which seek prey among the thousands of wintering wildfowl and waders on the Humber mudflats.

LOCATION

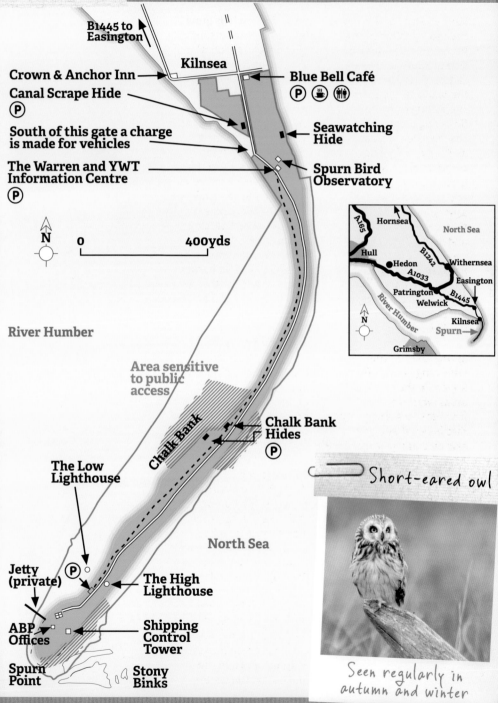

B1445 to Easington

Kilnsea

Crown & Anchor Inn

Blue Bell Café
Ⓟ ☕ 🚻

Canal Scrape Hide
Ⓟ

South of this gate a charge is made for vehicles

Seawatching Hide

The Warren and YWT Information Centre
Ⓟ

Spurn Bird Observatory

N   0 ————— 400yds

River Humber

Hornsea   North Sea
A165
Hull
Hedon   B1242   **Withernsea**
A1033
Easington
Patrington   B1445
Welwick
River Humber   **Kilnsea**
N   **Spurn**
Grimsby

Area sensitive to public access

Chalk Bank Hides
Ⓟ

Chalk Bank

The Low Lighthouse

North Sea

Jetty (private)
Ⓟ

The High Lighthouse

ABP Offices

Shipping Control Tower

Spurn Point

Stony Binks

Short-eared owl

Seen regularly in autumn and winter

EAST YORKSHIRE NATURE RESERVES   **181**

Harbour porpoise
Phocoena phocoena

Most easily seen on calm days

- [ ] **SPRING**
- [x] **SUMMER**
- [x] **AUTUMN**
- [ ] **WINTER**

- [ ] **GRASSLAND**
- [x] **BY THE COAST**
- [ ] **WETLAND**
- [ ] **FARMLAND**

Harbour porpoise, the UK's smallest cetacean, occurs all along the Yorkshire coastline. Our nature reserves at Spurn and Flamborough Cliffs offer the perfect platform from which to see this charismatic mammal. They are often viewed surprisingly close to shore and have even been sighted as far up the River Ouse as Selby!

Unlike dolphins, harbour porpoises are a relatively inconspicuous species, showing little of themselves at the surface. On calm days, when the sea is flat, look for a small, grey coloured, triangular fin breaking the surface. If you are lucky enough to see the head you will notice its blunt appearance, another key identification feature. They tend to be seen alone, or in small loose groups or as mother-calf 'pairs'.

Harbour porpoises occur along our coast year round but do undertake seasonal movements, with land-based sightings peaking between July and October. They feed on schooling fish, cephalopods such as squid, and crustaceans, foraging along the seafloor in search of their prey. Growing to a maximum size of 1.9m, harbour porpoises reach maturity between the ages of three and five years old. Most calves are born between the months of May and August and fully weaned after four to eight months. Thereafter, harbour porpoises have been known to live for 24 years.

Viewing harbour porpoises takes patience, luck, or a bit of both! Sea conditions are key as waves and swell make it extremely difficult to pick them out. Therefore, choose a nice calm day, settle down at your chosen vantage point and wait. Binoculars and a spotting scope are extremely useful and you can get some birdwatching in while waiting for a porpoise!

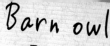
Barn owl
Tyto alba

Young barn owl

- ☑ SPRING
- ☑ SUMMER
- ☑ AUTUMN
- ☑ WINTER

- ☐ WOODLAND
- ☑ PASTURELAND
- ☑ WETLAND
- ☑ FARMLAND

There are few more inspiring sights than a ghost-like barn owl, floating across a summer meadow.

Barn owl activity peaks in summer, as short nights and hungry chicks mean they continue to hunt well after dawn and leave their roosts before dusk. Barn owls depend on small mammals for food and wherever these are abundant, this species thrives, providing that there are also safe roosting and breeding sites available.

Barn owls nest in cavities in trees and in old buildings and barns, but will also take readily to nestboxes, a feature that conservationists have exploited to help them colonise new areas. The reduction in small mammal numbers through the loss of habitat to agricultural intensification and increasing collisions with higher volumes of road traffic has led to a massive decline in barn owl numbers in the UK. In some areas, particularly East Yorkshire they have recovered and are doing well.

Hunting barn owls usually quarter areas of land (flying back and forth) a couple of metres above the ground. They listen and look for signs of mammal activity and once located will hover in order to pinpoint their prey, before diving headfirst into the grass in order to make final adjustments to their strike. At the last minute they swing their talons forward and throw their head back in order to catch prey with their feet. Prey is usually consumed whole immediately, with undigestible parts being coughed up later as a pellet. When feeding young, they will transfer the prey to their beak and then fly off with it to their nest site. Sometimes, barn owls will switch their hunting strategy to 'sit and wait' and can then often be seen perched on fence posts and low tree branches.

Barn owls are one of the world's most widespread bird species occurring in all continents except Antarctica.

STAVELEY NATURE RESERVE

This superb wetland site lying close to the River Tutt holds year round interest for visitors with regular sightings of otters and several orchid species among the highlights.

Common tern

Nest on floating rafts specially provided for them

Staveley Nature Reserve, formerly known as Staveley Carrs, has been renowned for rare plants for centuries. Today, this large, accessible site has been sculpted through quarrying activities followed by decades of work by Yorkshire Wildlife Trust and dedicated volunteers.

The site is in two parts; the East Lagoon edged with natural vegetation that was allowed to develop freely comprising of fen, reed swamp and flower-rich calcareous grassland, and the West Lagoons, landscaped with a limited number of trees planted and the rest sown down to pasture, which has since been intensively grazed. The nature reserve is bordered by the River Tutt on its northern boundary and there are footpaths and hides from which to observe the varied wildlife.

Small areas of fen are home to several relic species which were once

Marsh helleborine

A beautiful flower to be found in the fen areas

widespread before the carrs were drained and transformed into farmland. Locally scarce species such as water violet, marsh helleborine and meadow rue can be found.

Common breeding birds include summer visitors such as sand martin and several species of warbler, with common tern breeding on the rafts put out for them. There have been 22 species of damselflies and dragonflies recorded in the main

SPRING	SUMMER	AUTUMN	WINTER
Otter	Marsh helleborine	Teal	Red kite
Common tern	Common spotted orchid	Shoveler	Tufted duck
Sand martin	Bee orchid	Greenshank	Reed bunting
Large red damselfly	Barn owl	Migrant hawker	Tree sparrow
Orange-tip	Peacock butterfly		

lagoons or the small ponds and ditches.

Mammals are well represented with roe deer and fox amongst the larger species and water shrew and harvest mouse amongst the smaller species. Otter are seen regularly, quite often in the middle of the day, particularly in the East Lagoon.

Management of the nature reserve is designed to maintain the site's important habitats of fen, flower-rich grassland, open water, wet pasture and ponds by clearing encroaching scrub, mowing and grazing.

Staveley hide

Visit the new hide for wonderful panoramas

NEAREST POSTCODE
HG5 9LQ

GRID REFERENCE
SE 369 630

RESERVE SIZE
79.11 ha

PUBLIC TRANSPORT
Bus routes pass through Staveley village.

DIRECTIONS
On the northern outskirts of Staveley, 2.5 miles south west of Boroughbridge. Car park just out of the village on the Minskip road and also disabled access via radar key from the track next to the church on Main Street. Public footpaths cross the site from Staveley Main Street next to the pub and from the Minskip road.

Otters

Frequently seen in the East Lagoon

Six-spot burnet moth

A day flying moth commonly seen feeding on scabious during summer

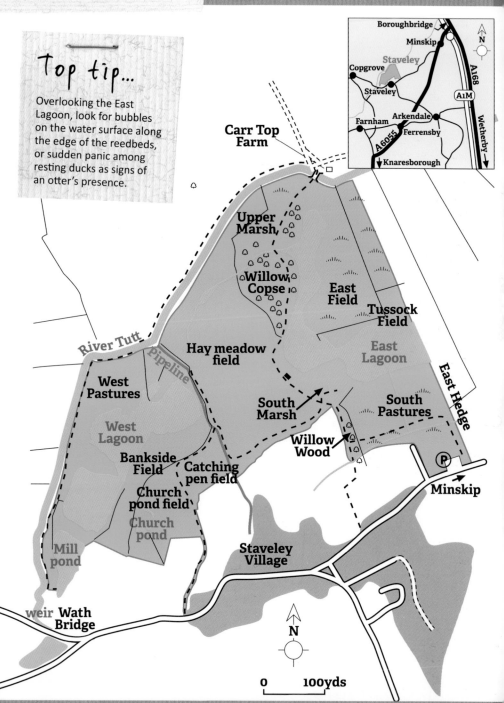

Top tip...

Overlooking the East Lagoon, look for bubbles on the water surface along the edge of the reedbeds, or sudden panic among resting ducks as signs of an otter's presence.

Boroughbridge
Minskip
Staveley
Copgrove
Staveley
Arkendale
Farnham
Ferrensby
A6055
A1M
A168
Wetherby
Knaresborough
N

Carr Top Farm

Upper Marsh

Willow Copse

East Field

Tussock Field

River Tutt

Pipeline

Hay meadow field

East Lagoon

West Pastures

West Lagoon

South Marsh

South Pastures

East Hedge

Bankside Field

Catching pen field

Willow Wood

Church pond field

Church pond

Minskip

Mill pond

Staveley Village

weir Wath Bridge

N

0   100yds

STOCKSMOOR COMMON

Tree pipits and linnets sing from the trees in the young woodland at Stocksmoor Common Nature Reserve. Wavy hair-grass may be found in the acid grassland – a habitat produced by rough grazing which has been all but lost in the modern intensively-used landscape.

Broadly split into two parts the nature reserve is home to rough acid grassland, which covers approximately half of the area. Moist for most of the year, one or two marshy areas exist within this grassland. Woodland has encroached on to the rest of the site, establishing after grazing ceased.

Mat grass, wavy hair-grass and tufted hair-grass dominate in the damper grassland areas – a plant community that demonstrates a halfway house between the extensively sheep-grazed uplands of the Pennines and the drier lowland acid grassland and heaths of the Vale of York. In the more grassy areas, adder's-tongue fern, common spotted orchid and common fleabane can be found.

The woodland is made up of pioneer birch, with oak, willow, gorse and hawthorn regenerating. This site is a good place to see a range of birds such as tree pipit, linnet, yellowhammer, willow tit and long-tailed tit.

In 1997 a new pond was dug and since then it has been gradually colonised by a range of invertebrates, which are an important feature of the nature reserve. Bracket fungi on the short-lived birch and the leaf litter that forms amongst the tufted-hair grass are just two of the micro-habitats that are important for a variety of beetles, flies and other types of insect. These in turn are fed upon by small mammals such as bank voles and wood mice, which themselves are food for foxes and tawny owls.

The Trust manages the site through a programme of grazing to keep down the coarse vegetation and invading scrub. Bracken is also controlled. The Trust has been involved on site since April 1965 when it was leased from Messrs Job Earnshaw and Bros. Limited.

NEAREST POSTCODE
WF4 4HZ

GRID REFERENCE
SE 275 150

RESERVE SIZE
11.9 ha

PUBLIC TRANSPORT
Bus services to Midgley available from Wakefield.

DIRECTIONS
Stocksmoor Common is situated five miles south west of Wakefield and not far from the M1. It is close to the village of Midgley. The B6117 runs alongside the nature reserve.

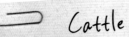

Cattle

Rare breed white park cattle grazing the nature reserve

Oak bush-cricket

Resting on a whitebeam leaf

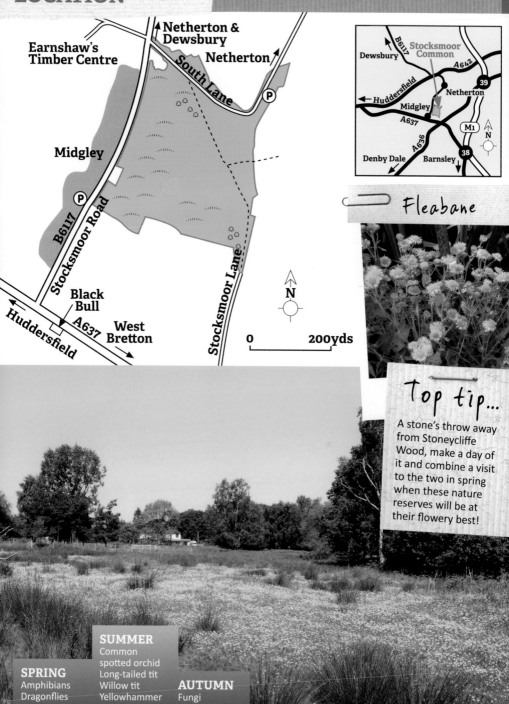

Netherton & Dewsbury

Netherton

Earnshaw's Timber Centre

South Lane

P

Midgley

B6117

Stocksmoor Road

P

Black Bull

A637

Huddersfield

West Bretton

Stocksmoor Lane

Stocksmoor Common

Dewsbury

B6117

A642

Huddersfield

Netherton

Midgley

39

A637

M1

A636

Denby Dale

Barnsley

38

N

N

0   200yds

Fleabane

Top tip...

A stone's throw away from Stoneycliffe Wood, make a day of it and combine a visit to the two in spring when these nature reserves will be at their flowery best!

SPRING
Amphibians
Dragonflies

SUMMER
Common spotted orchid
Long-tailed tit
Willow tit
Yellowhammer

AUTUMN
Fungi

STONEYCLIFFE WOOD

A stunning woodland with meandering beck trickling through – step into Stoneycliffe Wood, a semi-natural ancient woodland site, to enjoy bluebells and ramsons in spring, breeding birds in summer and fungi in autumn.

Chiffchaff

Listen out for their eponymous song

Oak and birch regenerate freely at Stoneycliffe Wood nature reserve, whilst holly, hazel and, in one area, heather form an understory. Historically managed for timber production, some areas have since become dominated by sweet chestnut. Invertebrates thrive here, providing food for the many breeding birds. Benefitting from adjoining woodland to the north and south this collection of woodlands forms a significant tree-covered belt in the wider landscape.

In spring there are magnificent displays of bluebells and wild garlic or ramsons, with yellow archangel in summer, all of which are ancient woodland indicators. Streamside plants include wood club-rush, hemlock water-dropwort and Sprengel's bramble. A wide range of woodland birds can be seen. These include a variety of summer migrants such as chiffchaff,

Bluebells

Provide a beautiful carpet of blue in spring

Ramsons

Also known as wild garlic

SPRING
Bluebell
Ramsons
Green
woodpecker
Chiffchaff
Lesser spotted
woodpecker

SUMMER
Butterflies
Dragonflies

AUTUMN
Fungi

STONEYCLIFFE WOOD

garden warbler, lesser whitethroat and spotted flycatcher, all of which breed. All three species of woodpecker frequent the woodland, feeding on the invertebrates in dead wood, which is an important feature of the site. Several rare species of spider have been recorded. Mammals are widely recorded with bank and short-tailed voles, shrews, wood mice, stoats and foxes all noted.

The nature reserve slopes down steeply from east to west, extending across Stoneycliffe Beck in the southern half. In places the slopes expose outcrops of sandstones of the coal measures which provide further diversity on the woodland floor.

In recent years the Trust has been improving footpaths on site to provide good access for visitors. Practical conservation includes woodland thinning to increase structural and age diversity and to create more varied dead wood for invertebrates. Bracken and Himalayan balsam are controlled annually to prevent them from invading the site and swamping the woodland flowers.

NEAREST POSTCODE
WF4 4NF

GRID REFERENCE
SE 274 161

RESERVE SIZE
40.13 ha

PUBLIC TRANSPORT
Buses that run from Wakefield to Huddersfield pass through Netherton. Exit on Upper Lane (Coxley View).

DIRECTIONS
The nature reserve is on the western edge of the village of Netherton. A footpath enters the site near the Star Inn. Another entrance is alongside Netherton Cemetery and a third footpath enters from the signposted entrance road to Earnshaw's Timber Centre, almost in Midgley.

OTHER INFORMATION
Footpaths can be muddy.

Spotted flycatcher

This declining summer visitor can still be found

Top tip...

A visit in spring provides huge variety with the carpet of bluebells providing a picturesque backdrop to the meandering beck.

LOCATION

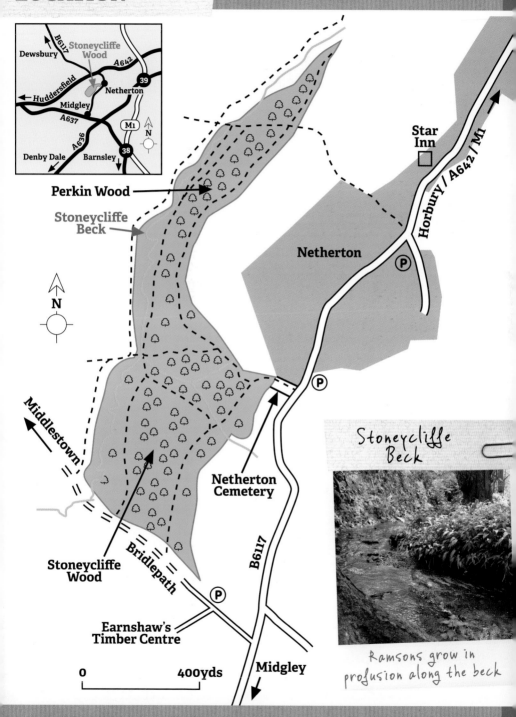

Dewsbury
B6117
Stoneycliffe Wood
A642
Huddersfield
Netherton
39
Midgley
A637
M1
N
A636
Denby Dale
A642
Barnsley
38

Perkin Wood

Stoneycliffe Beck

N

Netherton

Star Inn

Horbury / A642 / M1

P

P

Middlestown

P

Netherton Cemetery

Stoneycliffe Wood

Bridlepath

B6117

P

Earnshaw's Timber Centre

0   400yds

Midgley

Stoneycliffe Beck

Ramsons grow in profusion along the beck

STRENSALL COMMON

Strensall Common is a fabulous large heathland close to York where the pink heads and grey green leaves of cross-leaved heath intermingle with the purple spikes and green foliage of ling heather. Common lizards bask on the stumps of silver birch.

Strensall Common forms part of a larger tract of internationally important lowland heath that lies within the Vale of York.

Close to the City of York, the nature reserve supports a mosaic of wet heath, dry heath, mire, open water, woodland and acid grassland. Over 150 plant species grow here including marsh cinquefoil, the beautiful blue marsh gentian and carnivorous round-leaved sundew. Ling heather and cross-leaved heath turn the heathland purple in August. Less showy, but just as pretty are the flowers found within some of the drier grassland; pinky-red sheep's sorrel and the tiny white crosses of heath bedstraw can be seen if you look closely.

The Common is home to a host of insects including a nationally important population of dark-bordered beauty moth. Green and purple hairstreak butterflies occur here and bog bush-cricket live in the rushy grassland.

Birds using the site include woodlark, green woodpecker, stonechat, coal and willow tits. Cuckoo breed and hobby sightings are increasing.

Conservation management here aims to maintain the open areas of heath. Grazing using Hebridean sheep has helped control birch seedlings. Bracken is controlled along with invasive coniferous species that are not native to heaths in this part of the UK. Ponds are cleared out from time to time, which maintains patches of open water.

NEAREST POSTCODE
YO60 7QY

GRID REFERENCE
SE 647 615

RESERVE SIZE
41.57 ha

PUBLIC TRANSPORT
A regular bus service from York runs to Strensall.

DIRECTIONS
Follow the A1237 from York into Strensall village, follow the signs for Flaxton. After a mile you cross a cattle grid onto Strensall Common. The nature reserve is to the left. There are various parking areas within the common – a central parking point is by the Common Road level crossing.

SITE DESIGNATION
SSSI, SAC

Dark-bordered beauty

The caterpillars feed on creeping willow

Cross-leaved heath

Gives the Common its grey-pink colour in August

Top tip...
Visit on a warm August afternoon to enjoy the purple heather which carpets the common at this time of year. Bold Southern hawker dragonflies patrol sheltered sunny areas and common lizards lazily bask on old birch stumps.

Beck Wood

The Bungalow Farm

Walbutts

Ebor Way

Sewage works

The Sike

bor Way

℗

Common road crossing

Flaxton

Moorside Farm

Cattle grid

Strensall & York

N

0   200yds

Inset map:

Sheriff Hutton

Strensall Common

Flaxton

Strensall

Towthorpe

A64

A1237

York

N

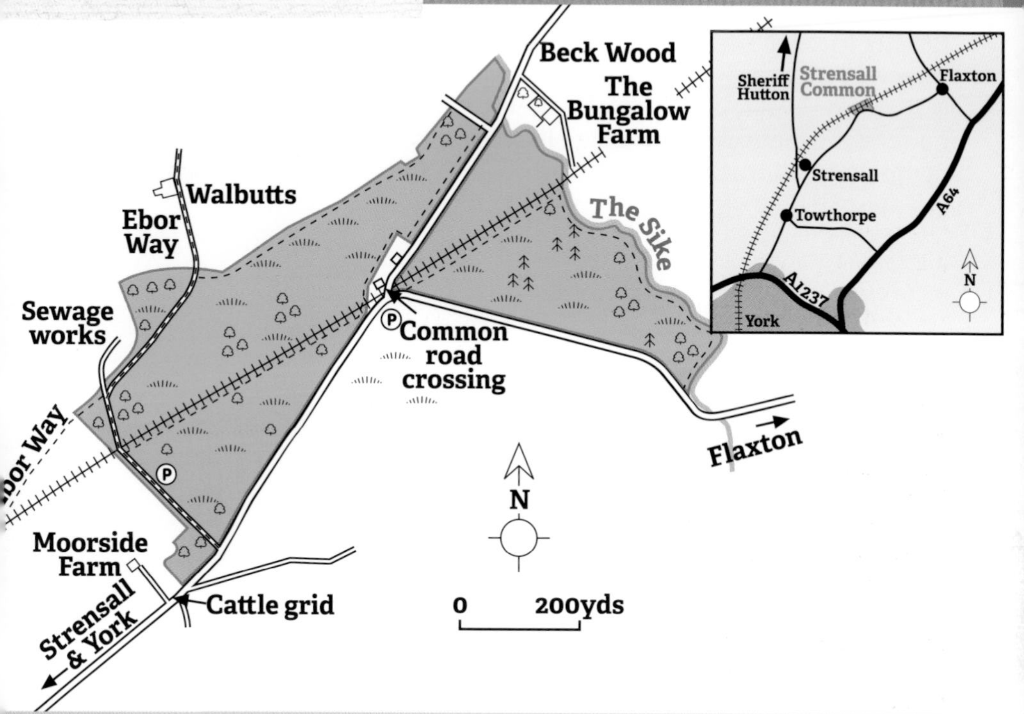

SPRING
Cuckoo
Woodlark
Common lizard
Four-spotted chaser

SUMMER
Green woodpecker
Hobby
Black darter
Marsh gentian
Flowering heather

AUTUMN
Siskin
Hoof fungus
Fly agaric
Oyster fungus

WINTER
Brown hare
Stonechat
Willow tit

SUNNYBANK

Despite its small size and location behind a petrol station at the end of Ecclesall Road, Sunnybank is Sheffield Wildlife Trust's most visited nature reserve. It is a hugely valuable green space where people can find trees and tranquillity, away from the noise of the ring road.

Sheffield & Rotherham

NEAREST POSTCODE
S10 2DF

GRID REFERENCE
SK 346 864

RESERVE SIZE
0.8 ha

PUBLIC TRANSPORT
From Sheffield city centre take a bus towards Bakewell, Castleton or Matlock and alight on Eccleshall Road.

DIRECTIONS
From Sheffield city centre, turn off the A61 onto Ecclesall Road (A625); follow round so heading back to the A61 but turn left into William Street. Turn right onto Exeter Drive. Metered parking is available in the area.

SITE DESIGNATION
LNR

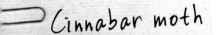

Cinnabar moth

See this day-flying moth between May and July

The pool at Sunnybank is surrounded by aquatic and wetland plants and is home to several types of dragonfly, pond skaters and common frogs.

The scrubby woodland and hedgerows provide plenty of food and shelter for the many birds that feed and nest here, while butterflies abound on the hay meadow in summer. Species to be found include small skipper, green-veined white, red admiral and common blue, while six-spot burnet and cinnabar moths have also been sighted, along with foxes, hedgehogs and common pipistrelle bats.

Wood mouse

Commonly found on the woodland floor - food for tawny owls

Top tip...
Because of its closeness to the city centre this is a great and tranquil place to spend a lunch hour or break from work.

LOCATION

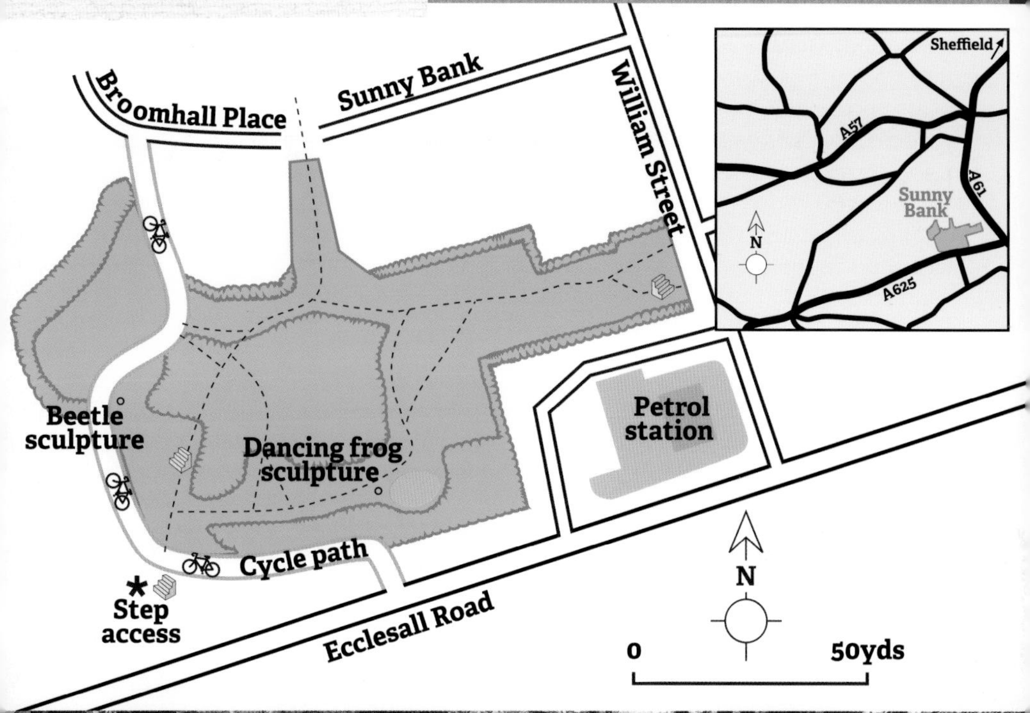
Broomhall Place
Sunny Bank
William Street
Sheffield
A57
A61
Sunny Bank
N
A625
Beetle sculpture
Dancing frog sculpture
Petrol station
Cycle path
Step access
Ecclesall Road
N
0
50yds

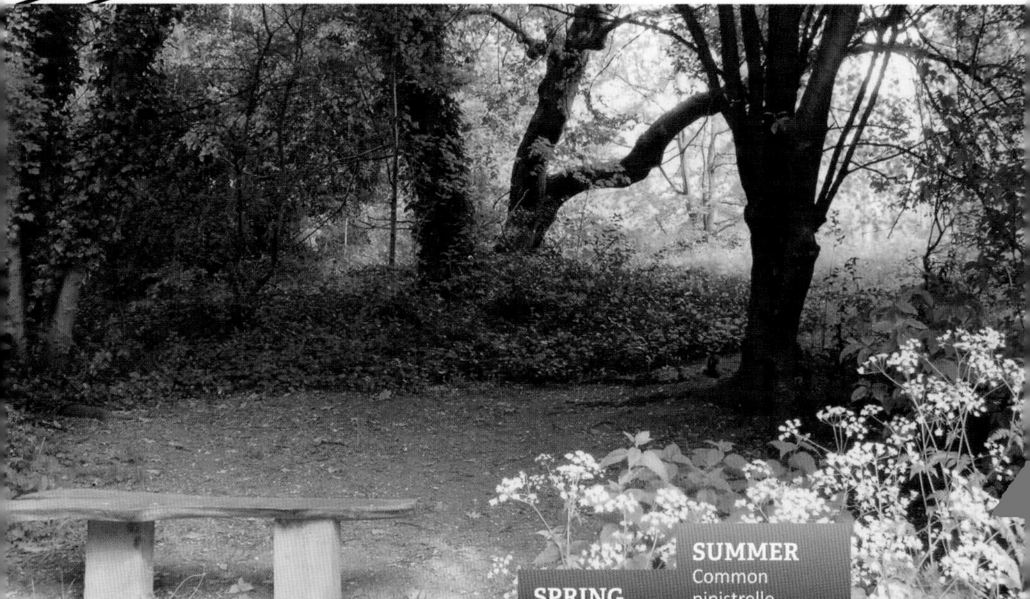

SPRING
Fox
Common frog
Yellow flag iris

SUMMER
Common pipistrelle
Dragonflies
Butterflies
Six-spot burnet

AUTUMN
Hedgehog

THORPE MARSH

Enjoy a peaceful walk around Thorpe Marsh Nature Reserve with pastures lined with hedgerows, ponds, lakes and small woodlands. With such varied habitats supporting a wide range of plants and animals you are guaranteed to see or hear something of interest.

On the east bank of the River Don floodplain, Thorpe Marsh Nature Reserve is a mixture of semi-improved and unimproved grassland, small patches of woodland and open water. It was never intensively farmed due to the surrounding railway lines and Ea Beck, as well as being purchased by the Central Electricity Generating Board in the 1960s for tipping fly ash. This has meant that a great mix of plant species have flourished. Reedholme and Cockshaw Fields have centuries-old ridge-and-furrow corrugations with plants not now commonly seen in pastures – species such as adder's tongue fern, pepper saxifrage, devil's-bit scabious, great burnet and common figwort. Voles, mice and shrews thrive here and so do the owls that feed on them, including long-eared owls in winter.

The disused railway embankments, open in parts and wooded in others, give excellent views over the site and support many plants such as red and white campions, lady's bedstraw and broad-leaved helleborine and many insects and breeding birds. Hedgerows of varying ages provide food, cover and highways for insects, birds, mammals and grass snakes. Small patches of woodland and scrub with oak, ash, hawthorn, blackthorn, willow, birch and, in the wetter areas, alder, give many feeding and nesting opportunities for great spotted woodpeckers, long-tailed and willow tits, treecreepers and tawny owls, among others.

Long-eared owl

NEAREST POSTCODE
DN5 0LN

GRID REFERENCE
SE 594 088

RESERVE SIZE
77 ha

PUBLIC TRANSPORT
Catch the Doncaster to Askern service via Almholme from Fordstead Lane.

DIRECTIONS
The nature reserve entrance is at the Norwood Gate on Fordstead Lane, near the Norwood pumping station. Visitors may approach via Arksey or Barnby Dun. The public bridleway to the south of the ash-tip leads to the nature reserve and its permissive footpaths.

OTHER INFORMATION
Dogs must be under control on the bridle path only.

Thorpe Mere is the largest of the water bodies. Grey heron, geese and ducks are regulars but waders like oystercatcher, green sandpiper and redshank are often seen here. In winter wigeon and goosander are regulars. At the Mere Scrape little grebe, moorhen, coot and mallard usually breed and water rail are shy visitors too. Applehurst Pond is also worth watching with good views of water birds.

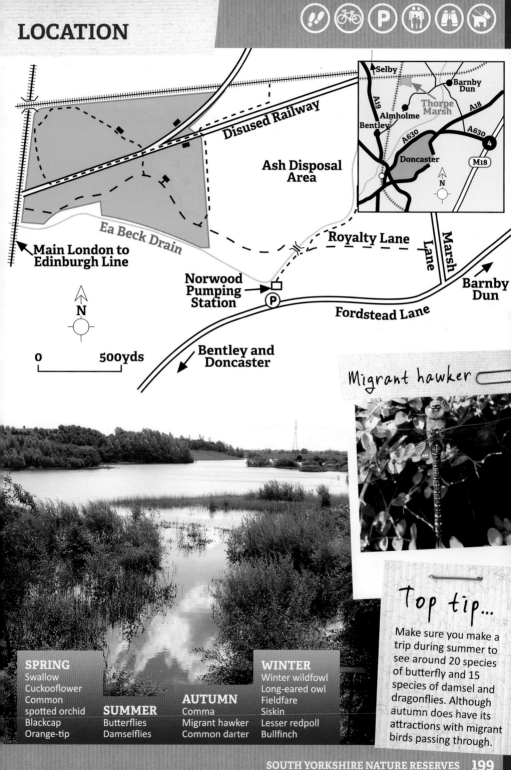

Disused Railway

Ash Disposal Area

Selby
Barnby Dun
A19
Thorpe Marsh
A18
Almholme
Bentley
A630
A630
Doncaster
4
M18
N

Ea Beck Drain

Main London to Edinburgh Line

Royalty Lane

Marsh Lane

Norwood Pumping Station → P

Barnby Dun

Fordstead Lane

N

0   500yds

Bentley and Doncaster

Migrant hawker

Top tip...

Make sure you make a trip during summer to see around 20 species of butterfly and 15 species of damsel and dragonflies. Although autumn does have its attractions with migrant birds passing through.

SPRING
Swallow
Cuckooflower
Common
spotted orchid
Blackcap
Orange-tip

SUMMER
Butterflies
Damselflies

AUTUMN
Comma
Migrant hawker
Common darter

WINTER
Winter wildfowl
Long-eared owl
Fieldfare
Siskin
Lesser redpoll
Bullfinch

TWENTYWELLSICK WOOD

Twentywellsick Wood is a small but fine example of ancient mature oak woodland with an abundance of woodland birds. Oak dominates the canopy with birch, rowan and some holly. Located on a steep slope the ground flora varies from bilberry at the top to other woodland species such as bluebell and wood stitchwort.

The nature reserve's strength lies in its role within a wider landscape which stretches from the Peak District to the city of Sheffield. It features a number of associated woodland bird species such as nuthatch, treecreeper, wren, robin and two species of woodpecker. Other species can often be seen passing through; for example, long-tailed tits flit from tree to tree as they move through the valley. The occasional hooting of a tawny owl can be heard in the autumn months as territories are set up in the area.

The steep bank is covered by thin acid soils giving rise to a ground layer dominated by bilberry and wavy hair-grass, with occasional patches of bracken. The high rainfall levels support a number of typical mosses such as *Hypnum cupressiforme* and *Dicranella heteromalla*. Other plants of note include the delightful hard fern. At the bottom of the slope the soils become deeper and more clay-rich on which bluebell, red campion and wood stitchwort grow. Here the canopy contains a number of large ash trees as well as an understory of hazel with occasional holly.

The nature reserve slopes steeply down to the railway. It is suggested that visitors keep to the upper part of the site and do not descend to the lower area. Most of the site can be adequately seen from the footpath. The oak woodland requires little day-to-day management. Practical conservation tasks include repairs to boundaries, removal of species such as rhododendron and sycamore and the disposal of litter.

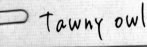

Tawny owl

NEAREST POSTCODE
S17 4QA

GRID REFERENCE
SK 325 809

RESERVE SIZE
0.51 ha

PUBLIC TRANSPORT
Train available to Dore rail station from Sheffield on the Sheffield – Manchester route. Bus routes from Sheffield centre available.

DIRECTIONS
Twentywellsick Wood is situated on Twentywell Lane above the Sheffield to Chesterfield railway line and close to the village of Dore, in south west Sheffield. By car, the nature reserve can be approached by taking the A621 Bakewell road from Sheffield. After a section of dual carriageway, Dore Railway Station is signed on the left. 200m after this a left-turn into Twentywell Lane should be taken. The road winds its way uphill, and the nature reserve can be seen on the right-hand side of the road. Continue past the wood as the road straightens out and Twentywell Road is on your right. Turn into this road and park safely to avoid any obstruction. Access is over a drop stone in the dry stone wall.

Inset map: Sheffield City Centre, Dore Lane, Dore Station, Twentywell Lane, A621 Abbeydale Road, Twentywellsick Wood, B6054 (A61)

Garden

House

A621 and Sheffield Twentywell Lane

N

Dore South Junction

P

Houses

B6054 (A61)

0   25yds

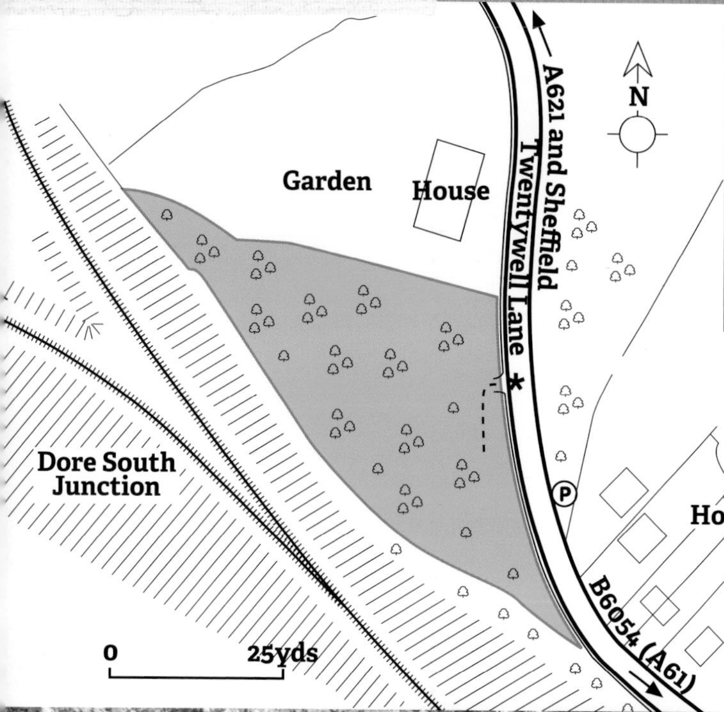

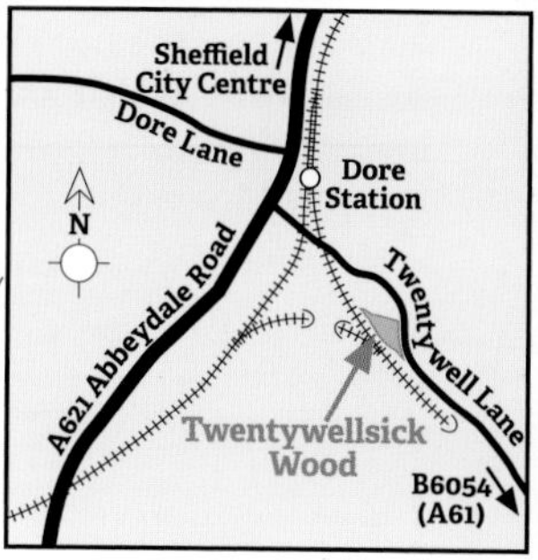

Robin

Top tip...

Stand behind the wall on the road and take in this diverse woodland whilst enjoying the delightful songs of resident birds.

SPRING	SUMMER	AUTUMN	WINTER
Bluebell	Bilberry	Tawny owl	Holly berries
Nuthatch	Treecreeper	Fungi	
Fox	Chiffchaff		

UPPER DUNSFORTH CARRS

A series of wet meadows and areas of wet woodland, supporting a wide variety of wetland plants and an interesting and diverse range of insects.

Willow catkins

A characteristic sign of early spring

Upper Dunsforth Carrs comprises of a series of habitats that are becoming increasingly rare in lowland Britain as a consequence of agricultural improvement and drainage. The permanently waterlogged soils over most of the site have produced a variety of wetland communities, representing various stages in ecological succession. Where the vegetation is summer grazed by cattle, diverse rush-pasture, fen-meadow, tall-herb fen and swamp have developed, whilst ungrazed areas support willow and alder carr. At the south end of the nature reserve, the lighter sandier soil supports drier grassland, similar to the hay meadows that would have once covered much of the Vale of York.

The site has many bird species characteristic of the farmed landscape surrounding the site, such as chaffinch, greenfinch and yellowhammer. Snipe may be found in winter, along with mixed flocks of lesser redpoll and siskin, whilst reed bunting are present all year round. Green woodpecker are a noisy inhabitant of the nature reserve.

Over 120 species of beetle have been found on site, including the nationally scarce diving beetle *Agabus uliginosus* and the large click beetle *Ctenicera pectinicornis*, which is an important indicator of damp grassland.

NEAREST POSTCODE
YO26 9RU

GRID REFERENCE
SE 440 631

RESERVE SIZE
10.21 ha

PUBLIC TRANSPORT
Bus services are available to the village of Great Ouseburn from Boroughbridge, York and Ripon.

DIRECTIONS
Heading south on the B6265, three miles from Boroughbridge, turn left following signs for Upper Dunsforth. Turn left again and parking is on the left after 0.6 miles, before you reach the T-junction at the end.

SITE DESIGNATION
SSSI

OTHER INFORMATION
Can get very boggy and wet in places.

Lesser redpoll

Flocks feed on alder seeds in winter

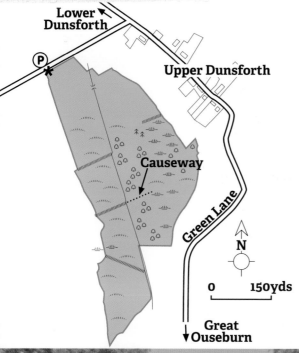

Top tip...

Look for flocks of lesser redpoll and siskin feeding on alder seeds during the winter.

SPRING	SUMMER	AUTUMN	WINTER
Great spotted woodpecker	Ragged robin	Migrant hawker	Snipe
Willow warbler	Yellow flag iris	Comon darter	Reed bunting
Willow tit	Dragonflies		
	Butterflies		
	Sedge warbler		

UPPER PARK WOOD

Visit Upper Park Wood for fantastic panoramic views of the 'Last of the Summer Wine' countryside of the Holme Valley – a colourful mosaic of meadows, woodland and moorland, as well as a chance to consider man's impact on the environment. A variety of habitats in the nature reserve support a great diversity of species.

Oak woodland with an understory of holly and a ground flora rich in bluebells, Upper Park Wood was probably once part of a game park for deer and wild boar, as part of the ancient Manor of Almondbury.

A good network of paths allows you to experience excellent views from the nature reserve, as well as encounter a wide variety of habitats; woodland edge, field and path margins, pond, wet areas, acid grassland, hedges and dry stone walls. The acid nature of the soil is reflected by the plant species growing on the nature reserve, including foxglove, heath bedstraw and sheep's sorrel which thrive on the site, along with bilberry and heather. The pond was created by damming a stream, and in one of the fields a shallow scrape has also been created.

The south facing hillside lies on the lower coal measures, made up of layers of shale and sandstone, with coal seams above some of the sandstone beds. Until the early 1900s the richer seams were worked along the valley. Evidence of two coal pits can be seen adjacent to the steps up the side of the wood, marked by the profuse growth of Western gorse.

Designated as a Local Nature Reserve in 1987, the site took its name from a tiny remnant of ancient deciduous woodland. Owned by Kirklees Metropolitan Council and managed jointly with Yorkshire Wildlife Trust, the site has grown with the acquisition of adjacent fields which have since been planted with a variety of native trees and shrub species. Much of the woodland management is carried out by a group of enthusiastic volunteers with the aim of maintaining and increasing biodiversity where possible.

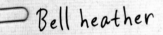
Bell heather

NEAREST POSTCODE
HD9 6QN

GRID REFERENCE
SE 145 130

RESERVE SIZE
4.8 ha

PUBLIC TRANSPORT
A bus service passes the nature reserve, or take a bus from Huddersfield to Holmfirth and alight at Honley Bridge then take Northgate. Nearest train station at Honley, an hourly service runs between Huddersfield and Sheffield.

DIRECTIONS
Approach via Northgate, a left turn off the A616 from Huddersfield, immediately after the A6024 turn-off towards Holmfirth. After a steep climb, of about 0.75 miles you reach a high wall which can be parked against.

SITE DESIGNATION
LNR

LOCATION

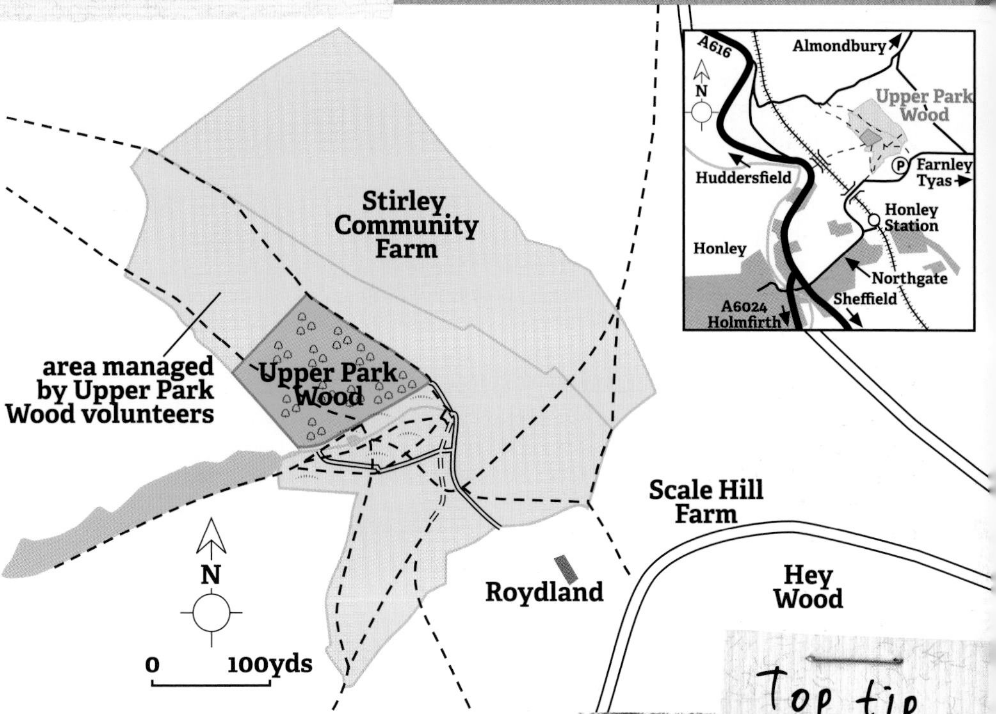

Map labels

Stirley
Community
Farm

area managed
by Upper Park
Wood volunteers

Upper Park
Wood

N

0   100yds

Scale Hill
Farm

Roydland

Hey
Wood

Inset map

A616

Almondbury

Upper Park
Wood

N

Huddersfield

Farnley
Tyas

Honley
Station

Honley

Northgate
Sheffield

A6024
Holmfirth

Top tip...

An excellent network of paths offers opportunities to explore the wider landscape, including Stirley Community Farm which is less than a mile away. A geology trail starting at Castle Hill passes through the nature reserve.

Foxglove

SPRING			
Blackthorn			
Western gorse	SUMMER		
Wild cherry	Butterflies	AUTUMN	WINTER
Bluebell	Buzzard	Bilberry	Roe deer

WELWICK SALTMARSH

Big skies, clouds of birds, raptors skimming past and a spray of purple flowering saltmarsh plants, all set against the landscape of the wide open mouth of the Humber estuary with views of the Humber Bridge in the distance.

Welwick Saltmarsh is the most extensive area of saltmarsh on the north bank of the River Humber. It is advisable to view this nature reserve from the riverbank as accessing the saltmarsh itself can be dangerous and would cause disturbance to wildlife.

From the floodbank you can enjoy spectacular views across the mouth of the Humber. Thousands of birds use the Humber estuary including large flocks of golden plover which appear bronze against the mudflats in the evening sun. Hundreds of large, curve-billed curlew feed on the edge of the saltmarsh whilst grey plover, knot and dunlin whir past and drop down to feed on the mudflats. Many of these flocks pass right overhead as they transfer to their inland roosting sites as the incoming tide pushes them from the river edge.

Welwick Saltmarsh is also a fantastic location to view wintering raptors and owls. Short-eared owl, merlin, peregrine, marsh harrier, hen harrier and kestrel are all regularly seen.

In spring scurvy grass creates hundreds of white tussocks across the marsh and mid-summer sees a real show of purple flowers from sea lavender and sea aster. The saltmarsh also supports sea purslane, sea arrowgrass and cord grass. On the land side of the saltmarsh a small area of relic dune containing two ponds supports common reed, bird's-foot trefoil, spiny restharrow and the curious non-native spring beauty.

Management of the saltmarsh involves some cutting and the Trust is trialling grazing in some areas of the nature reserve.

NEAREST POSTCODE
YO26 9RU

GRID REFERENCE
TA 338 191

RESERVE SIZE
44.12 ha

PUBLIC TRANSPORT
Nearest bus stop in Welwick village around 2 miles away.

DIRECTIONS
From Welwick village head south down Humber Lane which becomes Row Lane. At the end of the lane take a sharp right and park along Sheep Trod Lane. Walk south down a dust track to the site.

SITE DESIGNATION
SSSI

OTHER INFORMATION
Dogs only allowed on leads on public footpaths. Parking available at the top of Humberside Lane.

Peregrine

One of several raptors that can be seen in winter

Grey plover

Look for distinctive blac armpits (axillaries) in flig

LOCATION

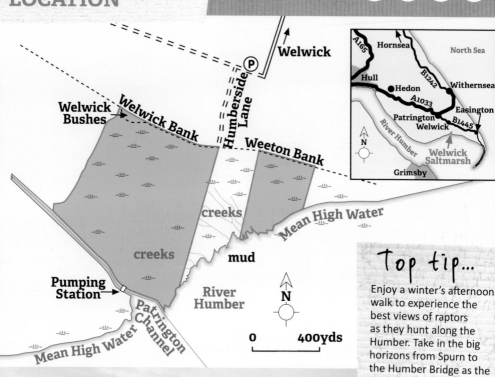

Welwick

Welwick Bushes

Welwick Bank

Weeton Bank

Humberside Lane

P

creeks

creeks

mud

Mean High Water

Pumping Station

River Humber

Patrington Channel

Mean High Water

N

0   400yds

Inset map
A165 · Hornsea · North Sea · Hull · B1242 · Hedon · A1033 · Withernsea · Patrington · Welwick · Easington · B1445 · River Humber · **Welwick Saltmarsh** · Grimsby · N

Top tip...
Enjoy a winter's afternoon walk to experience the best views of raptors as they hunt along the Humber. Take in the big horizons from Spurn to the Humber Bridge as the sun goes down.

SPRING	SUMMER	AUTUMN	WINTER
Marsh harrier	Scurvy grass	Short-eared owl	Barn owl
Skylark	Sea lavender	Hen harrier	Peregrine
Linnet	Sea purslane	Merlin	Golden plover
	Spiny restharrow	Curlew	Knot
		Dunlin	Curlew

Barn owl

WHARRAM QUARRY

A species rich chalk grassland, Wharram Quarry is home to many of the characteristic flowering plants that thrive on the thin Wolds soil. Butterflies flit from flower to flower and in the sky you may see and hear the buzzards that nest in the nearby woods.

NEAREST POSTCODE
YO17 9TW

GRID REFERENCE
SE 858 653

RESERVE SIZE
6.82 ha

PUBLIC TRANSPORT
Nearest train station is in Malton.

DIRECTIONS
At the crossroads on the B1248 in Wharram-le-Street, head west towards Birdsall and the nature reserve is about 0.5 miles on the left as the road descends. Parking is limited and in the gateway.

SITE DESIGNATION
SSSI

Woolly thistle

Large and impressive, often hosting parasitic thistle broomrape

The nature reserve was actively quarried for chalk between 1919 and the 1940s and was offered to Yorkshire Wildlife Trust in the 1960s by the owner Lord Middleton after he noticed bee orchids growing on the quarry floor.

The quarry floor has variable depths of soil and consequently different plant communities. In the west, where the spoil was deposited, is now dominated by coarse grasses and hawthorn scrub. Several species of grasses can be found including cock's-foot, meadow and false oat-grasses, red and sheep's fescues, and quaking grass. Glaucous sedge is widely distributed. The wildflowers present a beautiful scene, they include the yellow flowers of cowslip, rough hawkbit, mouse-ear hawkweed and bird's-foot trefoil; the purple wild thyme and clustered bellflower; the pink restharrow and the blue common milkwort. Common spotted, pyramidal and bee orchids can all be found in June and July. The quarry is one of the few Wolds sites for thistle broomrape which parasitizes woolly thistles. The endangered red hemp-nettle has been introduced from nearby populations along with small-flowered buttercup on the quarry face.

Butterflies abound on sunny days, including plentiful marbled white, small heath, meadow brown, ringlet and common blue. Dingy skippers can sometimes be seen, particularly in the north east corner.

In order to maintain the succession of plants areas of the floor have been periodically scraped back to the chalk. In order to prevent the succession from open flower-rich sward to dense coarse grasses and hawthorn scrub the quarry floor is grazed with the Trust's Hebridean sheep in winter and parts are mown in late summer.

Top tip...

June and July are the best months to visit; try to pick a warm and sunny day. A wet, warm evening in summer will bring out a multitude of snails.

LOCATION

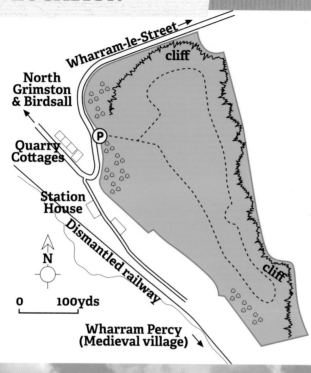

Wharram-le-Street →

cliff

North Grimston & Birdsall

P

Quarry Cottages

Station House

Dismantled railway

N

0   100yds

cliff

Wharram Percy (Medieval village) ↓

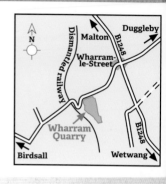

N

Malton   Duggleby
B1248

Dismantled railway

Wharram-le-Street

B1248

Wharram Quarry

Birdsall   Wetwang

Red hemp nettle

This endangered species now grows on the quarry faces

SUMMER
Marbled white
Small heath
Thistle broomrape
Woolly thistle
Pyramidal orchid

SPRING
Dingy skipper
Colt's foot
Cowslip

AUTUMN
Autumn gentian
Carline thistle

WINTER
Stoat
Fieldfare
Redwing

Yorkshire fog

Holcus lanatus

Common blue resting on Yorkshire fog

☑ SPRING
☑ SUMMER
☑ AUTUMN
☑ WINTER

☑ GRASSLAND
☐ BY THE COAST
☐ WETLAND
☑ FARMLAND

An attractive velvety grey grass which can be found across the county in damp meadows, woodland rides and other open areas. Whilst considered a pest in countries such as North America and Australia where it has been introduced, in its native range it is an important species within a number of different plant communities. This grass provides food for caterpillars of a number of butterflies, including speckled wood, wall and small skippers, along with a range of moths.

This species is easily recognised, with round, pink and white striped shoots – like stripy pyjamas – with grey-green leaves and purplish flowers. Where present in large numbers, the effect of the flowers can give a meadow a purplish sheen. The plants produce a large amount of seed which contributes to its ability to rapidly colonise new areas but it also spreads vegetatively, using runners along the soil surface. The runners then form clusters of leaves which take root to form a new plant. This vigorous behaviour can lead to the species dominating in certain habitats unless kept in check by grazing.

In the lowlands of Yorkshire, when hay meadows were traditionally cut, the regrowth of grass was known colloquially as 'fog' as it mainly consisted of this species. The fog was allowed to develop after the hay cut before turning out livestock such as sheep and cattle to graze.

Tansy beetle
Chrysolina graminis

Tansy beetle

- ☐ **SPRING**
- ☑ **SUMMER**
- ☐ **AUTUMN**
- ☐ **WINTER**

- ☐ **WOODLAND**
- ☑ **RIVERSIDE**
- ☐ **WETLAND**
- ☐ **FARMLAND**

This beautiful iridescent green beetle, about the size of a little finger nail, is one of Yorkshire's most treasured gems!

The reason the tansy beetle is so special is that currently it can only be found in small populations along the River Ouse in York. At present it is not recorded anywhere else in the UK and is declining elsewhere in Europe.

As its name suggests the tansy beetle relies on the tansy plant as its food source but, due to factors such as shading from riverside willows and Himalayan balsam, the tansy clumps are dying out and isolating beetle populations. Unfortunately the beetle doesn't help itself and although it has wings it has a reluctance to fly which restricts movement between the scattered tansy clumps.

Tansy plants grow alongside the River Ouse and from the public footpaths you may be lucky enough to see this endangered beetle, ideally on warm sunny days between April and May or August and September.

Yorkshire Wildlife Trust works with other conservation organisations to help conserve the tansy beetle, mainly through encouraging the growth of tansy plants. Riverside willow and Himalayan balsam are removed, and new tansy plants are planted to help encourage the beetles to spread. In addition, the Trust has been helping to create safe havens for the beetle away from summer floods which can cause high mortality and by reducing the grazing pressure on tansy plants by livestock.

Tansy flower

WHELDRAKE INGS

Big skies, often full of whirling flocks of birds, stretch out above you, while the wide green expanse of floodplain meadows go for as far as the eye can see. The Derwent flows quietly by, reeds rustle in the breeze and a mysterious 'plop' in the ditches might signal a pike, water vole or even otter. In fact, at times in the centre of Wheldrake Ings, it can be so peaceful and remote that you feel like the only person on earth.

Snipe

Snipe can be heard drumming in spring

For centuries Wheldrake Ings, at the heart of the Lower Derwent Valley Living Landscape, has been managed in a traditional way, which means you can still see habitats that have been here for centuries.

Spring is a time of vibrant growth on the Ings. As winter floodwaters recede the rich meadows begin to grow and plants such as marsh marigold and cuckooflower are the first to add splashes of colour to the fields. Tucked within the growing grassland waders such as lapwing, redshank and curlew start to raise their young. Flotillas of young duck families scoot into the overhanging willows around the pool edges. Late June sees the meadows at their best with some of the

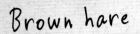
Brown hare

Look for females boxing males in spring

Lapwing

Waders such as lapwings raise their young in the grassland

SPRING	SUMMER		WINTER
Whimbrel	Great burnet		Otter
Cuckoo	Meadowsweet		Whooper swan
Brown hare	Meadow		Wigeon
Marsh marigold	vetchling	**AUTUMN**	Teal
Cuckooflower	Banded	Roe deer	Peregrine
	demoiselle	Barn owl	

finest areas supporting up to 25 plant species per square metre. Look for the crimson raspberry-like heads of great burnet and the cream sprays of meadowsweet. This type of meadow community is uncommon now and the area at Wheldrake Ings is of international importance. In early July the land is dry and the meadows are ready to be cut for hay.

By August sheep and cattle are turned out to graze the re-growth of grass or 'fog' as it is known. In autumn, the meadows start to flood and impressive expanses of open water attract a spectacle of thousands of ducks, geese and waders. 40,000 birds use the Lower Derwent Valley each winter, with a significant proportion of these at Wheldrake.

The wetlands attract a wide range of birds. Spring and autumn can be exciting as migrant waders, terns and raptors pass through. Spotted crake, water rail and willow tit all breed along with many common waders and ducks. Marsh harrier, hobby and peregrine are all seen regularly with the chance of an osprey or black tern during migration.

The site also supports a host of grassland and wetland insects including some very rare beetles. Fish such as pike and rudd can be glimpsed in the ditches and otter have bred on the nature reserve on several occasions in the past few years.

Management here is a fine balance of controlling water levels to support the wintering, passage and breeding birds, whilst also creating the right conditions for the rare floodplain grassland to thrive. On top of this regular maintenance and cleaning of the ditches and pools is required, which each winter receive silty deposits as the River Derwent bursts its banks and spreads across its floodplain.

NEAREST POSTCODE
YO19 6AS

GRID REFERENCE
SE 694 444

RESERVE SIZE
156.88 ha

PUBLIC TRANSPORT
York to Selby buses stop on the Wheldrake to Thorganby road 25m north of the top of the entrance road.

DIRECTIONS
Eight miles south east of York, four miles east of the A19. From Wheldrake follow the road (Carr Lane) towards Thorganby and out of the village where the road takes a sharp right turn. 0.5 miles further on a narrow road to your left (after the Yorkshire Water compound) takes you down to the nature reserve. Park on the stony area next to the bridge over the River Derwent.

SITE DESIGNATION
SPA, SAC, RAMSAR, SSSI, NNR

OTHER INFORMATION
The paths are muddy after wet weather. Special access kissing gate allows buggy entrance.

Migrant birds

Clouds of ducks and waders make a fine sight

Top tip...
Enjoy a post-Sunday lunch stroll on a crisp, sunny winter afternoon. There's a great chance of spotting a hunting peregrine creating a mass whirling spectacle of thousands of teal, wigeon, golden plover and lapwing – an exhilarating spectacle. Stay until dusk when whooper swans fly into roost on the floodwater. Magical!

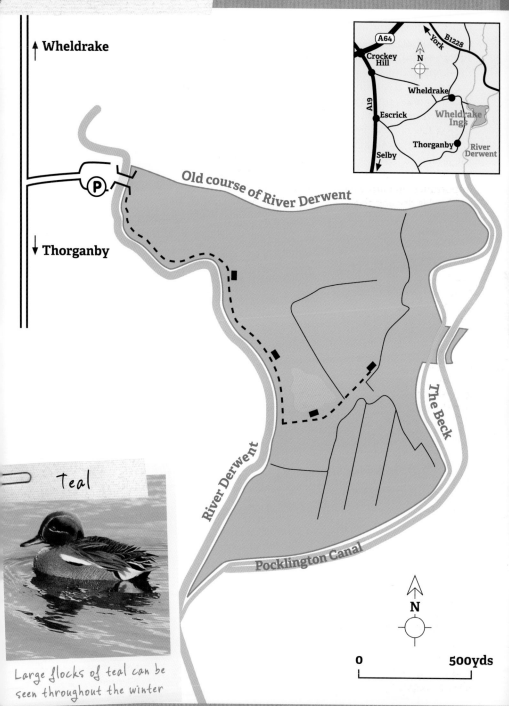

↑ **Wheldrake**

↓ **Thorganby**

Old course of River Derwent

River Derwent

Pocklington Canal

The Beck

A64
Crockey Hill
York
B1228
N
A19
Wheldrake
Escrick
Wheldrake Ings
Thorganby
Selby
River Derwent

Teal

Large flocks of teal can be seen throughout the winter

N

0   500yds

WILLOW GARTH

This page is sponsored by Croda International P

Willow Garth Nature Reserve provides a window to the past, to a time where the countryside was a mosaic of different habitats each varied in their structure. Lying in the floodplain of the River Aire, the open water and marsh make it ideal for wading birds.

A myriad of wetland habitats including open water, marsh and willow carr has resulted from the generally flat and low-lying nature of the land. This site, excellent for willow, was in fact a commercial osier bed in the past where willow was grown to make baskets and furniture.

Marshland species can be found in the central and western areas of the site, whereas woodland and scrub exists in the north east corner. Close to 140 species of birds make use of these habitats, many of which have been recorded as breeding on site. Reed and sedge warblers, great spotted woodpecker and green sandpiper are amongst the birds that can be found. The variety of habitats also supports a diverse mix of flora including water chickweed, common meadow-rue and alder buckthorn. Crack and grey willow make up the majority of the woodland on the nature reserve with some silver birch and hawthorn. Mammals recorded on site include the harvest mouse, bank vole, common shrew, pygmy shrew, roe deer and fox.

Owned by Croda and managed by Yorkshire Wildlife Trust, the key management aim is to continue a traditional willow coppice. The rest of the site is managed less actively with footpaths kept clear for visitors. Invasive Himalayan balsam is controlled in the summer months and reedbed cutting occurs around the ponds. Ditch maintenance is also undertaken to ensure water is able to flow around the site.

Top tip...

A trip in early spring will provide the ideal conditions to see both emerging and returning wildlife before the vegetation grows up restricting some views.

NEAREST POSTCODE
WF11 9AA

GRID REFERENCE
SE 513 240

RESERVE SIZE
5.3 ha

PUBLIC TRANSPORT
Buses and trains to Knottingley from Leeds, Castleford and Pontefract Monkhill.

DIRECTIONS
Willow Garth is situated almost due east of Knottingley off the A645. From Knottingley, head eastwards along the A645, crossing the Leeds to Goole Canal (very near the former works of Croda). Almost at the bridge, turn left into un-metalled Trundles Lane (a bad junction, use extreme caution). After 200m, where a narrow footbridge crosses a canal ahead, turn sharp right. The unfenced canal is now on the left, the Croda works on the right. Continue for ⅓ mile until it leaves the works fence. Park here on the roadside. The nature reserve entrance lies 200m ahead, on the right.

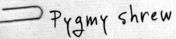

Pygmy shrew

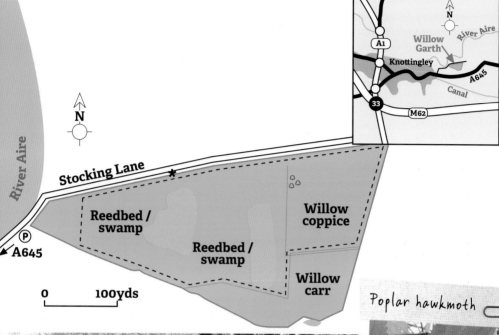

A1

Willow Garth

River Aire

Knottingley

A645

Canal

33

M62

N

River Aire

N

Stocking Lane

Reedbed / swamp

Reedbed / swamp

Willow coppice

Willow carr

P

A645

0   100yds

Poplar hawkmoth

Reed warbler

Present between April and September

SPRING	SUMMER		
Reed warbler	Butterflies		
Sedge warbler	Dragonflies		
Butterflies	Poplar	**AUTUMN**	**WINTER**
Amphibians	hawkmoth	Fungi	Snipe

WOODHOUSE WASHLANDS

Woodhouse Washlands are an ever changing tapestry of colours and textures throughout the seasons. The winter wetland attracts flocks of lapwing, which give way to a spring buttercup meadow. Then the early summer grassland and riverbank provides insects for swallows, swifts and martins, which feed over the area, giving spectacular displays.

Lying in the floodplain of the River Rother, the nature reserve straddles the boundary between Sheffield and Rotherham. This suburban site, whilst surrounded by roads, housing and industry, has a rich and varied history. Until the 1950s the river meandered through extensive marshland and flooded on such a regular basis that a rowing boat was kept at the Methodist chapel to transport people between the housing and factories. The disruption resulted in a flood alleviation scheme being put into operation and by 1960 the river channel had been straightened, flood banks built and ditches dug to control the water. Since then the river has only flooded the washlands three times; lastly during the major floods in June 2007.

The scheme transformed the widespread marshland into a rich mosaic of grassland, marsh, ponds, ditches and temporary pools with willows and remnant hawthorn hedges dotted across the site creating additional habitat features. The River Rother was once one of the most polluted in Europe, a legacy of the industrial past. Today, the river supports a good fish population as well as a range of invertebrates and plants. Watch out for the occasional flash of turquoise as a kingfisher flies past. In winter, see ducks including goosander and gulls. The nature reserve is managed by a mixture of cattle grazing and periodic maintenance of the ditches, ponds and hedges. The land is divided by the river and a railway viaduct which helps create the distinct characteristics of the different compartments. Metal sculptures have been installed along the route, giving information on the industrial history as well as the plants and animals that can be seen.

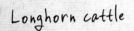

Longhorn cattle

Put to graze on the grasslands to maintain the wildlife's habitat

NEAREST POSTCODE
S13 9WG

GRID REFERENCE
SK 438 852

RESERVE SIZE
73.33 ha

PUBLIC TRANSPORT
Nearest bus stop Furnace Lane; Woodhouse Railway Station within ½ mile of entrance.

DIRECTIONS
The nature reserve has three main entrances. The entrance on Furnace Lane leads to a small section of the nature reserve with a walk along a tree-lined path. The other entrances are on Retford Road via a public footpath, part of the Trans-Pennine Trail, and on Rotherham Road accessible from Beighton and Swallownest.

SITE DESIGNATION
LNR

OTHER INFORMATION
The Trans-Pennine Trail, running along an edge of the site, allows easy access for cyclists and wheelchair users in good weather (it can get very muddy in wet weather).

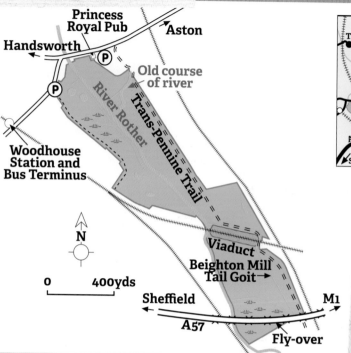

Princess Royal Pub

Aston

Handsworth

Old course of river

River Rother

Trans-Pennine Trail

Woodhouse Station and Bus Terminus

N

0   400yds

Viaduct

Beighton Mill Tail Goit

Sheffield

A57

M1

Fly-over

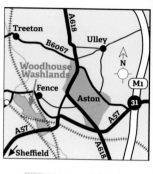

Treeton   A618   Ulley

B6067

Woodhouse Washlands

N

M1

Fence

Aston

31

A57

A57

Sheffield

A618

Top tip...

In early summer, skylarks are singing and the grassland is full of wildflowers, grasses, rushes and sedges attracting a wide range of insects. The jewel-like banded demoiselle holds territory over the river and emperor dragonflies cruise over the ponds.

Alder

SPRING	SUMMER	AUTUMN	WINTER
Skylark	Butterflies	Fungi	Winter migrants
Pignut	Dragonflies	Goldfinch	Hawthorn berries
Cuckooflower	Damselflies	Teasel	Lapwing
Orange-tip	Great burnet	Rosehip	Goosander
Marsh marigold	Green woodpecker		Alder

WYMING BROOK

A little bit of wilderness on the edge of Sheffield, this site is enjoyable for both its landscape and rich wildlife.

Once set aside for the exclusive use of the nobility, when it was part of the hunting and hawking grounds of Rivelin Chase, Wyming Brook's babbling streams, mossy crags and sweet smelling pines are still protected today as a valuable home to wildlife.

Red cracking bolete

Have tubes and pores instead of gills

Today, all visitors can enjoy this little bit of wilderness on the western edge of Sheffield, with easy strolls by the streams or higher, rockier routes with dramatic views of the Rivelin Reservoirs, the source of the brook, and the city beyond. Part of the Eastern Moors SSSI, there is an abundance of wildlife at this nature reserve, including bizarrely named moths: the common lutestring and Northern spinach.

The nature reserve is also home to many kinds of birds, including pine-seed-eating crossbill, which breed in late winter and then can be seen in noisy family parties among the pines. Listen out for

their sharp 'chip' calls as they fly overhead. Nearby, resident dippers sporting smart white breasts forage for aquatic insects including caddis fly larvae along the fast flowing stream.

In autumn the mossy banks, dead wood and boulders become coloured by the fruiting bodies of many fungi, including the wonderfully named plums and custard and amethyst deceiver.

Top tip...

Keep one eye on the sky particularly in spring when ospreys may linger over the nearby reservoir and sometimes pass over the nature reserve.

THE wildlife TRUSTS
Sheffield & Rotherham

NEAREST POSTCODE
S10 4LJ

GRID REFERENCE
SK 269 858

RESERVE SIZE
69.8 ha

PUBLIC TRANSPORT
Buses from Sheffield City Road/Stafford Road and from Eyre Street, along Redmires Road.

DIRECTIONS
From Sheffield city centre take the Manchester Road (A57) towards Rivelin Dams. Just past the dam turn left onto Wyming Brook Drive. Follow this to the end. Parking is available on Redmires Road and car park.

SITE DESIGNATION
LNR, SSSI

Dipper

Look along the brook for this dapper bird

LOCATION

Head Stone Bank

Reddicar Clough

New Hagg

Wyming Brook Dr

A57 Manchester Road

Rivelin Dams

Tunnel entrance

Bird feeding station

Wyming Brook

to Redmires Reservoir

Redmires Road

to Sheffield and Fox Hagg Nature Reserve

Soughley Lane

N

0   800yds

Damflask Reservoir

A6101

Wyming Brook

Rivelin Dams

Redmires Reservoirs

Sheffield

A62

N

SPRING
Dipper
Nuthatch
Treecreeper
Great spotted
woodpecker

SUMMER
Blackcap
Chiffchaff
Speckled wood

AUTUMN
Fungi

WINTER
Crossbill

YELLANDS MEADOW

A traditionally managed hay meadow set amid steep hills in the beautiful limestone landscape of Swaledale in the Yorkshire Dales National Park.

Yellands Meadow is a tiny meadow lying next to the River Swale and is one of twelve included in 'The Muker Meadows' SSSI. A stream, lined with alders, runs diagonally across the meadow. There is a small stone barn on the western boundary containing the original stone cow stalls.

The meadow has resulted from traditional management in the harsh climate of the hills. It is of a type that is now almost entirely restricted to a few valley heads in the North of England. The flowering plants in the meadow include an abundance of pignut, lady's mantle, meadow buttercup, wood cranesbill, clovers and hawkbits. Other flowers include yellow rattle, cuckooflower, meadow vetchling, bugle, eyebright, bird's-foot trefoil and common spotted orchid. Along the moist banks of the stream are meadowsweet, melancholy thistle and marsh-marigold. There is a range of grasses in the sward with sweet vernal-grass, the grass that gives cut hay its characteristic and evocative smell, predominant.

There are no clearly defined footpaths on site. To enjoy the meadow it is suggested that visitors cross the bridge over the stream to the right of the entrance gate and, keeping close to the boundary wall and river fence, go clockwise around the meadow, return across the footbridge at the eastern end and then walk back along the stream.

The meadow has been managed in a traditional way by the same tenant family for a number of generations and is grazed in the autumn and early spring and a hay cut is taken in July.

NEAREST POSTCODE
DL11 6QJ

GRID REFERENCE
SD 918 977

RESERVE SIZE
1.14 ha

PUBLIC TRANSPORT
A very limited bus service runs along Swaledale.

DIRECTIONS
Situated between the River Swale and the B6270, about one mile east of Muker. A small parking area exists in an informal lay by near the field gate on the B6270.

SITE DESIGNATION
SSSI

Yellow rattle

Partially parasitic on grasses

Top tip...

To see the meadow at its colourful best visit from late May to early July. With the flowers in bloom, the meadow is alive with the sight and sound of bees, grasshoppers and butterflies.

Meadow buttercup

Enjoy a fine display throughout spring and summ

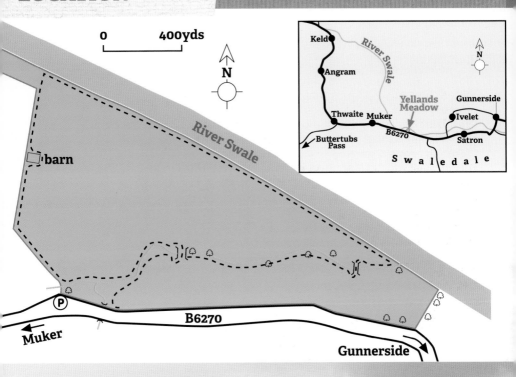

0   400yds

N

River Swale

barn

Keld

River Swale

Angram

Thwaite Muker

Buttertubs
Pass

Yellands
Meadow

B6270

Gunnerside

Ivelet

Satron

Swaledale

N

P

Muker

B6270

Gunnerside

SUMMER
Eyebright
Yellow rattle
Meadow vetchling
Lady's mantle
Common spotted
orchid

SPRING
Marsh marigold
Cuckooflower

LEEDS SITES

These sites are owned by Leeds City Council and managed in partnership with Yorkshire Wildlife Trust. Work carried out on the sites includes habitat management, improving access and interpretation, as well as some survey and education work. For details of the fun and varied events programme on these sites check out the Trust's website ywt.org.uk/whats-on.

❶ Rothwell Country Park

A reclaimed colliery site from the 1990s that has been transformed into a mosaic of woodland, meadow and ponds with fantastic views of the surrounding area. This site can be easily accessed from the Trans-Pennine Cycle Way as it is conveniently right next to the Aire and Calder Navigation Canal. The site has lots of paths to help you explore. Look out for the dragonflies emerging from the ponds and thriving on the insect-rich grassland hunting areas.

❷ The Lines Way

A disused railway line that runs from Garforth through to Allerton Bywater. This 4 mile stretch provides easy access for cyclists, walkers and horse riders along a superb wildlife corridor, which is home to glow worms. Use the Lines Way to visit Townclose Hills and Owl Wood.

❸ Townclose Hills (locally known as Billy Wood)

This SSSI gives a stunning show of wildflowers, thanks to its magnesian limestone soil. Glow worms abound during humid summer nights. The woodland is traditionally coppiced with managed scrub edges adding to its appeal for nesting birds.

❹ Letchmire Pastures

A wild reclaimed former colliery site, with a young woodland and meadow where bee orchids are now plentiful.

6 Rothwell Pastures

This site is based around a network of streams, meadows and a disused railway line. Many people don't realise the former importance of this area as a manorial hunting estate. These days however there are water voles rather than wild boar at large!

7 Owl Wood & Pit Plantation

These two semi-mature woodlands located just off the Lines Way are connected and former woodland management has meant there is plenty here for local wildlife. There are a couple of paths to explore.

8 Hollinghurst Wood

This stand of woodland located in Great Preston provides a haven for nesting birds who also use the nearby St Aidans wetland areas. There is an area of meadow and scrub which is being managed to provide a diverse structure. Paths lead through this area from adjoining roads.

9 Water Haigh Woodland Park

This mosaic of woodland and meadow areas is located next to the Aire and Calder Navigation with access from the Trans-Pennine Cycle Way. There are paths all around the site and a picnic area next to the canal.

10 Ledston Luck

This site is easy to drive right by, but then you would be missing out on a quiet haven.

5 Kippax Meadows

Tucked away next to the village of Kippax. This mix of meadow and scrub provides a small network of paths to gain some fresh air and exercise. Enjoy the show of Southern marsh and common spotted orchids.

Photograph Credits

Amy Lewis
Red Admiral – title page
Skylark – page 17
Corn bunting – page 18
Gatekeeper – page 45
Sedge warbler – page 58
Whitethroat – page 61
Hare's-foot clover – page 61
Common pipistrelle – page 70
Small copper – page 78
Tree sparrow – page 81
Water vole (main) – page 87
Holly blue – page 88
Ringlet – page 110
Buzzard – page 115
Dunlin – page 118
Blackcap – page 128
Hobby – page 141
Meadow pipit – page 167
Sea buckthorn – page 179
Chiffchaff – page 190
Spotted flycatcher – page 192
Reed warbler – page 217

Alistair Campbell
Peacock butterfly – page 99

Amy Hattersley
Bluebell woodland – page 137

Andrew Barraclough
Chafer Wood – page 69

Andrew Gallon
Rob Stoneman (headshot) – page 8

Andrew Mason
Gannets – page 25
Green woodpecker – page 176
Barn owl (main) – page 183
Long-eared owl – page 198

Barry Flude
Barn owl – page 207

Barry Greenacre
Saltmarshe Delph lake – page 163

Bob Coyle
Blue tit – page 21
Tufted duck – page 58
Long-tailed tit – page 160
Lesser redpoll – page 202
Common blue on Yorkshire Fog – page 210

Brian Lavelle
Yellow rattle – page 222

Bruce Shorthand
Eyebright – page 125

Carl Lewis
Tansy flower – page 211

Carl Watts
Bee orchid – page 17
Redshank – page 102
Otter (main) – page 146
Dark green fritillary – page 171
Great crested grebes – page 175
Six-spot burnet moth – page 186
Lapwing – page 213

Carol Wootton
Stoat – page 15
Adders – page 35
Grass snake – page 72

Caroline Comins
Askham Bog pond – page 40
Marsh orchids – page 40
Yellow flag iris – page 41
Water violet – page 42
Pond and yellow flag iris – page 43
Fen Bog – page 77
Wood sorrel – page 90
Marsh valerian – page 114
Longhorn cattle – page 115
Kiplingcotes flower meadow – page 121
Cowslip and burnt-tip orchid – page 124
Leyburn Old Glebe – page 125
Bloody cranesbill – page 156
Rifle Butts Quarry – page 156
Cross-leaved heath – page 194
Strensall Common – page 195
Woolly thistle – page 208
Wheldrake Ings – page 212

Yellands Meadow – page 223

Catrin Rees
Visitors at Potteric Carr – page 153

Charlotte Holgate
Veg box – page 28

Chris Jones
Common gorse – page 35

Claire Jackson
Raking cuttings at Foss Island – page 20
Lake – page 49
Upper Dunsforth Carrs – page 203

Claire Marshall
Azure damselfly, Common toad, Kestrel,
Puffin – all on title page
Little owl – page 8
Kingfisher – page 31
Large red damselflies – page 154

Colin Speedie
Harbour porpoise (top left) – page 182

Damian Waters (drumimages.co.uk)
Curlew – page 52
Avocet – page 139

Dave Appleton
Little ringed plover – page 138
Grey plover – page 206

Dave Key
Pyramidal orchid – title page
Dyer's greenweed – page 106
Hoary plantain – page 107

Dave Wilkinson
Rhododendrons – page 133
Stinkhorn – page 134

David Adams
Black darter – page 173

David Evans
Emperor moth – page 173

David Martin
Redstart – page 88
Red-veined darter – page 180

David Nichols
Flamborough cliffs – page 24
Spurn Point – page 178

Denis Matthewman
Robin – page 201

Derek Haslam
Common lobster – page 25

Des Ong
Adder (top left) – page 36

Elizabeth Round
Harland Mount – page 105

Ellen Fairbank
Cattle – page 168

Emma Bradshaw
Bat detecting – page 27

Erik Paterson
Palmate newt – page 80

Faye Palmer
Pygmy shrew – page 216

Fiona Shipp
The Lines Way – page 224
Rothwell Pastures – page 224
Hollinghurst Wood – page 224

Frank Vassen
Wood warbler – page 96

Gary Cox
Shoveler – page 48
Whinchat – page 85

George Stoyle
Lightbulb sea squirt – page 84

Gillian Day
Hedgehog – page 21
Goosander – page 48
Razorbill – page 83
Coal tit – page 127

Gordon Scaife
Bird's-foot trefoil – title page

Harriet Linfoot
Garden – page 27
Vegetable patch – page 27
Bee keeping – page 27

Helen Gottschalk
Green crafts – page 29

Helen Percival
Broadhead Clough – page 53
Cotton grass – page 53
Burton Riggs – page 59

Ian Jelley
Fen Carr meadow – page 79
White park cattle – page 188

Ian Rose
Jay – page 108

James Ferguson
Sycamore leaves – page 62
Dog violet – page 105
Early purple orchid – page 126
Lesser celandine – page 174

Jamie Hall
Black-tailed skimmer – page 139

Janet Packham
Brimstone – page 142

Jayne Lilywhite
White-letter hairstreak – page 56

Jenny Hayward
Work party at Ellerburn Bank – page 75
Water avens – page 92

Jess Bersey
Crab – page 26
Rockpooling – page 26
Filey Dams – page 81
Kirkstall Valley – page 123

Jim Horsfall
Columbine – title page
Café and Tofield Room – page 29
Sphagnum squarrosum – page 31
Tormentil and cross-leaved heath – page 32
Devil's bit scabious – page 32
Agden Bog – page 33
Brockadale – page 55
Purple milk vetch – page 55
Purple loosestrife – page 66
Pepper saxifrage – page 78
Common cow wheat – page 99
Toothwort – page 107
Common twayblade – page 108
Adder's tongue fern – page 113
Thimble morel – page 130
Columbine – page 130
Oak bush-cricket – page 188
Woodhouse Washlands – page 219

Jo Clegg
Yorkshire fog (main and top left) – page 210

Jo Meays
Ox-eye daisy – page 104
Common frog – page 122
Banded demoiselle – page 152
Tansy beetle (main and bottom right) – page 211

Joanna Richards
Pond at Adel Dam – page 31
Royal fern – page 42
Grass Wood – page 94
Hetchell Wood – page 106
Stoneycliffe Wood bluebells – page 191
Beck – page 193

John McArthur
Little grebe – page 80
Black-necked grebe – page 151

John Shephard
Thistle broomrape – page 158

Jon Hawkins
Fallow deer stag – page 38
Roe deer – page 129

Jon Traill
Emerald damselfly – page 23

Jonathan Bliss
Common darter – page 58

Jonathan Leadley
Family walk – page 10
Red grouse – page 12
Dunlin – page 25
Kilnsea Wetlands – page 119
Meadow vetchling – page 159
Migrant birds – page 214

Species Index

Join us

Yorkshire Wildlife Trust

Join Yorkshire Wildlife Trust today and help protect Yorkshire's wildlife and wild places

Yorkshire Wildlife Trust is a local charity working to protect and enhance Yorkshire's wildlife and wild places for all to enjoy. We care for over 90 nature reserves many of which you can read about in the pages of this book.

We also stand up for wildlife where it is threatened and work to influence landowners and other decision makers to encourage them to manage land and progress developments in a way that is beneficial to wildlife.

The Trust runs lots of events and activities across Yorkshire in order to inspire people about nature and spread our messages about our work to create a Living Landscape and Living Seas in Yorkshire. It is thanks to the fantastic support of our members, volunteers and supporters that we are able to continue with this work.

Why not join us?

For a small monthly donation you can directly support the nature reserves found within these pages and all the wildlife that finds refuge within them.

We will keep you informed with our superb full-colour magazine, *Wildlife Yorkshire*, which contains news of all our work, the latest wildlife stories from around the county and information to help you experience the best that Yorkshire's countryside and wildlife has to offer.

Joining is easy. We prefer to sign you up by Direct Debit as that is cost-efficient for us to deal with and protects you with the Direct Debit guarantee.

To join:

Call 01904 659570 and ask to speak with the membership team. You will need your bank details or credit card.

Log on to www.ywt.org.uk and sign up online.

Pop in to one of our centres (The Living Seas Centre at Flamborough, Potteric Carr, Spurn or our York office)

Thank you!

f ⓔ You Tube

www.ywt.org.uk